"*Dr. Wang is not only a dear friend and the very best eye surgeon; he is also one of the greatest people I have ever known.*"

—Dolly Parton

"*To try to put my feelings about Dr. Wang, his accomplishments, his courage, his iron will and his faith into a couple of sentences would be tantamount to packing a Mack truck into a burlap bag. This remarkable man overcame all but impossible odds to become the best in his field, and this world is a better place for having Dr. Ming Wang pass through it.*"

—Charlie Daniels

"*I have known Dr. Wang for nearly two decades; he is a respected eye surgeon and friend. What Ming has done with his life since arriving here in the United States as a penniless student over 30 years ago exemplifies the true essence of the American dream, and the freedom that we enjoy in this great country. I highly recommend his autobiography,* From Darkness to Sight.*"

—Senator William H. Frist, MD,
former U.S. Senate Majority Leader

"*If I didn't know Ming, it would be hard to believe the story of his life. But I do know him, and his life truly is a remarkable story of faith, persistence, and excellence.*"

—Bill Haslam,
Governor of the State of Tennessee

"*Ming Wang is well known for the eye surgeries he's performed to give countless people better sight. And it's hard to forget that he's also a ballroom dancer, once you've seen one of his ads on TV. But what many people don't know is that Dr. Wang also gives very generously of his time and talents so that blind children in other countries can regain their sight. What better gift can you give someone? Nashville is lucky to be able to count Dr. Wang as one of our own.*"

—Karl Dean,
Mayor, Nashville

"My deeply respected friend, Dr. Ming Wang, has topped the heights of human achievement. Through his personal and professional triumphs, Ming has captured the essence of what it means to be free and to be a loving humanitarian. The story of his unique life, as only he can tell it, will be a blessing and an inspiration to all who come to know it."

—Dr. Winfield Dunn,
former Governor of Tennessee

"From Darkness to Sight is an inspiring story that shows how hard work, optimism, and faith can not only lead to personal success, but also make our country stronger. Dr. Ming Wang's journey from dark days in Communist China to his career in the United States as a physician and philanthropist is a testament to the possibilities of the American Dream."

—Senator Lamar Alexander

"The story of Ming Wang's journey from the severe hardships of the Cultural Revolution (U. C.) in China to becoming one of the most accomplished doctors in the U.S. will make you a believer that all things are possible."

—Dr. Rice Broocks,
Senior Minister of Bethel World Outreach Church in Nashville,
co-founder of Every Nation Ministries,
bestselling author of God's Not Dead

"Dr. Wang performed LASIK eye surgery on me in 2000 and we have been friends ever since. It has been a pleasure to serve on his Wang Foundation Board, and to witness the generous application of his talents and skills giving the gift of sight. Ming Wang's life story is unique and inspirational, as is he. I am indeed thrilled that he has shared it in his new book!"

—Shirley Zeitlin, Owner, Shirley Zeitlin & Company

"I have known Dr. Ming Wang for many years. He is a highly respected eye surgeon, writer, award-winning ballroom dancer, philanthropist, and dear friend. Dr. Wang is the epitome of the Renaissance Man. His skill as an eye surgeon is legendary, his empathy and concern for patients worldwide is noteworthy, and his Christian faith guides and drives him!"

—Colleen Conway Welch, PhD, CNM, FAAN, FACNM, Nancy & Hilliard Travis, Professor of Nursing, Dean Emerita, Vanderbilt School of Nursing

"It was a great pleasure having Dr. Wang work in my laboratory while he was a student at Harvard Medical school. He managed to explore cutting-edge science and publish in the top journal Nature while excelling in his clinical duties and other pursuits. He has continued this path of technology development in laser applications in eye surgery ever since then and his new book captures a truly touching and amazing story of a multifaceted life."

—George Church, PhD, Professor of Genetics, Harvard Medical School

"From Darkness to Sight is a roller coaster of emotions! Once I picked up the book I couldn't put it down, each page dripping with humanity in the face of life's most difficult circumstances. This is a story of tenacity and determination, an odyssey of searching through great darkness to find a sliver of light that would ultimately become a wave of grace and mercy. Dr. Wang writes, 'Over the years of my life, I had learned again and again that it was often in these especially difficult situations, where human capability seems to have reached its limit, that we really have the chance to encounter God's true power.' And isn't that the story of all of our lives? We struggle for meaning *and understanding amidst the highs and lows that we share with our loved ones, with our colleagues, with our God. We reach to discover our purpose in this world. Dr. Wang's journey is one of self-discovery crowned with the humility to reach out beyond himself to find true peace and freedom. I would highly recommend this book to everyone. And as an executive producer in feature film and television, I look forward to seeing* From Darkness to Sight *come alive on the silver screen!"*

—David Fischer, JD, Chief Financial Officer,
Kingston Road Pictures

From Darkness to Sight

From Darkness to Sight

*A Journey from
Hardship to Healing*

Ming Wang, MD, PhD

From Darkness to Sight
© 2016 Dr. Ming Wang

Hardcover ISBN: 978-1-939447-95-1
Trade Paperback ISBN: 978-1-939447-913
Ebook ISBN: 978-1-939447-920
Library of Congress Control Number: 2015940520

Printed in the United States of America

Dedication

To my father, Dr. Zhen-sheng Wang, my mother, Dr. A-lian Xu, my brother, Dr. Ming-yu Wang, my wife, Anle Wang, my son, Dennis Wang, and my godparents, Misha Bartnovsky and June Rudolph, and my entire family, as well as my teachers, mentors, colleagues, and friends.

To my patients, with whom I have shared the journey from darkness to sight.

To China, my birth country, which shaped my character.

To America, my adopted country, which gave me freedom and the opportunity to serve.

To God, the Creator of all.

Contents

Foreword by
Senator Bill Frist, MD

I first met Ming Wang in 1999, during my U.S. Senatorial re-
election campaign. As a fellow physician and Harvard Medical
School alumnus, it was with a sense of camaraderie that I learned
of his many accomplishments in science and ophthalmology, but
what I remember most about that first meeting is Ming's love for
our great country that he now calls his own.

Most of us cannot imagine what it would have been like
to grow up without the freedom we enjoy as Americans. Ming
grew up in China during the tumultuous Cultural Revolution,
a period when millions of youth were deported to some of the
poorest parts of the country to endure a lifetime of hard labor and
poverty. The opportunity for education was stripped from Ming
when he was only a teenager. It looked as though his dream of
joining his family's long line of physicians was dead. Yet through
his tenacity and his parents' tireless efforts to instill hope where
it could be found, Ming fought the communist regime and made
his way to the United States to gain freedom and build his future.

Over the years, Ming and I have kept in contact. When I
was the U.S. Senate Majority Leader, he visited D.C. and we
discussed issues of culture concerning the East and West. When

I was teaching at Princeton University, we discussed commerce in China.

We are all capable of making a profound difference when we work hard and put the needs of others before our own. As long as I have known Ming, he has worked hard and selflessly. He has built a prominent ophthalmology practice, and people travel from all over the globe to consult with him about their vision. Many of my own family members have had laser vision surgeries performed by Ming. He also established the Wang Foundation for Sight Restoration, a 501(c)(3) nonprofit charity that has helped many patients—including children—regain their sight. Without Ming's efforts, many of these patients would have lived in total darkness for the rest of their lives.

I, too, have peered into the darkness that is lit only by the hope of healing. In Sudan, on the last day of one of my medical relief trips, I was called in to see a patient recovering from a horrific injury. When I walked into the one-room building where he was recovering, I found him huddled in the corner on a bed. He caught my eye, and his smile pierced the shadows in the dim room. I asked what I could do for him, and he told me that two years before, his wife and two children had been murdered during the civil war in Sudan. He had lost his leg and hand to a land mine only eight days before our conversation. What struck me the most was that even in that moment of devastation, this man had called me in to thank me for being there. He said to me, "Everything I've lost—my family, my leg, my hand—will be worth the sacrifice if my people can someday have what America has: freedom! Thank you ... not for being a doctor, but for being an American."

I carry that man and his story with me, a symbol for what my work as a doctor and a Senator—and what Ming's work as a doctor and a philanthropist—is all about: the freedom, opportunity, and compassion at the heart of who we are as Americans. I consider Dr. Ming Wang a friend and a fine American.

From Darkness to Sight chronicles Ming's remarkable journey from the search for freedom as a teenager in China to building a new life in America, escaping deportation, fighting racial discrimination and financial hardship, and ultimately becoming a world-renowned eye surgeon and philanthropist. His is an inspirational story of moving from East to West, from atheism to faith, from fear, poverty, and discrimination to healing—for himself and others. *From Darkness to Sight* challenges us to imagine a life without freedom, and shows how hope, determination, and faith helped one man take it back.

William H. Frist, MD
Former Majority Leader, United States Senate

Introduction

You can tell a lot about a person by looking into his or her eyes. Think about it. Eyes are the first thing you look at when you meet someone. There is so much you can tell by the way someone looks at you. We make snap judgments about people based on what emotions we perceive through their eyes. Do they look loving, angry, surprised, or fearful? Do they invite you into a conversation or force you to be silent? William Shakespeare wrote that the eyes are the windows to our souls. I believe that! As an ophthalmologist who has spent decades studying eyes and seeking to understand what makes them work organically, biologically, mechanically, and even emotionally, I have learned to communicate with my patients and understand their feelings through their eyes. With God's grace, being able to restore their sight and bring them out of darkness and into light has been the most exhilarating and rewarding experience for me. It is what motivates me; I live for that moment!

For the past 30 years I have built a career out of helping people see, having performed over 55,000 procedures (including those on over 4,000 doctors), and have treated patients from nearly every state in the U.S. and from over 55 countries worldwide. I believe that this is much more than just a career; it is a calling, a calling to serve and give back.

At first, back in my early twenties, just after I had narrowly escaped the treacherous throes of China's Cultural Revolution, I pursued medicine as a family tradition. Having come from a long line of doctors, I had dreamed of being one myself since I was a child. As far back as I could remember, I had watched my grandfather, my father and my mother—who were all doctors—work tirelessly to help their patients. The desire to serve became ingrained in me, but China's Cultural Revolution nearly destroyed that dream.

If, however, you had looked into my eyes when I first arrived here in the United States in 1982, I'm not so sure you would have seen a twenty-one-year-old who had a desire to serve. I had just endured the most difficult journey of my life, nearly losing everything—my family, my education, my home, my dignity, and even my life. My eyes had been filled with fear. China's Cultural Revolution had almost stolen the happiness and freedom of my youth, along with the chance to be educated and to grow up with hopes and dreams. I came to America for freedom.

I'm not exactly sure to what I can fully attribute the dramatic change from darkness to sight in my life . . . but it happened. Maybe it was the determination that had been instilled in me when, as a fourteen-year-old, my education was suddenly cut short and I faced the devastating fate of deportation and a life sentence of poverty and hard labor. Or maybe it was the radical turn of events that occurred with the death of Mao the dictator and the end of the disastrous Cultural Revolution, which catapulted me into an impossible national exam that would determine my fate, once and for all. Or it could have been the tireless devotion of my parents, who fought valiantly to find a future for their son when there was almost no chance for one. Or perhaps it was the dramatic change in my life moving from the East to the West, venturing into the New World to find freedom with only fifty dollars and an English-Chinese dictionary in my pocket, but with a big American dream in my heart. Then again, it was possibly those precious and life-transforming moments, in which so many of my patients had been living in darkness—some even for decades—and had been told they were irreversibly blind and would never be able to see again, patients for whom all other human efforts had failed and I was their last hope, where by the grace of God, along with dedication and hard work, we were able to finally bring them out of darkness and into the light.

Like a grand tapestry, it was perhaps all of these interconnecting events and experiences that brought about dramatic changes in my life, and have been woven into a picture that I am grateful for and treasure more than words can say.

When I look back, I am drawn to remember the many people whose eyes have captured the stories of their lives, and mine.

I remember looking into the eyes of my father as we walked among the beautiful and idyllic landscapes of Hangzhou, prior to the sweeping and destructive Cultural Revolution. His gaze was strong, stable and loving, and he taught me the will to fight in life and never give up.

There were also the eyes of China's dictator, the Red Guards, and militia which were filled with hatred, anger, and violence. Under their repressive and cruel gaze, I almost lost my life at the age of eight!

I will never forget the fearful and wide-eyed stare of the female teacher—one of the few who risked their lives climbing over the school's high wall in the moonlight to escape—as she turned towards us when my dad and I approached her to see if she was my mom.

I am still haunted by the image of a condemned man, his desperate pleading and the distraught look in his eyes as he begged the crowd for mercy, followed by their shrieks and screams as the cardboard sign that hung over his neck was suddenly flipped at a bone-chilling moment of life or death.

I remember encountering the gentle and encouraging gaze of Professor McNesby, who helped me come to America. His eyes were filled with intelligence, care, and respect for equality. In contrast, there were also the prejudice-filled eyes of Professors Miller and Anderson. Fortunately, the discrimination in their eyes only fueled my determination to work harder to prove them wrong.

There were also the eyes of President Ronald Reagan who, like a grandfather, looked at me with kind, gentle, and supportive attention. In those eyes I saw leadership, strength, and vision.

I remember fondly the eyes of my son, so innocent and filled with longing for love; and the eyes of my mom, who was always smiling and encouraging; and the joyful and happy glances from my brother who, at the age of age six, looked up to me. Even though he played the same musical instrument as I did, he had no idea that I was actually playing it for a very different reason—I was fighting for my life!

There have been so many intent gazes, with so much emotion, from so many people throughout my life. I cannot help but consider each one of them an integral part of my life's journey. I am a product of not only the East, but also the West; traditions of both have deeply impacted me. After spending twenty years in China and over thirty years in America, I feel I am now ready to share my story with you. It is a story about survival and determination, from darkness to sight; it is a story about the preciousness of freedom and opportunity.

After having taken care of thousands of patients for nearly three decades, I have come to understand that people who live in physical darkness have the most intense appreciation for sight. This illuminates a common theme that I have experienced over and over in my life. As human beings, we tend to take for granted all the things we have until we no longer have them. In fact, many of us (myself included!) spend the rest of our lives trying to recover the things we have lost, dearly wishing we had treasured them so much more when we did have them.

Who appreciates sight the most? Those who are blind. Who appreciates freedom the most? Those who don't have freedom!

The challenge to all of us here in America today is simply this: can we transcend human history, overcome the inherent weakness of human beings to take things for granted, and become a people who truly appreciate something as precious in life as freedom, *before* we lose it?

If this autobiography inspires you to be more appreciative, and plants even the smallest kernel of hope in your life when it seems that all hope has been dashed, then the effort that was put into the writing of this book will be worth it.

My own eyes have changed dramatically over the years. From whimsical to heartbroken to fearful to intense to hopeful to joyful and full of love, many emotions have flooded my eyes. Today and forevermore, they are now filled with gratitude. I am thankful to those who have encouraged and helped me in the darkest hours of my life. My eyes are filled with appreciation for the cultural roots and traditions I was taught in China when I was young, and for the opportunity and the gift of faith I received here in the West, which has allowed me to see the heart of God and experience personal transformation over the years. Most importantly, I am indebted for the gift of freedom I received from this great country that I now call home. It is a gift not only for me, but for all of us. *From Darkness to Sight* is about how that gift of freedom was lost, and the long and hard-fought journey to gain it back.

Part One

Will She See?

Chapter 1

Maria, Part 1

Everyone in the exam room was hushed and tense, waiting for me to tell them whether Maria would ever be able to see.

My heart sank at what I had just discovered, and I wasn't ready to tell them the bad news. I looked into the damaged eyes of this beautiful young girl and wondered, "Do we really have any chance at all of restoring all of her sight?"

Across me sat Maria Morari, a fifteen-year-old orphan from Moldova in Eastern Europe. With porcelain skin and rounded features, Maria resembled a young Audrey Hepburn. But she had never seen her own face. As far back as she could remember, she had been blind. Even half-hidden behind the examination equipment, I could sense that Maria was tense and apprehensive. She had traveled nearly nine thousand miles to find out whether I could help her see. Having sight would mean freedom and the ability to function independently. Vision meant hope for her future, which was otherwise terribly bleak.

Maria had been living in an orphanage in Balti, Moldova since she was seven, left behind with many other children whose families were too impoverished to care for them. She never saw her mother again after she entered the orphanage. Maria's homeland, nestled between Romania and Ukraine, is one of the poorest nations in Europe. Such widespread poverty has not only torn families apart, but also left many people vulnerable to exploitation. Tens of thousands of women and children have been trafficked as sex slaves, never to be heard from again. Such horror was a likely fate for Maria as well, who would soon be sixteen, the maximum age allowed at the orphanage. Would she end up on the streets just like many other orphan girls before her? She wasn't just young and dependent; she was also blind. What would become of her? I didn't even want to imagine.

While I have never been physically blind myself, I have known all too well the desperate fear of a dark and uncertain future. I grew up in China during one of the most chaotic and dangerous eras in the nation's history—the Cultural Revolution. Like Maria, I was well acquainted with pervasive poverty and crushing hopelessness. I knew the longing Maria must have felt for opportunity and freedom. When I was her age, all my hopes for an education and a promising future were stripped away, and I was left fighting for survival. Maria's plight reminded me so much of those terrible and frightening years of my own life, and now I longed to be able to reassure her that everything would be all right. But all I felt in that moment was doubt and the slimmest hope that she would ever be able to see.

I would never have met Maria if it had not been for Steve and Lynn Hendrich, a couple who had gone to great lengths to bring her to Nashville, Tennessee for medical care. They were determined to pave a path for Maria that wouldn't lead straight to the streets.

During the summer of 2012, the couple and their children had traveled to Chişinău, the capital of Moldova, on a short-term mission trip with Justice and Mercy International (JMI), an organization based in Franklin, Tennessee. The organization exists to bring justice to the poor, the orphaned, and the abandoned—to children like Maria. The family served at a summer camp outside the capital city. Lynn described to me what they encountered. Beyond the field of yellow sunflowers at the camp's entrance were squalid conditions, where orphaned and abandoned children spent school breaks. The Hendriches are people of deep faith, and they believe that God loves and cares for orphans. The family wanted to connect with the kids at the camp and to extend this sense of divine love.

When Lynn first saw Maria, she was sitting alone on a bench while other children played nearby. Lynn told me that Maria just looked so dejected and alone. Lynn and an interpreter joined Maria on the bench, where she remained reticent and withdrawn, staring at the ground.

"Hi, Maria; I'm Lynn."

Maria kept her head down.

"Can I talk to you?" Lynn asked. "I want to see you. Let me see your beautiful face."

When Maria finally raised her head, Lynn noticed that something was terribly wrong with the young girl's eyes. No wonder Maria had sat silently in a corner, her head down and her face hidden from view. Her left pupil was lost behind a milky-white scar, and her right eye moved rapidly from side to side, unable to focus on anything. Through an interpreter, Maria told Lynn that as far back as she could remember, she had been blind. She could see nothing out of her left eye, and could see only shadows and light in her remaining right eye, which had also been diminishing rapidly in recent months. She was afraid that she would soon be plunged into total darkness. Being an orphan and having to leave the orphanage soon and being left on her own, the young teen was distraught and had little hope for any joy in her life.

Lynn's family bonded with Maria during their short stay in Moldova, and they were anxious to help her in any way possible. As soon as the Hendriches returned to the United States, they shared Maria's story with their local congregation, Rolling Hills Community

Church. One church member was so touched by Maria's story that he contacted his eye doctor, who put the Hendriches in touch with me. Besides my cataract and LASIK surgery practice, I also partner with thirty other eye doctors to provide free eye care through a nonprofit organization called the Wang Foundation for Sight Restoration. Foundation doctors perform complex sight restoration surgeries on patients who not only suffer from severe injuries and blindness, but also have no means to pay for the surgeries. I was deeply moved by what happened to Maria. When I was young, many generous people came to my aid when I needed help, and now I had a chance to do the same for this young teen.

Getting Maria to the U.S. wasn't easy. For more than a year, I worked with the Hendriches and JMI to complete all the required documents so Maria could be granted a medical visa. What's more, her mother was still alive, so she needed to be tracked down so we could get her consent. Finally the day came when Maria's school principal brought her the good news: she was bound for America! The Hendriches, whom she had met fifteen months prior, were going to help her come to the U.S. for medical care provided by the Wang Foundation, care that might allow her to see for the first time in her life!

I was thrilled to hear that Maria was finally on her way to the States, and I couldn't wait to see her. I had read her medical files and knew her condition would be very tough to treat, but I was determined to do my very best.

On Monday, October 21, 2013, I was sitting in my office when one of our technicians rushed in.

"She's here."

The technician didn't even have to say Maria's name. I knew. My heartbeat quickened. My entire staff and I had been anticipating this moment for more than a year. And here she was, at last.

I walked quickly to the waiting area, expecting to be met with excitement and enthusiasm, maybe even a big hug. But to my surprise, everyone was sitting so still and quiet. There was Maria, perched timidly on the red couch, hunched over and fidgeting with her fingers. Lynn leaned in as if to console her, and Steve sat nearby. He and Lynn looked up and smiled as I walked in.

"Dr. Wang, this is Maria," Lynn said.

A local interpreter from JMI spoke softly to Maria in her native Romanian tongue. Maria looked up timidly, her eyes white and scarred. She shook my hand feebly. I could tell she was very nervous.

"Welcome, Maria! Let me examine your eyes," I said.

I led the group back to the examination room, Maria clinging to Lynn's arm as she ushered Maria down the hallway.

From the limited medical records I had obtained from Moldova, I knew that Maria's left eye had a detached retina, likely caused by premature birth and malnutrition, which left no hope of any vision in that eye. Her right eye had an advanced, blinding cataract and a history of recurrent inflammation. But once I looked at her eyes through the microscope, I saw the truth. Even though I'd had a general idea of the damage to her right eye prior to her arrival, I wasn't prepared for what I saw. Maria's condition was much worse than I had feared. Besides the severe cataract in her right eye, she also had a scarred cornea, a deformed iris, a constricted pupil, and damage to the eye from long-term inflammation. It was practically a lost cause. What would I tell Steve and Lynn? I didn't want to disappoint them or Maria, since she had come such a long way and they had so much hope.

The examination itself was tough also. Her eyes fluttered rapidly from side to side, a common trait in people who have been blind since birth. Trying to focus on her eyes as they moved made me feel nauseous. Examining through the scarred cornea, I confirmed the retinal detachment in her left eye. I explained to Steve and Lynn that without a properly functioning retina, Maria would never see out of that eye. A surgical procedure to correct a detached retina would normally have already been done in countries more affluent than Moldova. It frustrated me to know that in some parts of the world, even today, so many people still lack access to such basic medical care.

Maria's right eye now remained our only hope. But the cataract was so dense and opaque that I couldn't see beyond it to assess the health of the inside of her eye, the retina, and the optic nerve. What's more, even if the inside of her eye was healthy, the scarred cornea, deformed iris, and inflammatory damage would also make any attempt to surgically remove the cataract very difficult and risky.

I took a deep breath. If I had known just how bad her eyes were, I might have said from the beginning that it wasn't worth bringing her nearly halfway around the globe. But she was here now, and there was no turning back. I just sat there, holding back the news I dreaded disclosing.

My biggest fear in moving forward with surgery was that I might let so many people down, including Maria herself and all her supporters. All the time and effort it took to bring her here, all the immense expectations, and yet it now seemed very likely that all of our efforts would be futile. But like so many other times in my life, I didn't want to give up. I had to trust that God must have arranged all this for a reason, even though that purpose wasn't clear to us just yet.

I sat there praying silently myself. "God, I can only assume you have something in store. You must have a plan for this young teen, who has come all this way and is now sitting here in front of me."

Looking up at Maria and the Hendriches, I said, "Let's finish the exam."

Since I couldn't see through the cataract, we would need to conduct an ultrasound test to see if the retina in her right eye was also detached.

"Is this the decisive test?" asked Steve.

"Yes, it is. If the retina is detached in Maria's right eye as well, then we will have no hope of restoring any sight at all. If the retina is still intact, however, we have a chance."

"Do you think it's likely to be detached?" he asked.

I paused for a moment, reluctant to admit what I knew. "It's highly likely, given her premature birth, malnutrition, poor vision in the right eye ever since birth, lack of adequate eye care, and the fact that she has already had a detached retina in the other eye."

We knew we were facing a nearly impossible situation. We huddled together in the exam room, and I prayed that God would help us accept His will for the outcome of the ultrasound imaging. I was essentially bracing myself and the Hendriches for what would most likely be the ultimate disappointment.

After about 30 minutes, the ultrasound test was completed. Before I examined the results, I took a deep breath. As I exhaled, I looked down at the printout. There was no retinal detachment in her only remaining right eye! Thank God! Relief washed over me. I snapped the folder shut and went to find Maria, Steve, and Lynn. We narrowly survived the first major test and our journey could now continue, but there were still more obstacles to overcome before we would have the chance to give Maria any sight.

I explained to the group that, by the grace of God, the first major step was a success, but it was only the first of ten steps in this extremely difficult process of restoring Maria's sight. I explained to them that the whole process was like tossing a coin; each time it landed, it had to be heads in order to continue to the next toss. And this had to occur ten times in a row. Each of the tosses had only two possible outcomes, success or failure. The failure of any toss along the way would end the entire effort. We had to make it through all the remaining nine tosses in order for Maria to have any chance of seeing again.

"What are the odds that this whole process will succeed?" asked Steve.

"Very slim."

"What happens if we fail?"

"She'll likely lose what little sight she has right now, and will be cast into total darkness for the rest of her life. Right now she can at least see light." Then I added, "However, if we're successful, Maria may be able to see the world around her, and herself, for the first time in her life."

Steve and Lynn looked at each other hesitantly. We sat in silence, feeling the gravity of the situation and the tremendous impact this decision would have on Maria and her future.

"You don't have to make a decision right now. Please go home and pray about it," I said.

I wish I could have been more reassuring, but I had to prepare everyone for the worst. Deep down, however, I was still harboring a slim hope that we might succeed. I had an inkling that God was up to something because He had brought us all this far. Though a successful outcome seemed nearly impossible through human effort alone, I believed God could step in and reveal His strength. Over the years in my life, I had learned, time and again, that it is often in especially difficult situations like this, when our own attempts seem to have reached their limit, that we really have the chance to encounter God's true power.

After days of praying and careful consideration, I have decided to recommend the surgery to Maria. She and the Hendriches concurred. Even though we were all aware of the risk of the surgery and that the chance of success was slim, we knew that God was in control!

On Thursday, November 7, 2013, a bit over two weeks after that initial examination of Maria's eyes, we came together again at an outpatient surgery center near my office in downtown Nashville.

We had arrived at a crossroads. Inside the surgery center, a bold red line on the floor marked the entrance to the operating room area, a line no one could cross unless properly scrubbed and committed to surgery.

"This is it," I said. "The point of no return."

After I went over the surgical plan one last time, everyone gathered in a circle and held hands around Maria to pray. Maria had been prepped for surgery and was lying on a gurney, wearing a powder-blue surgical cap and covered by a white blanket. Steve and Lynn prayed for me to receive wisdom and guidance during the surgery. Knowing that we had such a slim chance of success, I prayed in earnest that God would help us do our best and that He would grant us a sense of peace, regardless of the outcome. In essence, I was preparing the group to accept what was likely inevitable failure.

As I walked through the doors to the operating room, which was the color of soft sunlight, I let go of all the anxiety and nervousness I had been feeling. Now was the time for complete focus. Maria's vision and her future were in my hands. As I looked at Maria, blind and asleep on the stretcher, I was reminded of myself at her age, when my own future was crushed with little warning. I remembered vividly and painfully the darkness in which I was confined for many horrible years, and I resolved to do my best so that Maria would not also be trapped in such darkness.

I had suffered greatly during the Chinese Cultural Revolution, and I had gone through so much in my life that I wondered how I had been able to pull myself through all those difficulties. During the darkest days of my teenage years, while many others got crushed and even perished, I had fortunately survived. Why had God allowed so much hardship to take place, hardships that had at several points in my life nearly destroyed me? Did He have a purpose for me, and if so, what was it?

Sterile surgical gloves stretched over my hands. The tips of my fingers were still scarred from frostbite I had endured while playing the Chinese erhu violin during that bleakest winter of my life, nearly four decades earlier. I was reminded of the long and arduous journey thirty-four years ago that had brought me thousands of miles around the globe to America, from my hometown: Hangzhou, China.

Part Two

Growing Up in China

Chapter 2

Hangzhou

"What is my child doing out here on the street all by himself?" my mother asked in panic. My caretakers rushed outside, apologizing profusely. I beamed up at them from my high chair, oblivious to the adults' concern.

Since both of my parents had active professional lives, a local family looked after me while my parents were at work. This family had several kids of their own, so they just left me alone in a traditional Chinese high chair, a heavy mahogany cylinder that stood a few feet off the ground, with a wooden board midway inside that allowed a one-year-old to stand up and grab its rim without falling out.

Even at that young age, I wasn't content to be left in a dark corner of the house. I wanted to explore, to see the world around me. Although I was just a baby, I figured out a way to actually move the high chair forward by pushing my little body back and forth in circular motions, which caused the cylinder to make small forward movements. I worked at this all day until I moved the cylinder, inch by inch, across the entire floor of my caretakers' home, and eventually onto the street outside where my mother was shocked to find me. It must have been an amusing sight to behold—a little baby ferociously rocking a high chair back and forth and maneuvering it on the street through fast-traveling cars and bicycles. Needless to say, that family kept a much better eye on me from then on.

I was too young at the time to actually remember this incident, but growing up, my mom often told me the story.

"You were very different than other kids from the very start," she said. "You were always curious about things and determined to do your very best at whatever you set your mind to."

Many years later, that same kind of singular focus, innate tenacity, and relentless determination would help me wrestle myself out of much rougher spots than the dark corner of my caretakers' house.

My parents were both doctors, and my father came from a long line of physicians. My dad, Zhen-sheng Wang, grew up in Anhai, an ancient town in the Fujian Province on the southeast coast of China. My grandfather, Ding-pei Wang, was a famous doctor in Anhai and was renowned for his generosity. The mayor of Anhai named him a "Doctor with a Heart to Help," an official proclamation honoring his tireless dedication to the community throughout his career. When I was a boy, I often asked my grandfather to tell me stories of how he had valiantly treated wounded soldiers, displaced refugees, and countless peasants during the turmoil of the Second World War. As I listened, I often ran my finger along the wood grain of the plaques from grateful patients that hung on his walls.

All nine members of my grandfather's family were physicians. Growing up among healers, my father was a doctor at heart himself from a young age. He told me that when he was still in elementary school, he created a small clinic at home where he treated his young friends' minor injuries.

My dad met my mom, A-lian Xu, at Zhejiang Medical University in Hangzhou during the summer of 1953, when they were both first-year medical students. My mother didn't come from a family of doctors as my father did. Her inspiration to pursue medicine came from witnessing how severe illnesses ravaged villagers throughout the countryside near her hometown of Zhangzhou in the Fujian Province. In medical school, she chose to specialize in infectious diseases like polio, smallpox, and schistosomiasis, a disease caused by parasitic worms. She felt it was her duty—as did my father, my grandfather and my grandfather's family—to be part of the solution to such terrible afflictions that predominantly hurt the poor.

My parents graduated from Zhejiang Medical University in 1958. Both outstanding students, they were employed at the school and its teaching hospital immediately following graduation. They married later that same year.

I was born early on the sunny morning of October 24, 1960. At first, my mother wasn't sure what to name me. But as she lay in bed after delivering me, she saw the sun rising over the horizon, setting the town ablaze in hues of gold and pink, so she decided my name would be Ming-xu, meaning "bright sun rising in the east."

Despite the sunny morning on which I was born, I came into the world during one of the bleakest periods of modern Chinese history. In 1958, two years before I was born, Mao Zedong, the founder of modern China and the beloved leader of the Communist Party, had launched the Great Leap Forward. All of China's citizens were called upon to contribute to this aggressive attempt to catapult China into the modern Industrial Age. Farms were abandoned and peasants were put to work producing steel in backyard furnaces. The result was disastrous. By the time I was born in 1960, China was in the throes of the worst famine in human history. Within only three years, an estimated thirty-six million people perished.

While the famine was worse in rural areas, food was scarce everywhere, and poverty persisted for years after the devastating

Great Leap Forward was halted. Around the time I was born, my parents' combined monthly salary was only one hundred and six yuan, or thirteen dollars. I remember that, in my earliest years, our family subsisted on mostly rice and a few vegetables, since we couldn't afford meat. On one weekend, my parents used some of their savings to buy just one cookie. So rare and precious was this treat that they split the cookie in half, and gave me one half, and split the other half between themselves. My parents were always very loving and dedicated to my well-being, so although we had very little, they made the most of it. Additionally, it's hard to feel poor or unhappy when you grow up in Hangzhou, one of China's oldest and most beautiful cities.

Hangzhou, the capital city of the Zhejiang Province on the east coast, is located just south of Shanghai. My family lived on the north side of the city, at the base of a mountain near the remnants of an ancient city wall. My dad often took me on walks up that mountain after supper, when the town was quiet and crickets were singing. We walked among the dense trees, our path lit by moonlight. Dad walked slowly and patiently as I took tiny steps, jumping into shadows as if they were puddles that might splash into the light.

My father told me that our planet was a round ball orbiting in space around the sun. He pointed toward the night sky and explained that the moon traveled in circles around the earth.

"Daddy, why then doesn't the moon fall down?" I asked. I was just a toddler at the time, brimming with curiosity.

He thought for a moment. "The law of gravity keeps it there. When you're older, you'll understand." My father was a doctor, not a physicist, but he loved science.

"How come the moon is so bright?"

"The moon is like a mirror, reflecting light from the fiery sun," he said.

I imagined us walking atop this big ball of dirt, alongside a ball of fire and a shiny mirror suspended in space. My curiosity was insatiable, and for every question I posed, my dad offered a rational and scientific answer. There was never a mention of anything mystical, nor of a higher power or a creator. During these years, China had no God and virtually no religion, besides the doctrine of communism. My childlike questions about life and the world were always met with simple logic and science. My parents nurtured my curiosity and encouraged me to ask as many questions as I could come up with.

One day while walking through the city streets with my mom, I watched with fascination as construction workers dug into the ground, into this giant dirt ball that Dad called earth. I wondered what would happen if they just kept digging and digging straight down, and where they would end up if they reached the other side of the earth. Would people there walk upside down? What did they look like? I never imagined back then that one day I would actually live there, America, which was on the other side of the planet.

When I was four, my family moved to a three-story dormitory building about a mile from West Lake, the heart and soul of Hangzhou. Over the years, my parents and I spent many Sunday afternoons walking along the lake's tranquil shores. I ran ahead of them along the trails, running my arm through the long, wispy willow branches that drooped down to lotus pools and lily ponds on the water's surface. My dad told me that West Lake's stunning scenery had been a refuge and source of inspiration for poets and painters for thousands of years. He recounted the legends and histories of the ancient bridges, pavilions, and pagodas. The lake stretched far across the horizon, where misty hills and peaks rose up in the distance. Every spring, bright green camphor trees enlivened the hills, and in late summer, I would deeply inhale the rich scent of osmanthus flowers that bloomed in bursts of yellow.

Compared to the idyllic beauty around West Lake, our living arrangements were much less inspiring. We lived in a drab, concrete dormitory close to the medical school where my parents worked. In those days, it was dangerous to express anything that resembled a bourgeois aesthetic. The clothes we wore were all simple, utilitarian "Mao Suits," usually blue or gray. Buildings were uniformly boxy and gray. Despite the natural paradise nearby, no such beauty or elegant decor was allowed inside anyone's home. Instead, most homes had only reverent portraits of Chairman Mao, photos of workers laboring in the fields, and maybe a few black-and-white family photos. Everything had to be clean, bare, orderly, and strictly working-class.

Our young family shared a one-room apartment that was about a hundred and thirty square feet on the second floor of the building, alongside fifteen other families on our floor, with whom we all shared one single bathroom down the hall. The bathroom was a big room with three sinks on one end and three stalls on the other. The toilets had to be manually rinsed out a few times a day. There were no showers or baths. In warm weather, I simply washed off with a hose out on the street. When it was cold, we bathed at communal bathhouses or at home by filling up a large basin with buckets of cold water drawn from the communal bathroom down the hall, and then warmed on the stove outside our door.

Half the time our communal bathroom had no running water at all. In the winter, the pipes often froze, and in the summer, given the limited water supply and the large number of families consuming it, the water pressure was so low that the water flow often couldn't reach the second and third floors of the building. When that happened, all forty-five families in the three-story building would all descend and converge on the first floor's single communal bathroom. People held buckets and waited patiently for hours in long lines to get water. We also had no air conditioning or heat in our building, so the inside temperature was always the same as it was on the outside. In the summer, my father and I walked around our apartment and in the communal hallway bare-chested, and in the winter, I had to wear my thick quilted coat outside and inside, even in bed!

The window from our apartment looked onto a field full of lower-lying houses. I would often drag a little stool close to the wall and climb up so that I could look out. Since we had no television, I would cross my arms on the windowsill, rest my chin on my hands, and enjoy the "scenes" of the everyday life that I watched through the window. They were my TV shows as a child. What I saw was an area very crowded with buildings and people. I saw neighbors coming out of the back doors of their homes to beat the dust from clothes with wooden poles. No one owned washers or dryers, so clothes were cleaned by hand using soap and a washboard, and then they were rinsed and hung to dry. For our laundry, my father crafted a rectangular frame using wire and bamboo sticks that extended way out our window, before angling sharply back to the top of the window frame. We weren't the only family making such creative use of our window. All our neighbors had similar drying contraptions sticking out of their windows as well. On any given day, the dormitory's outer wall was full of makeshift flags of all colors and shapes, all waving patient allegiance to the rudimentary conditions in which we lived inside that building.

Being packed together so tightly, however, did allow us to know our neighbors very well. The building was filled with kids of all ages. There were no video games, electronics, or TV, and none of us owned any toys, but that didn't matter. In those barren times, my imagination came alive. When it was warm, I led groups of kids in games of soccer and hide-and-seek outside. When it was too cold to play outdoors, I told stories and staged shows inside our one-room apartment to entertain my friends. I used scissors to create a miniature kingdom—including city walls, houses, and a castle—out of cardboard and paper. I made hand puppets from fabric scraps and clay heads that fit over my little fingers. My parents' bed served as a stage, and mosquito netting that hung from the bedposts became the theater curtain. I tied a string across the front of the bed, on which I hung the bedsheet. I jumped onto the stage (the bed) and hid myself behind the bedsheet. Neighborhood kids gathered in front of the bed and sat on stools, watching the shows with fascination, as puppets dancing on my fingers acted out legendary Chinese tales. I particularly loved the Monkey King character, a fabled animal who was creative, tenacious, and overcame obstacles during his many adventures to the West. My mother often came home from work to find us huddled around her bed. She would wait patiently in the dark room until I had finished the show, clapping wholeheartedly when the makeshift theater curtain closed, the lights came back on, and my hand puppets took their bows.

My younger brother, Ming-yu, was born in the summer of 1968. One day I came home to see a bunch of grownups huddled around my parents' bed. I wriggled my way through the group, pushing my shoulders against their legs until I was right next to the bed. My new baby brother was bundled up in the middle of the mattress. He was born three weeks premature, so his face was full of wrinkles, and I couldn't understand why a newborn baby would have them, so I called him "little old man." But I also gave him his real name. My name, Ming-xu, meant "bright sun," so I suggested that my parents name him Ming-yu, meaning "bright universe." I was the sun, but I wanted him to be something even bigger.

Since I was eight years older, I often took care of my little brother, picking him up from daycare the way my mother used to come for me when I was a toddler. I had a key tied to a string that hung around my neck to let us into our apartment when my parents were still at work. My first task after coming home from school was to prepare the rice for dinner. We didn't have any kitchens in the building, but there was a small coal-burning stove in the hallway outside the door of each apartment. While little Ming-yu played, I washed the rice in a bowl of water, lit the stove, and placed the bowl on the flame to cook. At times I would leave the bowl on the flame longer and the water would boil over. The neighbor's grandmother across the hall would then call me, and I would return and lift the lid just in time to avoid burning the rice or overflowing the water that could extinguish the stove's flame.

In the evenings, my family ate dinner together, sitting on small stools around a square wooden table. After dinner, my parents pored over the mounds of books that were crowded among the sparse furniture in our apartment. There were only two kinds of books, though: my parents' medical textbooks and communist books like *The Quotations of Mao Zedong*—also known as his "Little Red Book"—and other selected works by Mao. No other books were allowed—no literature, no poetry, no art—nothing that failed to promote the prevailing Marxist ideology.

But my dad and I shared a little secret. We had one other little book in our house hidden behind the red books on the shelves, a book of poetry featuring the four famous poets of China's Tang Dynasty. Dad wanted me to learn and relish the ancient verses of our culture. One of the four poets was Li Bai, who lived in the eighth century and often wrote of finding companionship with the moon, that celestial body that had so captured my young imagination. I read those poems so often that I can still recite them today, fifty years later.

One of Li Bai's verses says, "If one wants to enjoy life, one has to make the best of it." My spirit of making the best of any circumstance was embedded in me in childhood and would carry me through the many years that laid ahead. We were materially poor, yet we were rich in love and affection for each other. My parents nurtured an environment where I was not reprimanded or restrained for being different from other kids, and where I was allowed to explore and ask questions freely. It gave me the emotional security to dream about the future. I imagined myself one day wearing the same white coat my father wore in the hospital where he worked. I put together a little medical kit that I carried with me everywhere. My parents brought me old instruments, medicine bottles, and other supplies, and I also filled my tin box with tweezers, iodine, cotton swabs, cloth bandages, and herbal ointment. I treated my young compatriots' injuries the way my father had done when he was a boy. Growing up to be a doctor was my constant childhood dream. During those years, I often thought what an honor it would be to continue my family's medical tradition.

Though I harbored these young hopes, what I didn't know at the time was that another impending disaster would soon follow the treacherous famine that had claimed so many lives across China. By the time I started elementary school, a fierce political storm was brewing. Its calamitous force would grow more powerful and widespread in just a few years, leaving a lasting devastation across the country. No family would be left unharmed—including ours.

Chapter 3

The Black Dot and My Mother

"**D**o you want to go to jail? What did you do in school? Don't you want to live anymore?!" My mother's eyes were wide with fear.

I had just arrived home from school. I climbed the stairs to the second floor of our dormitory building and was approaching our apartment when she emerged from inside, frenzied and upset.

My lower jaw trembled. I couldn't imagine what the matter was. How could I be in any trouble? I was a good student, held the high rank of class monitor, was well known and liked, and I hadn't done anything wrong.

I followed Mom into the apartment where Dad was pacing back and forth, agitated and nervous. He asked me to sit down and told me that my school had just discovered that a student had committed a treasonous and counterrevolutionary act . . . and I was found to be the culprit!

Being classified as a counter-revolutionary meant jail or even death, so I was petrified. I shivered and cried over the trouble in which I had found myself, and I had no idea at all what I had actually done.

During that time in China, trouble was everywhere. The disastrous famine and death brought about by the Great Leap Forward had proven Chairman Mao was tragically wrong. To salvage the country, several party leaders implemented a number of reforms, and within a few years the economy had started to rebound. But Mao feared he was on the brink of losing his own power, so in response he arrested his top lieutenants and reasserted his authority over the party. He then launched the infamous Great Proletarian Cultural Revolution to more forcefully purge all of his opponents, and pursue the creation of a society ruled by the working class, who would be loyal only to him.

The first goal of the Cultural Revolution was to eliminate higher education. Mao himself had received only an elementary-school education, so he hated anyone who was more educated than he was. He regarded knowledge and education as the source of evil and political dissidence, something that must be crushed. Just as I was starting elementary school in 1966, universities across China were all shut down. People with knowledge and education were labeled the "stinking ninth class," the absolute lowest social ranking, beneath even the criminals, prostitutes, and beggars. Education and urban living were believed to weaken the communist cause, so millions of young people who should have been attending colleges were instead forcefully deported to the poorest corners of the country and condemned to a lifetime of poverty and hard labor. To be deported for the purpose of "re-education through labor" meant working in harsh and impoverished conditions, earning only a dollar or two a month for the rest of one's life. Such meager wages might buy a spot in a room with a dozen other people and a bit of rice to eat every day. Deportation was a life sentence, with no chance of ever being allowed to return to the cities. Many of these bright young people were never seen or heard from again, and some even committed suicide to avoid such heartless deportation.

In my neighborhood, I watched the parents of an older teenager weep and beg as they pleaded with local communist leaders not to deport their daughter. I saw the father twist his cap in his hands, as the mother hung on him and begged him to do something. And then one day the teenager was gone. There was nothing the family could do, because the government had changed her so-called "registration" to an impoverished and distant area of the country, so she would be forced to live there forever. The registration process was strict, allowing the communist government absolute control over its citizens. A person could only be legally registered in one geographic location, and therefore had to live there. One had absolutely no right to live anywhere else unless the government actually changed one's registration site. If that teenager hadn't followed the deportation order and instead had stayed in our hometown, she would have been sent to jail. Food rations were also tied to these registrations, so if the teen tried to live anywhere other than where she was registered, she wouldn't receive any food rations, and would starve. No one could escape such deportation once the communist cadres changed the location of the registration that was designated by the government. One has no choice but to live in the registered town, and only there, for the rest of one's life. Over the course of the ten-year Cultural Revolution (or "Cultural Holocaust," as it is sometimes called), the lives of an estimated twenty million youth were destroyed by this deportation program.

The nation's young people were also called upon to revive the revolutionary spirit and help Mao get rid of his opponents. Young students had mobilized into a regimen of the infamous Red Guards, denoted by red cloth bands emblazoned with gold script that were wrapped around their left arms. This young Gestapo-like organization was charged with uprooting old traditions, customs, and ideas, and exposing anyone who showed any signs of capitalist, elitist, or bourgeois tendencies. Red Guard students destroyed historic monuments and sites of cultural heritage throughout the country, attacked and humiliated their teachers and principals by parading them through public squares with signs around their necks, spitting on them and kicking them as they passed by. Posters everywhere denounced teachers, and many were jailed or even executed, while others committed suicide. Mobs of kids in excited revolt excoriated and shamed the very people who had been preparing them for the future. Students burned their textbooks and boycotted classes. Schools across the whole country were in utter disarray.

By 1968, the effects of the Cultural Revolution had spread from higher education to all sectors of society. Red Guards, workers, and peasants had overtaken schools, factories, hospitals, and businesses. Those with expertise and authority to run these places were violently replaced with peasants and unskilled workers who were only equipped with their Marxist ideologies. My school, the Second Elementary School of Yan An, had also been taken over by uneducated factory workers who had no idea how to run a school. They ousted our principal and changed our curriculum; instead of science and the humanities, we could only study communist teachings.

Every day at lunchtime, my young classmates and I assembled in the track-and-field area to recite Chairman Mao's teachings and practice the "loyalty dance," demonstrating devotion to our beloved leader. Each session was an opportunity for the Red Guards to drill into us the principles of the party and the glorious attributes of its paramount leader. I took my place in one of many long rows of students, all of us dressed in blue pants, white shirts, and red neckties. We moved and marched and spoke in unison. Standing over us and shouting with enthusiasm, the Red Guards reminded us of how Mao had founded modern China, had saved us from the oppression of feudalistic lords and Western powers who had humiliated China for a century and a half, had united a country torn apart by civil war, and had championed the proletariat. We were therefore obligated to emulate him always, and to seek our country's greater good above all else, even our individual lives.

Living in a one-party system is difficult to imagine for anyone who is used to having choices. In the United States, people are allowed to have opinions about things; they can align themselves with any number of ideologies; and they can vote along a number of party lines. No such choices existed for us in China in those days. We couldn't even choose to be a member of the one ruling party, the Communist Party, as it was a very difficult yet desirable status to earn because of its privilege and the favors bestowed upon its members. As an ordinary citizen, it was dangerous to be considered at odds with the party. Either we supported the ruling party, or our lives would be at stake. Dissent was simply not tolerated, and dissidents were often executed.

Like all the other students, I couldn't help but be swept up in the hysteria. When the factory workers who had overtaken my elementary school targeted certain teachers, I had to go along with all the other students. One fateful day, on order of the Red Guards, I wrote on a classroom windowsill, "Down with Teacher Zhao! Long live Chairman Mao!" The Red Guards had singled out this teacher and ordered all of us to oppose and criticize him. I didn't know why we had to denounce a teacher who was so devoted to his students, but I had no choice except to obey the ruling authorities.

But when I got home from school, my mother's frantic, fearful questions caused me to regret what I had done earlier that day.

"What in the world did you do at school?" she asked, her voice high-pitched with fear.

She and Dad had heard from someone at my school that I had written something incendiary and counter-revolutionary on the windowsill.

"What did you write, Ming?!" Dad asked, his voice full of anger.

"Nothing bad!" I said. "Just revolutionary slogans."

"Your teachers found 'Down with Chairman Mao!' written in your handwriting. Did you write that?" he asked, his voice quivering.

My face became white and cold. Someone must have smudged the middle portion of the two sentences I had written in chalk on the windowsill!

The school was on the verge of declaring me a counter-revolutionary, an eminent danger to the beloved paramount leader, a threat to the proletarian society, a reactionary who should be jailed or executed!

I was only eight.

Shivering with fear, I re-wrote the two slogans on a piece of paper so my parents could see for themselves that what I had actually written wasn't counter-revolutionary at all.

Later that evening, after an intense and nervous discussion with Mom, Dad said, "We have to go and talk to the school. If we don't clear up this misunderstanding, Ming-xu will have a black dot in his file for the rest of his life."

The "file" was the official record of your entire life. You would never be allowed to actually see it yourself, since it was a secret document held by the Communist Party. Its content documented all of your actions in the past and determined your class and status, your eligibility for favors and promotions, and whether you were a threat to the government and the party.

"How big is the black dot?" I was afraid that this so-called black dot was going to follow me for life!

For many nights I had nightmares of a black dot forming and coming after me. I saw a large blob of calligraphy ink rising up from a bottle on a desk at the local party office, rolling along streets and through courtyards until it found my home, where it would swing itself up the side of the building, reaching the pants and shirts hanging on the laundry contraption, then through the window and into our room, where it would finally find me and haunt me, casting shadows on the wall, just like the puppets had done when they danced on my fingers. It would never, ever leave me alone!

Later on I learned that of course what my father meant by a black dot was not a physical dot, but a statement put in my personal file that would label me a reactionary. As a result, my future would be irrevocably stained. No educational institution would ever accept me, and no company would ever hire me. A black dot in my file in the communist system meant a future of utter darkness. This one accusation, this grave misunderstanding, was set to ruin the rest of my life!

My parents couldn't sleep for nights on end. From my little bed a few feet away, I could hear them toss and turn, whispering to each other, their voices strained and worried.

"We have another meeting with the school tomorrow," my mother said one night. "I hope they'll listen to us. They have to. We just can't let Ming-xu's life be ruined like this."

I couldn't sleep either. I lay in bed completely gripped by fear, staring toward the window to see if the ominous black dot had yet found me. I knew of older students who had been labeled counter-revolutionaries, had received the dreaded black dot in their files, and had committed suicide. I felt like I was in a free fall, scared and confused. But before I could completely fall apart, my parents quickly reacted to the crisis.

They took me with them to several meetings with school officials in an attempt to gain their pardon.

"Please accept our deepest apologies," my mother said. "Ming-xu is just a child. He meant nothing by these scribbles which someone else has altered to make them look bad."

"Whatever you do," my father pleaded, "please don't put a black dot in his file. Punish him in any way you deem necessary, but please spare him that mark."

The Red Guards left us waiting while they held a long, closed-door meeting in another room to determine the fate of the rest of my life. We were filled with dread. Every second we had to wait felt like an eternity.

Finally, one of the school officials returned. "We acknowledge that perhaps Ming-xu did not write these words intentionally," he said.

I felt as if a thousand pounds had been lifted off my shoulders. My parents cried tears of relief.

"But, this is still a very a serious offense," the official continued. "Ming-xu will have to face certain grave consequences if he wants to avoid a black dot in his file."

While I did narrowly escape being declared a counter-revolutionary and prosecution, my punishment was nonetheless very severe. Back at school, I was demoted to the bottom of my third-grade class. All of my honors were stripped from me. I was disqualified for a prestigious national award for academic excellence that I had worked so hard to achieve, and had already won in prior years. My classmates didn't quite understand what had happened, but they knew I must have done something really bad, so they avoided me for months, as if I had an infectious disease. While I was relieved that I was able to avoid the black dot, I still felt utterly humiliated and alone.

My family had always stressed the importance of study and knowledge. Even Chairman Mao himself once said, "Study every day and keep on improving." Working hard in school was a crucial key to good employment and a promising future. I clung to that belief and kept going even in those dark days, grateful for the love and support from my family. I may have been relegated to the bottom of my class, but together we had fought off the black dot! I figured that as long as I kept studying hard and maintaining top grades, I would be able to get back on my feet again.

My father continued to practice internal medicine at the hospital. In those volatile times, being a doctor who was loyal to the government and had no particular social or financial standing kept him safe and necessary to society. That is, until the Red Guards threatened to close the medical college where he and Mom taught classes.

One night during dinner, one of my mom's colleagues hurried into our house in a panic.

"We need your help, A-lian; the Red Guards are about to destroy the university and all the labs!" he urged.

Mom bolted up from her stool, ready to run out the door, but Dad held her back.

"Don't go, A-lian. It's too dangerous!" he implored.

"I have to go. I won't stand by while they destroy my lab and classroom."

She hurried out the door with her colleague. Shortly after that, Dad decided to go himself as well. He told me to stay home and quickly went out the door. He wanted to find Mom and keep her from danger. I ran out behind him and clung to his leg.

"Dad, please don't leave me alone!" I didn't understand what was happening and I was scared. Reluctantly he took my hand, and we hurried out of the building and made our way toward the university.

Along the route to the school, a parade of trucks full of Red Guards rolled by. They wore bamboo hard hats and waved metal clubs, shouting revolutionary slogans: "Long live Chairman Mao! Destroy the bourgeois schools! Down with teachers and the stinking ninth class!"

I could sense my father was becoming more nervous. His pace quickened, and I struggled to keep up with him.

"Quick Ming-xu, run!" he shouted over his shoulder. "We have to make it to the university before those trucks do!"

I ran as hard as I could, trying to keep up with his long strides. My lungs burned and my eyes watered. When we arrived at the university gate, my heart was pounding and I could hardly breathe. As I gasped for air, I looked around and saw that a sentry of Red Guards had already arrived and blockaded the entrance. Under a big, bleak, and glaring spotlight, as teachers emerged from inside the university, the Red Guards beat them with iron clubs until they were writhing on the ground and screaming in pain. And they then continued the beatings until the teachers' skulls cracked wide open. There was blood everywhere. I was so shocked that I squeezed my eyes shut and started whimpering. Dad snatched me into his arms and hurried away.

I peered nervously through squinted eyes to see where we were going. Dad ran to the back of the university, where we stood beneath high walls. It was very dark, but in the moonlight I could see the silhouettes of people climbing over the wall to escape for their lives. I recognized many of them—other professors who worked with my mom. Dad and I waited eagerly, scanning the faces of those climbing over the wall, hoping to see Mom among them climbing to safety. I would never forget the fearful wide eyes and scared stare of one of the teachers when we approached her to see if she was my mother. I had nightmares for weeks afterward, in which a ghostly woman stared at me with wide eyes and that petrified expression.

More and more people climbed over the wall and escaped, but Mom wasn't among them.

"Dad, can we please go home now?" I asked him over and over again, my voice quavering. I was frightened. What if the Red Guards found us here? Would Dad and I get beaten too?

"Ming-xu! How can we go home when your mom is still inside the school?" he exclaimed, his voice tense and angry. Then, sensing my fear, he patted my back to soothe me, and soon I fell asleep on his shoulder, totally exhausted.

When I woke up, I was lying on the floor of our apartment. I heard moaning and groaning, the sounds of someone in severe pain. I raised myself up and looked toward the direction of the sound, and saw my mom lying on the bed in agony, on top of bloody sheets. I froze, too shocked to know what to do.

When he noticed I was awake, Dad came over and told me that Mom didn't escape but instead chose to stay behind to protect the lab, which contained decades of her and others' medical research. When the Red Guards finally found her there, they beat her with their iron clubs until she collapsed in a bloody heap, and left her to die. Luckily, among the Red Guards was one of

Mom's own students who couldn't bear to see his teacher being beaten to death. Risking his life and reputation as a revolutionary, he carried my mom through a little-known exit and brought her home, where Dad was able to stop her bleeding and bandage her. This young man, to whom our family owed my mother's life, had already left before I awoke. He never gave my father his name.

The human cruelty that I witnessed that day is seared in my memory. The magnitude of what happened to those teachers and my mother—the atrocious behavior of the Red Guards who beat and killed so many of the teachers, and who broke and bloodied my mom's body and pushed her to the brink of death—stayed with me for many, many years.

For a long time afterward, Dad slept on the floor with me so Mom could have the whole bed to recuperate, as she was suffering from many fractures and bruises throughout her body and lay there paralyzed. After several months of convalescing at home, Mom needed more hands-on care than Dad or I could give her, so she was transported to my grandmother's home in the Fujian Province, a two-day train ride from Hangzhou. For two years, I only saw my mom during my summer breaks. She was bedridden most of the time, only able to get up and walk in the second year of her recovery. To this day, my mother still has chronic pain throughout her body, and the tip of her right index finger remains permanently crooked from the beating.

No sooner did my mom finally recover than we lost her again. One day, early in 1971, we received dreaded news. In retaliation for her attempting to protect the lab and classroom, my mother would be deported, taken from us forever. But one of the party officials made a show of leniency and said that since my mother had two children at home, they would demonstrate the great love and generous mercy of their beloved leader Chairman Mao. Instead of being banished for the rest of her life, my mom would only be deported for two years to the destitute countryside to work for little pay as a "barefoot doctor," one of many physicians who treated peasants in rudimentary facilities and worked alongside them in the fields.

My parents' combined salary around that time was one hundred and eighteen yuan, or fifteen dollars, a month. Though they fared much better than many one-wage families, they had to pour all their savings into paying an elderly woman to help care for my little brother. For two years my father lived without his wife, and my brother and I without our mom. She was only allowed to come home once a year, and we wrote letters in between visits. Our tiny home now had a gaping hole.

The inhumanity of the Cultural Revolution spared no one. The first five years had been especially cruel. As schools were shut down and millions of students deported, many young people committed suicide rather than be exiled from their families for life. To stem this terrible tide of death, the government had no choice but to ease their grip to some degree, and they revised the deportation policy so that parents with more than one child could choose one of their children to stay home. This "chosen one" would be exempt from deportation, provided the child could find gainful employment in the city within a short period of time. Forcing parents to choose one of their children to be protected, knowing the rest would be displaced to face a life of destitution, was cruel and inhumane. How could any parent make such an impossible choice?

Not long before I finished junior high, my father came home from the hospital looking exhausted and dejected. He had always been the logical, quiet, decisive parent. I had never seen him so down.

That night, I heard my parents arguing in desperate whispers.

"Ming-xu will finish junior high in just two months! We have to make a decision about which child to choose," my father stressed.

"Choose Ming-xu. Let him be the one to stay," my mother begged.

My brother, Ming-yu, who was eight years younger than me, was only six years old at that time, so Mom reasoned that she and Dad would still have eight years before Ming-yu was old enough to face deportation. She hoped things might change before then, or if not, it would give them time to figure out a way to protect him as well.

"But, if we choose Ming-xu, then in order for him to take advantage of this 'chosen one' policy, he would have to quit school immediately and not attend high school, because if he did, he could be deported right after graduation, since the government has stated that they may discontinue the 'chosen one' policy next year," Dad said. Then he added in a sad voice, "But on the other hand if Ming-xu doesn't go on to high school and earn his diploma, he'll never be able to find a decent job."

"That's still better than being deported!" Mom's voice edged higher.

"But it's so cruel to just cut off his education like this! He's a star student. When he grows up and wonders why his education got cut short like this, what will we say to him? He won't have a decent career, and it will be hard for him to have a family. He will hate us for the rest of his life, and I will hate myself."

"He won't hate you," she said. "He'll know that with the horrible choices you were given at this time, you made the best decision you could to protect him."

I had known my whole life that education and getting into high school and then college was the pinnacle of success, not just for me but also for my parents and for the Wang family as a whole. Winning a fiercely competitive spot in a university meant a guaranteed job at one of the state-owned firms. Since the universities were shut down due to the Cultural Revolution, a high school diploma was the highest education anyone could get at that time. Without a high school education, destitution was guaranteed in a life of menial labor, earning only thirty yuan— or four dollars—a month.

My father let out a deep sigh full of turmoil and heartache. "If he wasn't such a good student, this wouldn't bother me so much. But he's so motivated and has worked so hard, especially in the last several years, after being humiliated, demoted, and nearly declared a counter-revolutionary with that horrible school slogan incident! He has come back from all of that and now has a chance to have a good education, and we are going to intentionally destroy all of it, and his life?!"

We sat quietly at dinner, a simple meal of rice, vegetables, and scrambled eggs. My father looked at me, his eyes brimming with sadness and uncertainty.

"My son, never in my life would I have ever imagined I would have to intentionally cut off your education like this! I hope you understand how much it kills us to make this terrible decision to not let you continue your education into high school."

So in the spring of 1974, at the age of fourteen, my education came to an abrupt end as soon as I finished ninth grade. Even though I was the chosen one, I still had to find gainful employment within a year or two, or I could still face deportation. But, with only a junior-high education as such, finding a decent job would be nearly impossible.

My parents had always fought for me, even when it seemed that there was no hope of winning. Once again, they would come to my rescue, helping me out of this dark corner in unique, creative, and occasionally even illegal ways.

Chapter 4

Running from Ghosts

I walked outside just before dawn, carrying a small stool and my erhu, an ancient Chinese violin. I sat down on a street corner near the apartment building where my family and neighbors were still sleeping. The bitter wind blew falling snowflakes into swirls that whirled along the street like tiny white tornadoes. I wore my warmest clothes, but since we couldn't afford gloves, my hands were bare as I began to play. The small sound box covered in snakeskin rested in my lap, and my left hand held the erhu's long vertical neck. As I moved the bow across the two strings with my right hand, a deep and mournful sound emerged.

For my entire life I had been told that a good education was essential for a successful, happy life. Now my education had been completely cut off, and with it, all my hopes for the future.

Since I was unable to find a job with only a junior-high diploma, my parents said that my only hope to avoid deportation was to secure a position as a dancer or musician, talents that were useful to the communist government. National and regional song-and-dance troupes performed in public venues across the country to promote the party's ideals. Chairman Mao's wife, Jiang

Qing, had created eight model Chinese operas to dramatize the revolution, the victories against foreign invaders and bourgeois counter-revolutionaries, and the glories of peasants, workers, and soldiers. From an early age, the eight model performances were all I ever saw. The era that history refers to as the "Cultural Revolution" was, in fact, a cultural holocaust. No movies or creative performances of any kind were allowed in China, except for Jiang's eight model plays.

Like many young kids, I knew nearly every word and could sing almost every part of the eight state-produced plays, since we heard them daily from dawn to dusk. Innately I loved music and dance, a passion passed down from my father. When I was in elementary school, I performed principal roles in a song-and-dance troupe that re-enacted the famous tales for audiences in factories, companies, and public settings. In one performance, I danced the part of a soldier who oversaw young women washing clothes for the People's Liberation Army. In another, I played an old man driving a horse-drawn carriage that transported harvested rice to Beijing. I practiced my acting and dancing as often as I could, since I was thoroughly delighted when the audience enjoyed my performances.

After I was forced to leave school at age 14, I hoped that my prior experience in music and dance could somehow win me a coveted spot in a communist song-and-dance troupe and thus save me from the devastating fate of deportation and a lifetime of poverty and hard labor. Since I'd had a significant amount of previous dance training, I advanced successfully through several rounds of auditions for the Hangzhou Arts School. However, even though the dance moves were the same as those I had often performed as a child many years ago, the circumstances now were totally different. This time, every step I took, every turn I twirled, every movement I made was fueled not by a passion for the art, but by a desperate need to carve out a safe place in the chaos of the times.

As a backup to dancing, I also took up formal study of the erhu, which my parents bought for me for about two yuan, or thirty cents. This simple instrument can only be played one string at a time, so, by definition, it cannot produce harmony. But when played well, its music is rich and soulful, with a touch of melancholy. I had only played the erhu occasionally since I was young, but now I grasped it as if it were a life preserver. I figured that even if my dance plan failed, if I was fortunate enough to be chosen for a government performing troupe for erhu, I would still have a chance to avoid a hopeless, deported life.

Sometimes my little brother, Ming-yu, sat next to me, holding a smaller version of the erhu. He loved to be with me and do the same things I did. We played duets together for my family and my father's colleagues. When I looked at my then-six-year-old little brother, I felt such tenderness for him, as well as an intense longing to return to the carefree days of my own young boyhood. As Ming-yu slid his small bow back and forth, he thought we were just having fun. He had no idea that I was fighting for my life.

I studied the erhu tirelessly. Along with weekly lessons, I practiced up to fifteen hours a day. In the early mornings, I played on the street corner to avoid waking my neighbors. My left hand, held high on the neck of the instrument, would quickly become numb from the cold and I would have to stop playing. The long neck of the erhu rested on my shoulder, and the bow lay across my knees, as I blew hot breaths of air onto frozen fingers and rubbed my palms together. I watched my former junior-high classmates walk toward the high school, and my heart ached with anger, envy, and despair at the sight of them heading to the place where I longed to be going myself. I had been a star pupil with straight As, and I wanted to be walking to school alongside them! Many of them were their family's only children, so they were allowed to go to high school without risk of being deported after graduation. But, being from a family with more than one child, I had no chance to go to senior high or college, so my education was cut off permanently.

I went back inside once my neighbors were up and about, but without heat, the apartment was never any warmer than it was outside. The skin on my hands froze from exposure, and the pain was excruciating when my hands would begin to warm up, and frostbite caused severe blisters that ruptured and oozed. The ulcers lasted for weeks until the skin finally healed, which left faint but lasting scars that are visible to this day. But no amount of pain in my fingers could compare to the despair in my heart at the prospect of facing the utter anguish of an exiled life.

One of the most famous pieces of erhu music that I learned was "Two Springs Converging Reflect the Moon," composed by the blind folk musician Ah Bing. This song is one of the most treasured pieces of music in the Chinese repertoire. While Ah Bing couldn't see the scene he evoked through his music, he imagined the moon reflecting light from the heavens onto these two springs that converged into one. The music is haunting and beautiful and echoes with longing and unfulfilled desires, as the composer imagines how beautiful the scene would have been if he could see.

As I played that piece sitting outside on the stool, my soul resonated with the sounds of sorrow and longing. As a teenager, I should have been looking forward to a life of exciting possibilities. But instead, along with millions of other youth, I had been condemned to the bottom rung of society with no hope for happiness. The elderly composer couldn't see, but he could imagine beauty. I had seen beauty, but I couldn't imagine my own future. The strings of the erhu sung of the moon, that glistening mirror suspended in space that my father and I had gazed upon in the forest walks of my earlier childhood years. What light did this moon reflect for me now? I saw nothing, only darkness stretching on for the length of my life.

I poured my heart and soul into mastering dance and the erhu, as they were the only open doors left to lead me out of darkness.

My dedication and hard work paid off and my skill improved dramatically. My teachers were pleased with my progress and both my parents and I were thrilled to learn that there was a high likelihood that I would pass the performance exam and join the Hangzhou song-and-dance troupe and thus be able to finally avoid the devastating fate of deportation! I was so excited at that prospect that for weeks I could not sleep and was counting the days to the day of the performance exam!

But, one day my father came home from work and looked at me with profound sadness. He told me something that left me feeling colder and more bitter than the winter wind outside.

The government had discovered that thousands of young people were learning music and dance with an ulterior motive, that is, solely to avoid deportation. They considered it a blatant attempt by the teenagers and their parents to skirt the deportation policy. In response, the officials announced that they wouldn't select any musicians or dancers from Hangzhou at all that year!

Hearing my father's words, I could hardly breathe. I was devastated yet again. I had been practicing dance and the erhu for an entire year! All that practicing, the frostbite, the pain, was now all for nothing! For days after I heard the news, I simply wandered around our neighborhood feeling so empty. My life had lost direction, as if I were walking through dense and endless fog. From my youngest years I had been active and on the move, studying and working hard to have a future. Now I was forced into idleness and uselessness. What options did I have left now? If I didn't find gainful employment soon, I remained at imminent risk of being deported.

My parents were not willing to see me succumb to a life of destitution. Also they had to find a way to keep me active and off the streets, because if young people were discovered loitering with nothing to do, they too would be at risk of being arrested and sent to labor camps. So my parents came up with an idea to keep me out of trouble and to hide me away for a while at least—I would study medicine, albeit illegally.

During the second half of the Cultural Revolution, a small number of universities around the country were allowed to be reopened, including the medical school where my parents worked. The college entrance exams had been discontinued since the start of the Cultural Revolution, so the only students admitted were those who did not actually have to take or pass any exam, mostly children of Communist Party officials or others with government connections.

My parents urged me to consider studying medicine at their university, even if only for the sake of knowledge.

"Why should I study medicine when I have no chance at all of becoming a doctor?" I asked.

"Ming, remember that knowledge is good and will always be useful," Dad said gently. "Study anyway and maybe one day you'll be able to somehow use what you learn now."

I didn't really see the purpose of it, but I knew the risks of deportation that I faced by hanging out on the streets, so I agreed. When I asked my parents how I could be allowed to study medicine when I wasn't even enrolled as a student, they said they would figure out a way. My parents then alerted their colleagues that they planned to smuggle me into school, and asked the professors to look the other way.

One morning my father accompanied me to the medical school and into the anatomy lab. Along three walls were glass cabinets displaying jars of body parts—an amputated hand, a cancerous foot, a human head—floating in foul-smelling chemicals.

"My son wants to study medicine here," my father said to the lab teacher. "Will you tutor him so he can catch up with the other medical students?"

The teacher looked at me. "But he's so young!"

"Try him. He may surprise you."

Another professor's child in hiding—a girl a few years older than I was—studied alongside me. For several weeks, the two of us huddled around the teacher in the lab as he pulled out from jar after jar parts of human bodies and explained them to us. The sight of specimens was unnerving, but floating limbs weren't the worst part. In another part of the room was a large bookcase that stood several feet from the wall. Behind the bookcase were coffins, and inside the coffins were dead bodies that were typically the remains of those who had been executed after being declared counter-revolutionaries in the public square. The corpses were given to the medical school, since most families of the deceased feared being labeled counter-revolutionaries as well if they were to claim the bodies of their loved ones.

As we studied the contents of the jars, I fixated on how close these dead bodies were to us behind the bookcases. As the anatomy teacher droned on, I would listen attentively for any bit of sound coming from the coffins. Whenever I thought I heard something, I would jump in my seat. I worried incessantly that one of the corpses would rise from its resting place in the coffin, but to my relief, none came back to life . . . except at night in my dreams! I had nightmares for months on end. The more time I spent studying the structures of the dissected, disintegrated human bodies during the day, the more vivid these dreams became at night. The corpses would come out of their coffins, plaintively seeking their missing parts. Handless, footless, and headless beings, their festering skin falling from their frames, would reach for me until I woke up gasping, sweating all over, the smell of death still lingering in my nostrils.

I was deeply relieved when we finally finished our anatomy sessions and I could escape the horrors lurking in the lab.

My tutor overflowed with praise when he discussed my progress with my parents. "You have a young genius on your hands!" he declared. "He has caught up with the other students in just two months and is ready now for regular classes in human anatomy."

I then started attending medical school every day, although still doing so illegitimately. I sat in the back row of a large lecture hall trying to blend in with the students who were authorized to be there, most of whom were much older than I was. My mom and dad sometimes taught at the podium themselves as well. When they did, they expected to see me there, and I always was. I had nowhere else to go and nothing else to do anyway. I tried to listen to what the instructors were teaching, but it all seemed to me so meaningless, since I knew clearly that there was no chance that I would never be allowed to become a doctor. I stared out the windows at other people living their everyday lives in a society that had no place for me. Though the nightmares eventually faded, no new dreams took their place. There was nothing but emptiness in my life as far as I could see.

I never saw the girl from the lab again, but I did start to notice an older girl who always sat in the front row of the lecture hall. She was in her twenties, so beautiful, and since I was a teenager, I was more interested in studying live human anatomy than the dead kind. I stared at her throughout class, unable to focus on the lectures. If she ever looked back and offered me even the slightest smile, the moment would carry me through the entire day. That would be the closest I ever got to her—or any girl—for many years to come. Throughout my schooling in Communist China, girls and boys were strongly discouraged from forming friendships, and dating was strictly prohibited on school or college campuses. Even the eight model plays—the nation's only entertainment for years—were devoid of any love stories. To be romantically or sexually involved before marriage was considered bourgeois, and not in line with proletarian values. The communist government classified any romance or marriage as a "personal problem" that needed to be "solved" before one could move on and do more important things to serve the Communist Party. Romance was foreign to me at that time, a luxury I simply couldn't afford anyway. I was overwhelmed with simply trying to survive. All of my time and energy were spent in desperate attempts to find a future with some semblance of hope and happiness.

My father was a well-known cardiovascular doctor and an expert in hematology. Along with other medical students,

I sometimes accompanied him as he made his rounds at the hospital. He took us to see patients, and he would ask questions and then listen and respond to the students' answers. As the professor's son, I was treated with respect, even though I was young and my oversized lab coat draped to the floor. For the first time, I had a taste of what it might truly be like to be a doctor. From my place in that circle, I beamed with pride at my father. I longed to be like him and to be a part of our family's profession.

Slowly but surely, I became more and more interested in the medicine that I was studying. I found it fascinating how human body worked, and how we could actually understand it and find a way to cure illnesses and help people. Though I was not studying medicine legally and had no chance to become a doctor, in my own heart I was dearly hoping that if I did master the material well, really well, I might have perhaps the slimmest chance of being allowed to become a doctor one day!

One morning, as I got ready to leave for school, my father stopped me. He again had to inform me with a profound sadness that another door had been closed on my future.

"Ming-xu, starting today, you will no longer be returning to medical school," he said with a heavy sigh.

For the second time in my life, my dad had to discontinue my education! He said that as soon as the medical school administration discovered I was attending classes without permission, they threatened to fire my father unless I left immediately.

So I was expelled . . . from a school at which I wasn't even enrolled!

For days I stayed home, lying in bed and staring at the ceiling.

I had embraced my father's challenge to study medicine "simply for the sake of knowledge," and now I couldn't understand why that was not even allowed. Unlike many medical students who got into the school through communist family connections and hence did not really care about studying at all, I did care and wanted to learn! I had been getting so excited lately about the medical knowledge that I was learning that I began to dream that there might just be a chance that I could be allowed to become a doctor one day! Now even that hope was completely crushed and the harsh reality sunk in. I realized that even though I had been a good student with straight As, without the right connections to communist cadres, I would never ever be allowed back in any school or given any further chance to learn!

My father saw how despondent I was.

"Ming, remember that life's path is hardly ever a straight line. There are always lots of zigzags before you find your way," he said. "Always have hope. Never give up hope."

From my bed, I watched shadows lengthen across the floor. I remembered the silhouettes my childhood puppets used to cast on the gray walls around me. The happy childhood memories faded with the shadows into the approaching darkness of the night. Were all my happy memories relegated only to my earliest years? Would there only be darkness ahead for me? I was gripped by a familiar fear as I tossed and turned, unable to sleep. I realized that no matter how hard I tried to fight back against misfortune, the darkness always seemed to be able to catch back on me, the black dot, the cadavers, the ever-present risk of deportation. I wanted so much to escape from these ghosts, and run to light and freedom.

Some time later, a former classmate from junior high, Hui Liu, introduced me to a young man named Tian-ma Wu, whose father had been killed during the Cultural Revolution. Prior to his death, he had been a famous playwright, the Arthur Miller of China. His most famous play featured an ancient city whose citizens rioted against its rulers. The play was interpreted by the communist government as an attack on the current regime, so Tian-ma Wu's father was declared a counter-revolutionary, arrested, and executed.

On execution days, the city held a ceremony in the public square. The accused stood on a stage wrapped in robes, with large cardboard panels hanging around their necks that displayed their names. Soldiers held the prisoners' heads down, and as each prisoner's name was announced, the panel was flipped around. If each character of the person's name was crossed off one by one, that prisoner could live and would be sent to prison for life. But if the characters were crossed with a long, singular red mark, the prisoner was condemned to immediate death. Large crowds, sometimes as many as several thousand people, gathered to watch these public spectacles. Each turn of the panel was a bone-chilling moment of life or death, followed by a collective shriek from the crowd.

The doomed were then driven in military trucks to the base of a hill at the edge of the city. There they sunk to their knees, and each one fell forward as shots rang out from guns pointed at the back of his or her head.

When I first met Tian-ma, I wondered if he had stood in one of those crowds of people in the public square. Had he seen the mark as it was written across his father's name?

I thought of the coffins at the medical school.

Tian-ma was seventeen, I was fifteen, and neither of us were allowed to go to school, nor could we find jobs, so we both faced deportation. But with the loss of his father, he carried a sorrow even much deeper than mine.

Like his dad, Tian-ma was a talented writer and had composed many poems. Together with Hui Liu, another gifted scribe, we gathered in Tian-ma's tiny bedroom, where each wall was covered from top to bottom with pages of our novels, poems, and drawings.

"Ming, how can we make a life for ourselves?" Tian-ma wondered. "Hui and I are writers. What can you do?"

"I can dance and I love music. I can also play the erhu."

"You should learn music composition," he said. "Then we might be able to find work if we can compose songs together."

I immediately delved into the art of music composition and put melodies together for many of Tian-ma and Hui's verses. One such piece was "A Prisoner's Song," written by Tian-ma. It described a city deprived of freedom and joy: "At the foot of the mountain, there's my hometown. There is no water, no sunshine. People walk through town listless, expressionless, without joy or happiness. Let's do it; let's break through the handcuffs on our hands and let's break through the prison, for freedom! We are prisoners. We have to fight for our freedom."

We worked hard, filling our days with writing and composing. We completed about fifty songs and even an entire opera. We submitted several works to music magazines, but nothing was ever published. Years later I realized that, given the subject matter of our songs, we were actually quite fortunate that no one paid close attention to them. Through our music, we expressed our longing for freedom, education, and opportunity. I didn't realize at the time just how daring our songs were. "The Prisoner's Song" alone could have gotten us jailed or put on the stage of the public square and executed.

We were so young, and yet our short lives had already been so scarred, full of tragedy and heartache. And the future offered no promise, no relief. I had tried everything I could think of, and it had all failed. The fighting spirit expressed in those songs was on the brink of being extinguished.

My parents, who had fought alongside me as I sought a career of any kind, were also on the verge of giving up. My mother despaired that deportation awaited me no matter what we tried.

"You have to find a job," my father insisted. "Just go find something, anything, or the government will find you idle and deport you immediately."

So after all of these years fighting and trying, I finally gave up trying to craft a career, and instead took a job doing the lowest-paying work available in the city.

Early each morning I rode a wobbly, rusty bike through the streets of Hangzhou, alongside hundreds of other commuters. A flood of people on bikes merged at each stoplight. It was summertime and everyone wore white, short-sleeve shirts or

T-shirts, as color of any kind was not allowed. I waited at the light with them, gripping my handlebars, my foot on the ground, poised and ready to go. When the light changed and it was time to move forward, we surged ahead like a tidal wave flowing through the streets, everyone pedaling as quickly as possible.

A half hour later, I arrived at a publishing factory and entered through an enormous steel gate. The factory had recently published *The Selected Works of Mao Zedong, Volume 5*. I joined a dozen older women at a table to wrap bundles of books in heavy brown paper, which were then stacked on carts to be shipped across the country.

Once a bright and promising student, now I was at the lowest pay rate, stuck at the bottom rung of society with no hope for advancement. Sadness overwhelmed me as I realized that all my efforts to hold onto the hope of having a future had failed—playing the erhu, practicing dance, studying medicine, and composing music. I couldn't imagine doing the mind-numbing, repetitive, low-paying work for the rest of my life. Wrapping stack after stack of books caused my hands to cramp and my back to slouch and stiffen, and my toil only produced enough money for a nightly meal of rice and vegetables.

I was paid the equivalent of ten U.S. cents a day, and my first biweekly paycheck amounted to just one dollar. Regardless of the meager pittance, I was relieved that I was finally able to contribute something to my family after more than two years of feeling useless and unproductive.

But that first paycheck ended up being the last one I would receive from wrapping books, as fourteen days after I started that job, my dad came home with a shocking news that would change the course of history in China. The newspaper headline was minor, the announcement only a few lines long, but the implications were enormous. The stoplight had finally changed to "go." Finally, I and the rest of China would be moving in an entirely different direction.

Chapter 5

New Hope Dawns

"Do you hear that?" I whispered. My friend and I were sitting on the floor of my family's apartment. We had been looking at the colorful collections of stamps, candy wrappers, and cigarette packs that I had carefully amassed and arranged into homemade albums since I was a young boy. I held a page by its corner, my hand suspended above the book. My friend cocked his head to listen. His eyes widened.

The sound was the unmistakable tune of a funeral procession. The music wafted from radios in every room along the hallway. Without a word, my friend got up and ran to his own family's apartment, with me following close behind him. We entered to find his family hushed and apprehensive.

The reporter announced, with an unemotional tone, "Chairman Mao is dead."

I quickly left my friend's apartment and made my way outside.

It was a warm afternoon on Thursday, September 9, 1976. I raced through the streets of Hangzhou to Tian-ma's apartment and into his tiny bedroom, with its verse-plastered walls.

He was napping, but I shook him awake and told him what had just happened. For a moment he looked pensive, but then a smile slowly appeared on his face.

"That's the best news I've ever heard," he said with a grin.

Mao's Cultural Revolution had destroyed China. It cut off the future for nearly twenty million young people and claimed more than a million lives. With Mao now dead, the madness finally came to an end. Government officials realized they wouldn't be able to hold on to power any longer if people were forced to continue to live in such a misery, poverty, and chaos. Deng Xiaoping rose to prominence and defeated Mao's followers, who had insisted on political ideology over the well-being of the people. The new pragmatic administration under Deng launched a series of unprecedented social and economic reforms that resulted in several subsequent decades of renewal and economic transformation in China.

On the evening that I brought home my biweekly one-dollar paycheck from the printing factory and proudly showed it to my mom, my dad came home, carrying a newspaper as if it were a winning trophy.

"Look at this!" He pointed to a tiny, two-inch announcement in a corner of the page. When I saw what it said, I gasped.

"So it's true then?" I asked, almost afraid to hope.

"Yes! The college entrance exam is coming back!"

For ten years (1966-1976), the national college entrance exam had been shelved, and students had been denied any higher education—including me. With Mao now gone and the Cultural Revolution finally over, China's leaders realized how tragic a mistake that was, and Deng Xiaoping made the decision to resume university admissions testing. All the universities that had been shut down during the Cultural Revolution would now be back in business.

I returned to the factory for the last time, since I was now allowed to go back to school, and told the people at my workstation that it was going to be my last day. They regretted seeing me leave, but gave me their best wishes. They told me they were sure I was meant for something bigger and better. Even though I had never enjoyed the type of work I did there, my fellow employees were gentle and caring, so I knew I would miss them.

At the end of the day, as I headed for the door, I shouted back to my coworkers, "I'll see you all in fifty years!" What would my life look like decades from that moment? I had no idea, but what I did know was that I finally had the hope that it could be more than what I had been allowed to imagine. I left that job not really knowing if I would get into college, but at least now I had a chance!

That night at dinner, my family was buzzing with excitement at the possibility that someday I might actually be going to college.

"In hindsight, I so wish we hadn't taken Ming-xu out of high school," my mom said. "Now it will be so much harder for him to do well on the college entrance exam, since it requires a high school education."

My goodness, Mom was right. In all the excitement, I hadn't thought about how much more difficult it would be for me now to get into college than for others who had not missed out on the past two years of high school education. Catching up on that much material in a short period of time would be nearly impossible. The regret my mother had just expressed washed over me and left me feeling overwhelmed. I had wasted the past two years desperately trying to find a profession to avoid deportation when I should have been in high school, studying. I would have had a decent chance of making it into college had I actually gone to high school, but now it seemed nearly impossible!

"Wait, can't I just start where I left off, right after the ninth grade?" I asked. I assumed that I would start the tenth grade and proceed through high school to the twelfth grade, as usual, taking the college entrance exam three years later.

"No, Ming, you need to jump up straight into the twelfth grade right away," my dad said, "since only the twelfth-grade graduating class will be allowed to take the national college admissions test."

"He's right," my mom agreed. "You'll have to catch up on those years of school that you missed between now and the day of the exam."

"But the exam is in two months! How can I possibly do that? And even if I can somehow magically jump instantaneously more than two years ahead into the twelfth grade, what are my chances of actually getting into college as a twelfth-grader?"

Dad was quiet for a moment. Then he spoke slowly, knowing that what he was about to say was not good news.

"Given how many people are vying for the very few spots available this year, twelfth-graders probably only have about a few percent chance of getting into college."

Dad explained that 1977 would likely be the single most difficult year to get into college in modern Chinese history. The lack of entrance exams for ten years created a ten-year backlog of students, and therefore ten times more applicants for college that year.

I gaped at my parents, wide-eyed and speechless.

"There's no way I can pull this off!" I cried, and buried my face in my hands.

I hadn't received any schooling in more than two years. How was I supposed to learn the entire high school curriculum in just a few months, and then compete with millions of other twelfth-grade students for such a small number of university openings? Surely my parents couldn't be serious. I was in tears.

"Can't I just start my tenth-grade in high school now and take the college exam in three years?" I begged.

"No, my son," Dad said, his voice tender but serious. "Remember: this is not a free country. No one can guarantee that the government won't shut down colleges again next year, for another decade! So you have to try your best to get into college this year, because you may never get another chance like this."

My parents had lived their entire lives watching China convulse and shift through numerous drastic changes caused by government dictatorships. They knew we couldn't count on any lasting freedom or stability. They had no confidence in the system and feared that such an opportunity for me to go to college would never come around again.

I knew they were right. I thought about how much I had struggled during the last few years to avoid the feared deportation. Everything I tried had failed—dance, erhu, medical classes, and music composition. I resolved that I would do whatever it takes now to avoid having to suffer such deep distress and hopelessness ever again.

I sat quietly as the weight of having to learn so much material in such a short amount of time, and to score in the top few percent of the twelfth-grade class, bore down on me.

"So how can I possibly do all of that?" I was perplexed.

"Leave that to us." My dad glanced at my mother. Joy lit up her face and her eyes danced.

Though my parents were optimistic, I was not, at all. I was facing perhaps my only shot to escape darkness and find hope for my future, but now I realized what an impossible shot it was! I felt the weight of my entire future and my family's legacy on my shoulders. I was burdened and afraid, but I had no choice but to fight with my "back against a river," as the Chinese proverb says. I could not retreat because if I did, I would "fall into the water" and lose all hope of a better life.

One of my father's patients happened to be Teacher Yang, the vice principal of Hangzhou No. 11 High school. My father approached Teacher Yang and asked for her help. Not long afterward, I was back in a classroom, sitting among other regular twelfth-grade students. Teacher Yang simply told school authorities that I was a transfer student from the twelfth-grade class of another high school. None of the students knew me, and no one asked any questions.

Soon after I started school, Teacher Yang took me aside and said there would be an important math exam in just two weeks. It was imperative that I pass this test or I might fail the class entirely. If I couldn't stay enrolled, then I wouldn't qualify to register for the college entrance exam.

I panicked and felt weak. I had to learn two-and-a-half years of math in just two weeks! As always, my parents came to the rescue. Dad reached out to several of his patients who were educators. He offered free medical care to them and their families in exchange for tutoring me in math and other subjects, such as physics, chemistry, biology, Chinese, politics, and English.

The tutors came to the house several times a week to drill me on their designated subjects, strategically attacking selected portions of mountains of material. I studied day and night, fifteen to eighteen hours a day. When I thought my brain would melt, I would switch subjects and study something else. If my eyelids started to droop and I felt I was falling asleep, I would splash cold water on my face and plunge back into the topic at hand.

Luckily, I did manage to pass the math exam, my first victory! But math was actually one of my easier subjects, since I enjoyed it the most. Like physics, it was logical and suited my style of thinking. Passing that test was like conquering only the lowest hill of a very high mountain range that I would have to scale in the coming weeks.

My family supported me wholeheartedly. My mother walked in from work one day clutching a huge stack of papers to her chest. She had borrowed old college entrance examinations— from before the Cultural Revolution—from colleagues and friends. My father came home with his share of practice tests as well. Since there were no copy machines at the time, the two of them sat at the table after dinner and spent countless hours writing out every question and problem set by hand.

My parents then took turns coaching and quizzing me on various subjects from science to the humanities. When we got closer to the date of the actual college entrance exam, my parents staged mock exam sessions, assuming the roles of exam officer and assistant exam officer.

"Pretend this is the official exam," my dad would say. "Remember that you cannot leave the room for any reason other than a bathroom break. No papers can be removed when you leave. Okay, ready? Now begin!"

My mother would come in hours later and call "time." Though they were only mock exams, we took them very seriously. There was no letting down of our guard. I knew that the actual college entrance exam would be the toughest test of my life.

After my parents and little brother had gone to bed, I sat at my wooden school desk, awash in dim light from a small lamp, continuing my studies deep into the night. I slept for only a few hours each night. I grew thinner and thinner because I was too busy to eat and wasn't getting enough rest. I was weak and utterly exhausted, but that didn't matter. The thought that I might fail— that I might be thrown back into the despair and hopelessness of the past few years again—truly motivated me. For once in my life, I actually saw a sliver of light beaming into the prison cell of darkness that had encased me for years, so I was determined to do my utmost to wedge that door open and get free.

But I knew also that the ten-year backlog of students was going to make the competition for the small number of the freshman spots extremely fierce. The acceptance rate for the 1977 college season would only be three or four percent, the lowest in the history of the People's Republic of China.

All over the city, thousands of students were anxiously studying and preparing. I went to school during the day, and at night I rode my father's rundown bike to group review sessions at local universities. Large lecture halls, like the one in which I had illegally audited medical school classes two years prior, now brimmed with hundreds of students and young people who had been displaced for up to a decade and were now fighting for the chance of a lifetime.

Riding home, the roads were empty. Kids had all disappeared from the street corners and courtyards. Inside our apartment building, the halls that normally brimmed with laughter, young voices, and the sounds of family life were hushed and still. The silence across the city was the sound of long-harbored hopes and dreams for the future—for millions of youth and their families—being miraculously resurrected.

As my classmates and I studied with feverish intensity, the qualifications for test registration were suddenly changed. My parents were right—there was no counting on stability in a communist country. Over the next few weeks, I would constantly be trying to regain footing on ever-shifting ground.

As the number of registrants for the first college entrance exam in ten years in China far exceeded expectations, officials decided that the qualifying pool of candidates allowed to take the exam had to be reduced substantially. There was simply no way everyone could take the test that year. Those of us in the twelfth grade—the youngest class qualified to register—would bear the brunt of this reduction. Just a few weeks before the university entrance exam, the government decided that the nation's entire twelfth-grade class had to be sifted through a strict selection process, and only a very small number of us would be allowed to participate in the exam. In each round of the elimination process, a day-long exam further reduced our numbers.

Hangzhou had about fifty high schools, with an average of three hundred seniors at each one. Only ten students would be selected from each school to move to the next round of testing. Those five hundred selected students were then have to compete at the district level, and only twenty from each district would make it to the next round. The final round of testing would reduce the total number of twelfth-graders from the initial pool of fifteen thousand from the entire city of Hangzhou . . . to only ten!

I advanced through each grueling round of the elimination process, exhausted and relieved each time I made the cut. In the end, I somehow managed to survive all three rounds, and I was honored and elated to become one of the only ten seniors from the city of Hangzhou selected to take the college entrance exam.

On the big day of the 1977 national exam, a clear, cold December morning, I left home and and rode my bike to my designated exam site at a local high school, one of several dozen test locations in Hangzhou. I was exhausted before we began the exam, so I had no energy left in me even to be nervous. Months of studying, weeks of testing and competing, the long hours, and the lack of sleep had all taken their toll. I barely had enough strength to pedal my bike, and I was in a daze by the time I arrived at the test site—and it was for the most crucial test of my life! I had conquered three enemy defense lines by this point, but I had little strength left for the fourth and final battle . . . the most important of them all!

For the next three days, from eight in the morning until five in the evening, several hundred of us at our test site sat hunched over long exams and endless questions on physics, math, chemistry, geology, biology, English, Chinese literature, history, and politics. The exam room remained quiet, as we were all too worn out to be excited or focused, I felt numb and half asleep, as if I were merely going through the motions of answering all the questions. I was only mildly confident that I had done well.

At supper the evening after the last day of testing, Dad asked me how I had done.

"I probably did all right," I said halfheartedly, as I was totally exhausted and ready to collapse and sleep for weeks.

Checking with the parents of other kids, and seeing that many of them did not feel that they had done as well, my parents felt optimistic and a new hope had risen in our family that perhaps I finally had a chance now of being able to go to college! All of our struggles and hardships over the years might finally pay off!

A few evenings later, there was a knock on the door. Like most families in China at that time, we didn't have a phone so we had no idea who was visiting, but we assumed it was probably another of many colleagues and friends who were stopping by to inquire about my performance on the exam. This time, however, it was Dr. Liu, a physician who had been assigned to provide medical care to the educators sequestered on a nearby mountaintop, grading the thousands of exams.

"The government has changed the rules again!" announced Dr. Liu.

My heart sank. Each time the officials changed the rules, it nearly toppled all my efforts, and I would have to struggle much harder to survive the next round. So what would it be this time?

Dr. Liu explained that the number of seniors who would be accepted into college would be further reduced significantly now to just four of the top students from the entire province of fifty million. "How did little Ming do?" asked Dr. Liu.

"He thinks he did okay," my dad replied. "But my goodness, it may not be good enough now since the chance of getting in has been even more drastically cut!"

I was shaken as I saw my dad look at my mom. They both looked disheartened.

Dr. Liu said goodbye and left, leaving us all feeling stunned by the news. After making it through all the grueling rounds of the intense selection process, I thought I would finally have the long-awaited chance to go to college. But it seemed that my chance was slashed yet again, and it would be nearly impossible for me to get into college now!

All the enthusiasm that had buoyed our family these past few months, the devotion and hard work fueled by renewed hope—hope that had been denied for ten years, hope for college and a promising life—all dissipated the instant Dr. Liu delivered this bad news.

In a few weeks would be the Chinese New Year. Except for the early years of the Cultural Revolution, when it was suppressed as a feudalistic tradition, the New Year has been China's most important holiday for thousands of years. Factories and businesses completely shut down for an entire week to celebrate. No matter how poor or prosperous, families across the country spend days cleaning, shopping, cooking, and preparing for the festival.

My brother and I usually enjoyed helping our mom prepare the special dishes we loved and waited for all year long. One of our favorites was *zong-zi*, delicious rice dumplings filled with pork, wrapped in large bamboo leaves shaped like cones and tied with string. The dish took a lot of time to make, but my little brother and I had fun joking and playing as we worked alongside Mom.

But this year the joy was gone, the preparations felt meaningless, and our favorite foods were tasteless, since our New Year prospects were bleak. Our family simply went through the motions during the festival that year.

Weeks went by with no word. It seemed as if I had indeed fallen through the cracks during this last and most crucial round. Only four seniors would be admitted to college from the entire province of fifty million people! Being one of the top four among all high school seniors seemed utterly unlikely, especially for someone like me who had just "jumped" three years ahead into that twelfth grade. I really should have felt more concerned, but I was so weak from exhaustion that I slept heavily for weeks.

I thought of returning to the publishing factory where I would again earn ten cents a day. I imagined both the joy and disappointment that I would see on the faces of the older women when I arrived to work alongside them again. Then I began to think about the darkness and hopelessness that had enveloped me during my teenage years, and could still return to hold me captive in darkness forever.

Then one day, Mom rushed into the apartment with a letter in her hand, waving it toward me. Too excited to speak, she pointed to the envelope, on which I saw the insignia of the Ministry of Education.

I leapt out of bed. This was it, the moment I had been waiting for all my life, the moment I had both anticipated and feared.

My hands shook as I slowly peeled open the envelope and pulled out the paper that laid inside.

The strokes of each Chinese character spelled out my future. "Ming-xu Wang has been accepted into the University of Science and Technology of China to study analytical chemistry."

My mother and I shrieked with joy. My little brother giggled and clapped his hands.

I paused for a moment. "But where is the University of Science and Technology of China?" I hadn't applied to that school at all; in fact, I had never even heard of it. On the day of the national college entrance exam, I had listed only three medical schools as my preferred institutions, including the one where my parents worked and where I had illegally attended classes two years earlier. I wanted to be a doctor; that was what I had always wanted. I later learned that China's college admissions system in 1977, wildly disorganized after a decade of disuse, had simply ignored most students' personal choices. Instead, top-tier schools were given first picks of the top-scoring students in each province.

So this meant that not only was I one of just four seniors accepted into college from my entire province, but I had apparently been the first choice of an elite school in China—the University of Science and Technology of China—the so-called "MIT of China." My parents were elated. Even though I hadn't gotten into medical school as I desired, I was going to college . . . something I thought would never, ever happen in my life!

My heart could barely contain the happiness I felt. The New Year celebration now had all-new meaning for me. The famous dragon in Chinese New Year parades represents the monster Nian, a legendary beast that would come out once a year to feast on villagers. According to tradition, the monster could be scared off by the color red, loud noises, and fire. I reveled in the waves of red across the city, a symbol of happiness and prosperity. The terrible darkness that had enshrouded me for so long was now lit up by flashes of light from fireworks exploding everywhere I looked. In Chinese, *nian* means both "monster" and "year." The monster of my life, the dark years that had devoured my hopes and dreams, had been vanquished at last.

Chapter 6

Little Bird Flies

The smell of firecracker smoke had barely cleared the air the day my family took me to the Hangzhou train station to see me off to college. I was unprepared for the pandemonium that awaited us. For nearly a mile, students and their families and friends queued through the station like the body of an immense black dragon. I felt anxious at the sight of so many people. How could a train hold so many passengers, and how would I possibly make it on board?

When the train pulled into the station and the compartment doors opened, the long black dragon undulated forward. A lot fewer passengers seemed to be disembarking than those who eagerly waited to board. The doors were crammed with people wedging themselves into any space they could find to push themselves onto the train.

I was pressed against masses of people, and I felt as if my ribs were about to crack.

"I can't get on the train!" I cried out to my parents, barely able to breathe.

"Ming-xu, this way!" Seeing that there was no chance for us to get onto the train through any of the cramped doors, my dad knocked on a window a few cars down and convinced a passenger inside to lift up the window to help him get me on board. My father lifted me up to the edge of the window so the man could pull me inside the train.

The stranger's helpful attitude turned sour as soon as he saw the luggage coming in through the window behind me.

"We don't have room for all of this!" he growled.

The benches of the train were full of strangers packed tightly together, and every inch of standing space was taken as well. Some passengers were even dangerously perched on the overhead luggage rack. There was barely enough space to expand my lungs and take in air.

I looked at the guy pleadingly. "But this is my luggage! I have to have it. I'm going to college."

He muttered something under his breath, and then reluctantly helped me pull my luggage through the window into the crowded train.

The siren sounded. I thrusted a hand out the window I had crawled through. Its glass was thick with steam from so much body heat. I waved to my parents and little brother, to Tian-ma and Hui Liu, and to all the other friends and relatives who had accompanied me to the train station.

I had promised my parents that I would make them and my teachers proud. "I will honor the Wang family name," I had said. In China, the family name is always written before one's given name, since it is considered more important. In China, I was "Wang Ming-xu," a member of the Wang clan, before I was an individual named "Ming-xu." If I did well in my life, I would bring honor to everyone who shared this family name. I felt the tremendous weight of that responsibility.

As I waved goodbye, I saw tears streaming down my parents' faces. Hui later told me that he had asked my father why he was upset, since it was such a wonderful occasion to send a child to college, the ultimate sign of success for every Chinese parent.

"Because we realize he's grown up now," my dad had responded. "He's gone from home forever."

My heart clenched, seeing their faces downcast and damp with tears. I would miss them terribly. I didn't have a chance to tell them how deeply grateful I was for their unwavering support and affection throughout my life. They had always believed in me and had been there for me. Without their tireless efforts, I would never have made it that far.

The train started its slow departure over the tracks and began snaking its way toward the north. As I listened to the click-clack of the wheels on the rails, a melody formed in my mind. The song was light and upbeat. As soon as I wiggled free enough to have some elbow room, I pulled out a pencil and started scribbling on a scrap of paper. The song I composed while standing on the train was called "Little Bird." I imagined a sparrow, once trapped in a cage, now free to fly into the open sky.

* * *

I entered collegiate life through the imposing north gate of the University of Science and Technology of China (USTC). I stood at the gate and asked a friend to take a picture, and I sent copies to my parents and all my relatives. After years of struggle with so little hope, I never believed that I would actually be able to go to college, so the moment felt surreal. After having my education cut off abruptly and facing the terror of impending deportation for so many years, I couldn't believe I was really standing in front of one of the finest universities in China! I felt so deeply grateful; I was finally embracing my destiny.

Before I arrived on campus, I found out that USTC was originally in Beijing. But during the Cultural Revolution, officials forced its move to Hefei in the Anhui Province, more than six hundred miles south of the capital city. Many professors who had refused to move had been prosecuted and jailed. The school suffered greatly during those harsh years.

I was now a member of the freshman class of 1977 that was entering school in the spring of 1978, consisting of top students from provinces across the country, students who would help revive the institution. I had been assigned to study analytical chemistry, which is the study of what elements are present in matter, and their function. But I was more inclined to pursue physics, which seemed more logical and made more sense to me. In analytical chemistry, you could mix a flask of red solution with a flask of green solution and get yellow results, based on the property of matter. From my perspective, there was little logic to it. I soon changed my major to chemical physics, a branch more involved with the laws and concepts of physics. Rather than flasks, Bunsen burners, and chemical solutions, I could use tools like computers, electrical circuitry, and lasers to evaluate the properties of a molecule or the structure of an atom.

Lasers had captured my imagination more than anything else. These focused beams of unified, monochromatic light weren't found in nature. When I was a boy, my dad told me that natural light was actually a blend of all the colors in the spectrum. To prove it, he showed me a prism and demonstrated how light passing through it was refracted into an array of different colors. As a kid, I discovered that diffused sunlight could be focused using a magnifying lens, setting paper on fire and sending tiny ants scurrying for shelter. As a college student, I learned that this fascinating technology extracts and directs singular colors of light by stimulating the release of energy from atoms, or rather, Light Amplification by Stimulated Emission of Radiation (LASER).

During my first year at USTC, I learned that the physics behind lasers dated back to Albert Einstein in 1905, and that the first working laser was built in 1960. By 1978, the year I started college, the application of this unique light source had begun to emerge in integrated circuit electronics, aerospace, construction, and even entertainment. I was enthralled by the lasers I later saw in the movie *Star Wars*, one of the first American movies we were allowed to see. I was fascinated by the Jedi, their magical lightsabers, and the spaceships fighting interstellar battles with such advanced laser weaponry.

Three years into my time at USTC, I had my first real-life encounter with lasers in the research lab of a professor named Xin-xiao Ma. Professor Ma was using lasers to study the chemical reaction of gas molecules. By changing the colors of the laser and monitoring the light emitted by the molecules, he determined the structure and density of his target molecule. As I stood in his lab, beams of green and yellow light shot across the room, bouncing off mirrors at sharp angles in various directions. I had never seen anything like it. As Professor Ma spoke, his face and lab coat reflected the hues of his laser. I was filled with a sense of magic and possibility. I believed science and technology could be a source of wondrous transformation, and the science of lasers quickly became my passion.

Toward the end of my first semester, I received some unfortunate and troubling news. My father came to campus to tell me that he was being sent to Mali, on the African continent. He didn't have much choice. He explained that China had been strengthening ties with the African nations and was providing social and economic help, including much-needed medical care. In the end, my dad would be gone for three years without any leave. When my mother had been deported to the countryside nearly a decade earlier, my dad, brother, and I had each other, but now two of us were missing from the household, so I was worried about Mom and Ming-yu.

One advantage brought by my dad's new post was that he was allowed to buy a number of valuable items that were hard to come by in China. He sent me a calculator and a small cassette radio that could record sound. So I was one of the few students on campus to have such high-tech gadgets. That little radio ended up playing a crucial role in my study of English, and later in my preparation for a future in America.

At USTC, I befriended a fellow student named Le-ping Li, who was five years older than I was. During the Cultural Revolution, he studied American English using smuggled textbooks, and now he spoke better English than most students on campus. Le-ping wanted to pair up with someone who would be willing to study and practice American English with him, as our English curriculum was limited to mostly reading and writing—with little conversational practice—and was mainly British English.

I was drawn to Le-ping and his intense pursuit of American English because I too was fascinated by America. My earliest exposure to the United States was back in elementary school, where we were taught that America was a "paper tiger"— seemingly menacing and imposing—but if you poked it with a pencil, it would tear straight through like paper. We were shown gritty black-and-white pictures of impoverished cities where the people looked unhappy and oppressed, including some African Americans who had been beaten or lynched.

"This is what all of America looks like. The water is deep, the fire is hot, and people live in poverty and eternal unhappiness," the teachers would tell us. "This is what it's like to live in a country where the wealthy exploit the poor. But here in China, the working class is the master. We are much better off here."

The official tone changed some years later. In February of 1972, President Richard Nixon visited China to meet with Chairman Mao and Premier Zhou Enlai for a week of talks aimed at normalizing relations with Beijing. After decades of estrangement and hostility between the two nations, President Nixon called his visit "the week that changed the world." Several months prior to Nixon's visit, my young classmates and I underwent a rigorous educational program intended to teach us about America. Officials were quickly preparing the people for the U.S. president's arrival. We were told that this president, who had previously been outspoken against communism, wanted to open Red China to the U.S., which would help his own re-election. We were instructed that if we met the President or one of his entourage, we should not speak or even smile, but simply be polite and formal.

I certainly didn't imagine that I would actually encounter President Nixon or his entourage in person. But when my school's song-and-dance troupe was recruited to receive President Nixon on the bank of West Lake in Hangzhou, I was among hundreds of youngsters who lined the streets that afternoon. We wore uniforms with blue pants, white shirts, and red neckties— clutching a Chinese flag in one hand and an American flag in the other—as President Nixon's motorcade slowly coasted by. Standing side by side in a black convertible with its top down, President Nixon and Premier Zhou smiled and waved to the crowd. I couldn't believe I had gotten the chance to be that close to an American president!

When the Cultural Revolution ended in 1976, China gradually allowed more books and movies from the West into the country. As a student at USTC, the first American movie I ever watched was *Futureworld*, a science-fiction film about robots in a fantasy theme park for adults. After being indoctrinated with negative propaganda about America since childhood, I was utterly shocked to see how modern America actually was. Nowhere in this film were the city streets filled with dirt and garbage, the people skinny like beggars, or the children dressed in rags. I began to question what I had been taught for so many years. Maybe I did not know the truth about America.

Like Le-ping and many other young people, I was hungry to know more about the West, especially this paper tiger, the United States of America. Le-ping introduced me to "Voice of America," a radio broadcast that came on every evening at eight o'clock. Thanks to my dad, I was one of the few on campus who had a radio, so just minutes before the program would begin, I'd walk outside to avoid disturbing students who were still studying. Streams of other students eventually poured out of classrooms and study halls onto the dark sidewalks, and all across campus small groups circled around those of us with radios as the voice of the broadcaster said, "This is the Voice of America."

For half an hour every evening, we listened to programs that had been specially designed so foreigners could learn American English. There was one called "Voice . . . of . . . America . . . Special . . . English . . . Program," which was deliberately spoken slowly. Another was called "English 900" and followed a textbook of colloquial American English. I soaked up these lessons week after week, and recorded the Special English programs so I could spend days listening to, transcribing, and memorizing them. Learning American English felt as essential as eating, and I was consumed by it.

But Le-ping had even more tricks up his sleeve.

"Ming-xu, the best way to learn is to listen to movies in English," he said.

"Where in the world can we get these movies?" I countered.

Le-ping told me the films were locked away in a storage room in the Department of English Language, but school rules restricted our access.

"We can get into the building after hours," he explained. "No one will ever know."

His plan was bold and could get us into trouble. I was wary, but my desire to learn English was stronger than my fear of getting caught.

One night after the eleven o'clock curfew, as lights went out and students went to sleep, Le-ping and I snuck out of our locked dorm and made our way toward the English department. The campus was pitch-black. My heart was pounding as I imagined getting caught and being forced to scrub the cafeteria floors on our hands and knees while other students laughed at us.

We climbed over a wall into the courtyard and snuck into the English department through a window. Le-ping had been inside the building during the daytime, and had left the window cracked just slightly so that we could pry it open that night from the outside. We pushed and pulled each other through the window, just as a fellow passenger had done to help me onto the train at the crowded station on my first trip to college.

The storage room was huge and filled with large, round steel disks. We had no access to the actual movies, only to the audio disks. The audio track for one movie would take four or five disks. We pulled out *Death on the Nile*, an Agatha Christie story, and loaded the first audio reel onto a machine the size of a suitcase. As we listened to the movie in a dark room in the middle of the night, my fears of getting caught for our illicit activity were compounded by the lethal actions unfolding in this unnerving murder mystery.

Many nights each week, for months on end, we risked getting caught and punished for the adventure of listening to the same movie over and over. We would pause the movie in different places each time, and re-enact the dialogue, trying to master the way the actors spoke. After every session, we would sneak back to the dorms at around two or three o'clock in the morning. Classes started at half past seven, so I usually ended up attending class half-asleep, but my English skills improved dramatically.

Movies weren't the only import I consumed with fervor. As China opened more to the West in the post-Cultural Revolution era, we were allowed to read more world literature. I discovered the wondrous works of Stendhal and Alexandre Dumas, nineteenth-century French writers whose novels drew me into my first encounters with religion, spirituality, and the concept of God. I marveled at how the Christian faith had influenced the great nations of the West. The demands of school kept me from delving more fully into these ideas, but they made an impact on me. The more I looked toward the West and America, the more it glistened like higher ground, a place of freedom to which I could run, a place where the black dots and ghosts might never find me.

In the fall of 1981, toward the end of my fourth year at USTC, the University made an announcement that created quite a buzz on campus. The school was going to send a small number of graduates to America. I couldn't believe the news. Maybe my chance of going to the U.S. had finally arrived!

Diplomatic ties with the U.S. had been formally established in 1979, and universities had been exchanging professional scholars for a few years. Not many Chinese students had yet gone overseas, but USTC told us they would be granting permission to a small number of handpicked students to study abroad, though those who were chosen would still have to secure acceptance and financial assistance on their own.

Each department was asked to nominate its top candidates, and I was one of many selected by the chemistry department. A highly competitive selection process—based on grades and a personal interview—would then narrow the applicants down to just the top five. While I couldn't have anticipated that the opportunity to go to the U.S. would ever arise, I had fortunately been diligently and passionately studying American English throughout the past four years. I was determined to convince my interviewers that I deserved one of the five spots from our department of over one hundred students. I explained that I wanted to more fully explore and master the sciences, especially laser physics. I pointed out that the U.S. had produced more Nobel laureates than any other country in the world, and I promised to represent our school and our country well if I was chosen to study in the U.S..

Shortly afterward, I learned that I had been selected to meet Professor James McNesby, a chemistry professor from the University of Maryland at College Park, who was coming to the USTC campus. This meeting would help the school decide on the final roster of five students who would be sent to the U.S. Apart from my brief and distant encounter with President Nixon, this would be my first up-close contact with an American. The night before Professor McNesby's lecture, I studied an English textbook so I could ask him a question after his presentation. I had to find a way to impress him so that perhaps he could not only help me get USTC's approval to study abroad, but also help me secure a teaching assistantship at his University. This might be my only chance to go to America and support myself there. I was so excited that I barely slept that night.

The next day, Dr. McNesby gave a presentation to a group of about one hundred students and faculty members. He looked so tall, and his nose seemed so big! His American features were so different from mine, unlike anything I had ever seen. Once Dr. McNesby finished his lecture, he asked if anyone had questions. While the other students remained formal and quiet, my hand shot up immediately. He motioned to me, and I stood up and asked him the question I had spent the night before preparing.

"Professor, what is the academic load of your school?"

Dr. McNesby looked puzzled. "Can you explain what you mean?"

"What is the academic load of your school?" I asked again.

"I'm sorry; I still don't understand. What do you mean by 'academic load?'"

I couldn't understand him clearly either, because despite all my previous English studies, my ability to speak the language was still very limited. To my horror, I realized I had only memorized that one question, but I failed to prepare for the possibility of needing to respond to Dr. McNesby's answer. So all I could think of to do in that moment was just smile and keep repeating the same question over and over.

"What is the academic load of your school?"

To make the matter worse, it dawned on me that perhaps the reason that he did not understand my question was because though I did pull out a English textbook to study and prepare my question the night before, I picked up a British English textbook, not an American one, so the expression "academic load" might not have as specific meaning in America as it did in Great Britain!

His confused look continued. I could see that my hope of impressing him was quickly waning, and I was about to sit down in total defeat.

"Ah, you mean 'what are the credit hours required for a doctorate degree?'"

Professor McNesby finally understood my question and gave me a response. Even though I didn't really understand his answer, I had nonetheless achieved what I set out to do; I had asked him a question! And just as I had hoped, the professor was indeed impressed, perhaps not by my rudimentary English but by my persistence in repeatedly asking him a question without giving up.

Before he left the podium, Professor McNesby pointed at me and said, "I want to see that kid in America."

Though I didn't completely understand what he had just said, seeing him smile gave me the feeling I had accomplished my goal. He would help me get to America!

Professor McNesby did help me secure a coveted opportunity to study in America, and as chairman of the chemistry department at the University of Maryland in College Park, he was also able to arrange a teaching assistantship not only for me but also for my classmates Jason Zhou and Ji-hong Dai, who were among the five chosen from our department to study overseas. The official offer from the University of Maryland and my student visa were secured by the end of the semester. Professor McNesby had also lent me fifty dollars, and relatives and friends gave me enough money to buy a one-way plane ticket to America!

I was visiting my grandparents in the Fujian Province when USTC's vice president called to confirm that all the paperwork had been finalized. My parents, aunts, and uncles surrounded me with exuberant cheers. "Little Ming-xu is going to America!" I promised them I would do a good job in America, and would honor China and the Wang family name. My family members' faces glowed with pride.

It was official; I was bound for America. Reflecting on my life up to that point, I was amazed that not only had I survived the devastating Cultural Revolution and gotten into college in the toughest year to do so in China's history, but now I was fortunate enough to be going to America for my graduate studies! How had I made it this far? Looking at the beaming faces of my family, I knew how much I was indebted to them for their love and support. My parents were dedicated to their children, and instilled in us from a very young age the desire to learn. Their encouragement sustained me during very trying times. Though I had suffered greatly during the Cultural Revolution, persevering through the difficulties had only made me stronger, and now I truly appreciated the opportunities of an education and freedom. I realized that it was the combination of my inner resolve and my parents' tireless advocacy that had helped me overcome these monumental challenges. In time, I would come to see just how much this upbringing shaped my character and influenced my life in America.

In January of 1982, I celebrated my last New Year at home with my family. In early February, in the dark hours of morning, an entourage of family members and well-wishers accompanied me as I began my journey overseas. I sat on the back of a classmate's bike, my luggage hanging from each side, as my parents, relatives. and friends rode alongside us through the streets of Hangzhou to the train station.

My dad accompanied me on the train to Shanghai, where I would depart the following day. He and I huddled tightly on the crowded train. My family had pulled together just enough money to buy a one-way airplane ticket to America, and now he was spending even more money to travel with me to Shanghai.

"You didn't have to come all this way with me," I said.

"I know," Dad said, "but I want to see you get on that plane."

Up until then, I had been so excited about America that I hadn't had much time to think about leaving my family so far behind. My lips started to quiver. The passengers across from me disappeared behind my blur of tears, which I then quickly wiped away.

At the Shanghai International Airport the next day, I stared up at an enormous Boeing 747, part of the fleet flown by the Civil Aviation Administration of China. A throng of people clustered on the tarmac as passengers made their way up the open-air staircase to get into the plane. As I reached the top, I turned around and looked toward the crowd in search of my father. I wanted to confirm that he had definitely seen me board the plane headed to America, and wave goodbye to him one last time. But the large crowd of family members was too far from the plane, so I couldn't see them clearly enough to identify anyone's faces. My stomach clenched, and a lump formed in my throat. My father had sustained me throughout this very long journey for so many challenging years, and now it looked like he would actually miss seeing me move on to the next stage of my life.

I waved in the general direction of the crowd, hoping my father might see me and wave back. But the hands of so many people were in the air, waving to their own friends and family; how would I know which one was actually my father's? As I put my arm down in disappointment, I noticed through the corner of my eyes that a person in the crowd put his arm down as well. Curious and excited that the person might be my father, I raised my hand again, and so did that person. I put my hand down again, and so did he. I waved again. He waved back. It finally dawned on me that that person was indeed my father! While I could not identify him in a crowd of people, he could actually see me standing alone on the top deck of the staircase, so he had figured out a clever way for him to stand out himself in the crowd by synchronizing our hand waves so we could identify each other from distance among all these people and wish each other a heartfelt goodbye.

I could now finally cross the threshold of the plane with peace of mind. I hummed the tune "Little Bird." In a matter of moments, I would be flying into the open skies to begin an entirely new chapter of my life, life in the United States of America.

Part Three

Life in America

Chapter 7

Three Musketeers

As the plane descended into the airspace of the San Francisco airport, I pressed my forehead against the oval window. The deep blue Pacific Ocean below me stretched and curved toward the horizon until it disappeared into a pale haze. Northern California's dark-green hills rolled outward into an ever-increasing expanse of land. I had never seen so much green in all my life, nor so many cars! I looked down at thousands of vehicles streaming through highways, and I couldn't believe I was finally about to step onto American soil. Tchaikovsky's symphony, *Romeo and Juliet*, wafted through my headset, a soundtrack to the scene I was beholding. If I could have gathered all my hopes and dreams for my new life in America, the glittering sea below me could not have contained them all.

Our route across the globe took us from Shanghai to San Francisco to New York City before we reached our final destination. I arrived in Washington, D.C. on Wednesday, February 3, 1982 with my USTC classmates, Jason and Ji-hong. It's a date I will never forget as long as I live. I was twenty-one years old. Everything I owned at that point I carried in my two hands, including two suitcases of clothing, a well-worn Chinese-English dictionary, and fifty dollars in cash.

We hailed a cab at the airport, excited and exhausted at the same time. The drive from Washington National Airport to the University of Maryland at College Park took us across the Potomac River and along the outskirts of the capital city. The three of us were crammed into the back seat, elbowing each other and pointing at sights like the gleaming dome of the Thomas Jefferson Memorial and the sharp point of the Washington Monument jutting straight into the sky.

The cab driver was from Africa. I was intrigued to meet another immigrant, and I asked him if it was difficult to drive in America.

"No, it's easier," he replied, "because the roads here all have lines and lanes."

This was true. Back in China, the roads weren't divided nicely with painted white or yellow lines like these orderly, American streets were, so driving on them in China was basically mayhem! I couldn't get over how immaculate the city looked with its trimmed lawns, clear sidewalks, and lack of leaves or garbage strewn throughout the streets. It was so clean that I was even attempted to just lie down and roll around on the ground. The difference between the pictures of America that I had been shown back in China and the reality I experienced from my cab window was so drastic that it left me disoriented. Nowhere did I see the widespread poverty and misery in which Americans supposedly lived. The real America wasn't at all the dark and unhappy place I had been told it was. I let out a sigh as I realized that everything I had previously been taught was now suspect. I would have to seek out the truth now for myself.

Jason and Ji-hong were no less surprised than I was. We marveled at our surroundings for the entire fifteen-mile drive from the airport to campus. As we unloaded our luggage outside the University of

Maryland at College Park, I looked around at the gently rolling grounds and the elegant, red-brick Georgian buildings with their stately, white column-lined entrances. Winter had muted the colors of the lawns and sky, which left the trees barren of any leaves, but I still reveled in the awe-inspiring beauty of our new school. Jason, Ji-hong, and I picked up our bags and made our way toward the chemistry building, occasionally asking for directions in our broken English. Each time we approached someone, the student or faculty member would stop and patiently explain the route, repeating it until we indeed knew where we were going. I was taken aback by the empathy and courtesy Americans expressed toward strangers. Such openness was foreign to me back home, and I was moved by it.

When we finally arrived at the large, boxy, brick complex, staff and faculty were trickling out the doors to head home for the day. We went inside and presented ourselves to the department secretary, who introduced herself as Marsha. She was a lovely woman in her mid-thirties who wore thick makeup—I had never seen ladies with such thick makeup in China before, and whose eyes smiled behind thick, gold-framed glasses.

"Welcome! Glad you made it safely," Marsha said. "You can go home now and rest for a day, and we'll see you back here on Friday."

Her accent sounded funny to me. I hadn't heard anyone speak English quite like that before. I stared at the abundance of red hair flowing around her face. I had also never seen that hair color previously in my life.

"But where is home?" I asked. "Where will we be staying?"

Her brow furrowed, and she looked at me curiously. "You're actually on your own for that, but I can recommend a hotel and give you a list of nearby apartments."

We thanked her and went back outside.

"What should we do now?" Ji-hong asked.

We didn't have enough money for a hotel. We had just spent more than fifty dollars for the cab ride from the airport. We were accustomed to the communist system in China and assumed that our housing would have already been arranged in advance and assigned to us by the university. We weren't prepared for this newfound independence and the responsibility that came with it.

I felt a strange, unfamiliar sensation, the first taste of freedom. For my entire life leading up to that moment, I had been told what to do. Now that I had arrived in America—the land of freedom—this new feeling of independence was refreshing, but it also left me a bit unsettled. Where would we stay?

Jason pulled out the phone number of a visiting scholar named Teacher Cai from USTC. We were relieved we were able to connect with Teacher Cai quickly, and he kindly allowed us to stay at his apartment for a few nights while we figured out our next step.

When I spoke to Professor McNesby later, he explained that graduate students were expected to manage their own affairs. "Our society is clean and civilized, as you have seen," he said, "and we're also highly individualistic. You have to depend on yourself to make a living. Everyone must pull their own weight here."

Once we had arranged to stay with Teacher Cai, I turned to Jason and Ji-hong, "You guys hungry?"

"Let's go find some food," Jason said.

We looked for a Chinese restaurant near campus, but there wasn't one within walking distance. We had no car, so we went somewhere close and cheap, a place a few broke students could afford. Our first meal in America was at a McDonald's right on the edge of campus. I was so hungry that I would have eaten anything. I ordered four Big Macs, but then immediately realized there was no way I was going to be able to eat it all. The Chinese diet is generally free of dairy, and I was about to eat double cheeseburgers slathered in mayo!

I expected the worst . . . but I loved it, I really did! So much so that I ate at McDonald's nearly every day, and in just three months, I had gained thirty pounds.

On Friday, Jason, Ji-hong, and I put on our best clothes. We wanted to make a good impression on our new colleagues and professors in the chemistry department. My parents had spent three months of their salaries to buy me an elegant three-piece suit, black with a white shirt and red tie. The three of us walked onto campus dressed head to toe in full formal attire . . . and immediately felt completely out of place.

All the other students and professors had on very casual clothes, like blue jeans, T-shirts, and polos. Some of them even wore shorts and sandals. People turned to look at us as we strolled by. We may have been nearly penniless, but we were certainly the best dressed. My face was burning with embarrassment. I had only brought two sets of casual shirts and pants. We had to go shopping as soon as possible.

Once we arrived at the chemistry department, I asked Marsha, "Can you give us some money? We need to buy some food and clothing." Seeing us standing there in fancy three-piece suits, I wondered if she really believed me.

"Your first paycheck will be in two weeks," she said.

"So, no money right now?" I asked.

She gave me a funny look.

I realized once again that we were on our own here in America. I had longed for independence, but now that I actually had it, I felt a bit lost. For years in college in China, I had relied on a national system of support. Being free and completely on my own in America would take a lot of getting used to.

During our graduate studies, Jason, Ji-hong, and I worked as teaching assistants to support ourselves. We hadn't yet been assigned cubicles, so we camped out that first day in the department chairman's conference room. My eyes felt heavy from lingering jet lag, so I leaned on the conference room table and propped my head up with my hand to keep from nodding off. But when Marsha entered the room and announced that we had to take a number of tests, I bolted upright. This was the first time since meeting her that she was not either sitting or standing behind her desk. She wore shoes with the highest heels I had ever seen in my life.

"These are subject matter tests," she explained, "that will determine what level of graduate classes you'll take."

I watched her walk around the conference table, marveling that she could move with such grace and effortless balance on heels that were so high, yet had such tiny points touching the ground.

We were sequestered in that conference room for the next six hours. Our studies at USTC in China had given us a very strong foundation in science, and my written English was now good enough to understand and respond to the questions without too much trouble. The tests covered several subjects, including analytical chemistry, physical chemistry, organic chemistry, and inorganic chemistry.

Marsha came in periodically to check on us. At around five o'clock, she returned one last time to collect our exams. "You guys ready for some pizza?"

We followed her to a party down the hall. I had no idea what pizza was, but I was starving and therefore open to anything. Once again, I was faced with another odd new food. I looked at the spread of food on the table and wondered who on earth would just throw meat and vegetables on a slab of dough like this and then just bake it? It seemed so uncultured and unsophisticated. The rich assortment of toppings could be made into a variety of so many nice dishes by a Chinese chef. But yet again, I ended up loving it anyway. At the pizza party, I learned that Marsha was Irish. Another immigrant! No wonder her English sounded so funny. As I introduced myself to others at the party, I soon discovered that people had trouble pronouncing the "xu" in my name so I decided at that point to just drop it to make things easier for everyone, so my new American name became just "Ming."

A few days later, our test scores were posted on a bulletin board in the hallway. My eyes widened when I saw the results.

Analytical chemistry: 93, physical chemistry: 91, organic chemistry: 100, and inorganic chemistry: 72. These subject matter tests weren't supposed to be easy, and a typical score was fifty out of one hundred. All three of us had received perfect scores on the organic chemistry test. We later learned that ours were the highest scores of any graduate student in the department in the past twenty years.

The news of our high scores quickly spread well beyond the chemistry department...and the University of Maryland. Back in China, newspapers across the country boasted bold headlines that read, "Three Chinese Students Stun American University." I imagined my family back home reading the newspapers, and I was delighted knowing I had honored the Wang family name across the globe. I hoped all the teachers who had worked so hard to help me pass the nearly impossible college entrance exam at the end of the Cultural Revolution years ago would see the headlines too. They would take such immense pride in the outcome of their extraordinary efforts. And such high scores weren't just about me; they proved to the world that China was emerging from the shroud of the Cultural Revolution, placing its students among the world's best. I felt the pride and gratitude of an entire nation surging through my body.

"Let's go celebrate!" I proposed to Jason and Ji-hong.

"Where?" they asked.

"Where else? McDonald's!"

* * *

During our first weekend in College Park, we set out to find somewhere to stay for the next few months. On the list of apartments Marsha had given us, we saw the odd name "Knox Boxes." I envisioned students living in actual boxes, and wondered how big these boxes were. In reality, the campus neighborhood was filled with small brick duplexes on a street called Knox Road. We ended up renting a windowless one-room basement apartment in a nearby house for about a hundred dollars a month, which we split among the three of us.

It turned out to be the perfect size for us. The university dorms back in China packed in thirteen students per unit, so a room with only two other people felt roomy and spacious to us. We shared the basement's bathroom with a couple who lived in an adjacent room, and when we wanted to cook, we had to ask the upstairs renters for permission to use their kitchen. But overall, we felt right at home.

"What should we do for furniture?" one of the guys asked.

As we strolled along Knox Road, we came across a dumpster brimming with things other students had discarded. Several twin-size mattresses were piled up against the metal bin. We took three of the better ones back to our room. After finding a few chairs and a roll of used carpet, we were all set.

Jason, Ji-hong, and I bonded in our tight quarters and went everywhere together. One of the visiting Chinese scholars, Ms. Jing-yi Hong, who was an expert in world literature, called us the "Three Musketeers."

"Like in the Alexandre Dumas novel!" I responded, recalling the literature I read back at USTC.

The name was fitting. The three of us became very close during those first two years together in a foreign land. Jason was three years older than I was, and he was the wisest and most diplomatic of our trio. If we had a conflict, Jason was the one to resolve it calmly and logically. He had been deported for several years to a poor region of western China during the Cultural Revolution, and the experience had given him his hard-earned maturity. Ji-hong was my age, and absolutely brilliant. He was the academic star of our trio. My unique quality was that I was well-rounded. I had the most diverse interests and often came up with fun things for us to do.

For the two weeks prior to our first payday, we pinched pennies in every way possible. I wore the same two or three sets of clothes over and over. We had no washer or dryer, so I washed my shirts and pants by hand in the bathroom sink. I tried to set up a laundry line outside our door—a contraption like the one my father had constructed in our window back in Hangzhou— but the homeowner here in America laughed and said, "No way."

After our first two weeks of work, I received my first paycheck of $198, which equaled about 1,600 yuan in China. I was so happy; I was speechless. In just two weeks I had earned as much as my parents made in more than a year. But while it amounted to a lot of money back in China, it wasn't enough to cover my living expenses in America, which were much higher than in China. So I had to take on some odd jobs like tutoring undergraduates, cleaning professors' houses, and working night shifts at Burger King and weekend shifts at the local Best Western for $3.35 an hour. Besides paying my bills, I had to save up enough money for the eight high-priced items that the Chinese government allowed overseas graduate students to purchase and bring home without paying customs fees. For the next three years, I worked hard to be able to buy these items for my family.

As soon as we cashed our first paychecks, Jason, Ji-hong, and I headed out to shop right away. I had budgeted fifty dollars for clothes, but when we arrived at the Salvation Army store, I realized I wouldn't need nearly that much. I spent only fifteen dollars and went home with two big trash bags full of all kinds of used clothes.

But this time, we turned even more heads than we did the day we showed up in three-piece suits. Evidently, all the clothes we had purchased at the thrift store were styles from the sixties and seventies—bell-bottom pants, brightly colored shirts, psychedelic patterns. So we had just morphed from yuppies into hippies. Our colleagues in the chemistry department were highly amused. They thought our formal attire had been strange, but now we had gone completely retro.

As a teaching assistant, part of my job was to lead evening recitation classes twice a week for undergraduate students. During these sessions, I would review material presented by the professor to ensure that the students had grasped the concepts, and help them work through difficult homework assignments. These recitation classes weren't mandatory for students to attend, but since they were quite helpful, there was usually a great turnout. Or so I had been told.

Before my first recitation class, I studied extremely hard, as I wanted to do a good job. Since my English was very limited, I decided to actually write down everything I planned to say for the entire two-hour session, and I memorized the whole thing the night before the class.

I arrived the next day well-prepared and excited to teach my first recitation class in America. There were one hundred and twenty students enrolled in the course, so I expected that many of them would come to my class. But when I walked through the doors, my heart fell to the floor.

As the doors slammed shut behind me, I stared up at the auditorium seats in disbelief. Only two people had shown up... two out of one hundred and twenty students!

It turned out that Jason, Ji-hong, and I were among the earliest exchange students from mainland China, so we were curiosities on campus. We wore silly clothes and spoke elementary English with heavy accents. In those first few weeks at school, my friends and I were regarded more as the Three Stooges than the Three Musketeers. That reputation had apparently spread to my undergraduate recitation class. The students heard that their new teaching assistant was foreign and difficult to understand, so nobody bothered to show up for my session.

I was humbled by all the no-shows. I was disappointed because I had done so much work to prepare, but I suppressed my chagrin and began to teach. The two students who did show up were happy to get the personalized tutoring.

The embarrassment inspired my desire to do a better job as a teaching assistant and improve my English as quickly as possible. To me a semester-long English class at the university would take too long, and in order to live and communicate in this country, I needed to learn the language more quickly than that. So I resorted to the tactic Le-ping and I had used back at USTC in China. I discovered a rundown movie theater called the Biography Theatre near Wisconsin Avenue in D.C.'s Georgetown district, at which I could watch two feature films a night for just a dollar. I went there at least once a week, mostly by myself, though occasionally I would drag one of the other Musketeers with me. I saw many classic American films there, like *Gone With the Wind, The Godfather, Some Like It Hot, Doctor Zhivago, On the Waterfront,* and *Breakfast at Tiffany's.*

The movies did help me improve not only my English, but also my understanding of American culture. My favorite movie was *It's a Wonderful Life.* I watched the main character, George Bailey, nearly give up on his life when he encountered seemingly insurmountable hardship. His guardian angel showed him that his life, no matter how difficult, had in fact made a positive impact on so many people. This story represented what impressed me most about American culture. Americans, as a whole, displayed an unbridled positivity toward life. I wanted to find the same freedom and confidence, and I wanted to make my life matter.

I remembered my father's words during the Cultural Revolution when I had lost all hope for my future. "Ming, you must always have hope," he said. Facing all the years of deprivation and repression back in China gave me a fighting spirit and a singular focus on whatever I set out to do. I was acutely aware of how precious this opportunity to live and study in America was, and I knew how hard I would have to work to succeed. I couldn't let the no-shows get me down, but the students weren't the only ones who saw me differently, as I would soon find out. Being accepted and respected in this new country was something I could never take for granted. I would be forced to prove myself again and again.

Chapter 8

The Yellow Dot

Not long after our scores on the subject matter tests were posted, Jason, Ji-hong, and I became the talk of the chemistry department. Professor McNesby was delighted with our performance on the tests, and later that week he addressed about one hundred students and faculty who had gathered in a lecture hall for a department meeting.

"We've got three smart cookies from China who are setting a good example for our students," he said, beaming from the podium.

My faculty advisor, on the other hand, wasn't convinced.

"You just got lucky."

His name was Jerry Miller, and he advised me on the required classes for my graduate program. He was tall, strong, and straight-faced. Professor Miller didn't believe that a minority student like me could succeed in American higher education. He made that clear in our first meeting with his dismissive response to my scores. It wouldn't be the last time I experienced his prejudice against me as a minority, nor would he be the last person to shun me based on my ethnic origin.

I was, however, very shocked to encounter such prejudice from my academic advisor. Being in America, I thought I had finally found the fairness and equality that had eluded me back in China. During the Cultural Revolution, I was part of a family of doctors and intellectuals who were reviled by the communists as the "stinking ninth class," the lowest rung of the entire social order. But I thought it was going to be the opposite in America; I was supposed to be respected for my knowledge and education. I could not get over how Professor Miller could be so contemptuous toward me simply because I was a minority. I realized that life isn't always fair, even in a great country like America.

On the other hand, many other professors were delighted at our academic achievement, and vied to be our thesis advisors and recruit us for their research teams. I went out to eat with at least four different professors, including Dr. McNesby, who hosted all three of us for dinner at his home one evening. Only one other faculty member, John Weiner, invited me to dinner at his home.

At the time, Professor John Weiner was not yet forty years old, but was already a rising star in laser applications in chemistry and physics. He had dark, curly hair and an intense gaze. He was curious, focused, and driven. While I owed so much to Professor McNesby for his assistance in getting me to the States, I was drawn to Professor Weiner and his intriguing work with lasers.

Professor Weiner and his wife, Denise, lived in a beautiful home decorated with reproductions of European art. Denise was French, and the couple had spent a considerable amount of time living overseas. They were lively and laughed a lot, and I felt at ease in their presence. After a hearty meal of homemade lasagna, Professor Weiner and I retreated to the living room to play a game of backgammon. He started lining up the red checkers on his side of the board, leaving me with the black pieces. I joked that we should switch colors since I was from Red China, to which he laughed.

"You could focus on any number of topics for your thesis," he said, as he moved one of his pieces on the board. He leaned forward, his elbows resting on his knees. "Why the interest in lasers?"

I told him about being wide-eyed in Professor Ma's laser lab back at USTC and in the movie theater watching *Star Wars*, and I added that I wanted to devote my life to this exciting, emerging technology.

"Are you ready to play *Star Wars* for real?" he asked.

"Yes, absolutely. That's what I've always wanted to do."

I was convinced that lasers would transform the world. Using lasers, we could better determine the safest and strongest materials for space shuttles and satellites, and the best elements for electronics and computer parts. Lasers would eventually be considered one of the greatest inventions of the twentieth century, and although I imagined so many inspiring possibilities, I didn't know then just how crucial lasers would later become to my career and my life.

"Welcome to the team," said Dr. Weiner. "We're going to do great things together."

The early years at the University of Maryland were spent mostly in classes for my graduate program or on the undergraduate courses for which I served as a teaching assistant. I juggled school, multiple side jobs, and occasional lab experiments. Despite my busy schedule, I still found time to pursue my favorite hobbies like piano, ballet, and ping-pong. I made many new friends, and for the first time in my life, I even fell in love.

Her name was Shu Chen. We met at a Christmas party at the end of my second year in Maryland, and talked throughout the evening. I found out that her family had come to the U.S. from Taiwan when she was in junior high. She loved science and was planning to go to medical school after her undergraduate studies were completed. I told her about the generations of doctors in my family and the medical school classes I had audited illegally back in China. She was lovely, lively, and intelligent, and I felt completely at ease with her.

Not long after our first encounter, Shu and I began dating. On the weekends, she often accompanied me to the rundown theater in Georgetown. I was a big fan of Bruce Lee, so we watched a lot of old kung-fu movies together. I didn't have any female friends growing up, and I had never had a girlfriend before, but our relationship blossomed over the next few years, and Shu and I were engaged by the time we finished school. I didn't know then that our relationship would fall on very difficult times because we were both too young to understand the balance between a healthy marriage and demanding careers.

Success in school was paramount to me and many other minority students fighting to prove ourselves at American universities. No matter how many As I got in my classes, Professor Miller was never supportive or happy for me, but when I got a B in a difficult physical chemistry class, he asked, "Sure you want to keep going? Can you handle the rest of your courses?" When it came time to formulate a doctoral thesis, Professor Miller doubted my ability to create and defend the proposal, or to conduct the experiments. I couldn't understand how he could still just fixate on my ethnicity and remain so blind to my actual abilities.

Miller had inherited a perception of the Chinese based on a century of fear and misunderstanding between our cultures. The only Chinese immigrants he was aware of weren't the visiting scholars or the capable students, but rather only the hundreds of thousands of poor immigrants from the Guangdong Province who first came to the U.S. in the nineteenth century. Those immigrants had come for the Gold Rush, and stayed on to build the transcontinental railroad, start businesses like laundromats and restaurants, and fight decades of extreme legalized discrimination. I didn't stand before Dr. Miller as a person in my own right; in his mind, I was apparently just one of many little "rats" that had jumped ship from China. I was endlessly frustrated that nothing I did—no amount of good work—could ever change his mind.

Fortunately, most of the other faculty members were not like Dr. Miller. They were open-minded and supportive toward students of all ethnic origins. Contrary to Professor Miller's predictions, I did successfully defend my doctoral thesis proposal, and research with Dr. Weiner began in earnest during the second half of my graduate program. With basic coursework completed, I spent much more time in Dr. Weiner's laser lab.

The lab was an immense room with thick concrete walls and flooring made of dark brown anti-corrosive tiles. One side of the room had windows that were kept permanently draped, but the room would light up from all kinds of laser beams bouncing off mirrors from different angles. The main attraction was a stainless-steel gas chamber that was hooked up to a variety of electronics. The contraption was as big as a king-size bed and stood at chest level. Panes of glass allowed us to observe what was happening inside the chamber.

Weiner's research team included me, two other graduate students named John Keller and Regina Bonanno, and a postdoctoral fellow named Mattanjah de Vries. We studied the interaction of colliding atoms in this huge laser-lit machine. The goal of our work was to create the most conducive environment for getting one atom to bond with another. Atoms that have bonded into molecules create a lot of the matter in the world, as when two hydrogen atoms bond with an oxygen atom to produce a water molecule. We used the sodium atom as our experimental model, and our endeavor was to create dimers, structures made up of two sodium atoms bonded together. We considered ourselves "molecular matchmakers," since we were studying lonely atoms traveling through space and evaluating how we could set a mood that would encourage these singles come together and settle down into more stable molecular pairs.

If we were molecular matchmakers, conducting these experiments was like staging singles parties. We inserted a block of sodium into a metal cylinder, and then warmed them up using electrical wires wrapped around the cylinder. As the heat increased, the atoms would vaporize and begin to move very quickly, until they shot out of the tiny opening at one end of the cylinder into a large reaction chamber. These atoms' intended partners were beamed into the same chamber from a second cylinder oriented at a 90-degree angle. The laser was key to increasing a single atom's receptivity to another. It was like introducing two people who each had their arms folded tightly across their chests. The yellow laser was used to help a lonely sodium atom "unfold his or her arms" and thus become more receptive to another atom, so they could have a chance to become a sodium couple.

Over and over again, we threw these atomic singles parties with various configurations, trying to see if a couple would form from each effort. We would know when it happened because the newly formed pair would emit a distinct yellow light.

Many evenings each week I would key up the atom beams, set up the electromagnetic components, and fire up the laser. Once everything was ready, the rest of the experiment was conducted in the dark. The only light came from the lasers traversing the room, bouncing from one mirror to another. The laser light would pulsate, making a tap-tap-tap noise, like incessantly dripping water. I was like a ghost in the dark, hovering over the machine until two or three in the morning, tortured by that repetitive rhythm. I remembered experiencing a similar rhythm when I was wrapping books at the factory at the end of the Cultural Revolution in China, but the difference was that back then I was sad because I had no hope for a future, but now I enjoyed it since there was a greater, more exciting purpose.

It was a long, tedious, often frustrating process, but thinking back, my Eastern upbringing and work ethic helped to sustain me. Dr. Weiner was pleased with my efforts. During a faculty and student party at his house, he told colleagues about the diligence and creativity that I regularly applied to the tasks. But once again, my faculty advisor, Professor Miller, was not impressed at all. When he heard Professor Weiner's complimentary remarks about me, he turned around and asked, "What do most Chinese do in this country anyway?"

"They're in the restaurant business," answered another professor.

"Exactly," said Miller. "Weiner is just using Ming to do some precision cooking."

I stared at him in disbelief. An awkward silence hung over the group, and then Professor Miller started laughing at his own joke.

Regardless of my performance, from record-high test scores to extremely delicate atomic experiments, Miller would never perceive me as a fellow scientist standing equally shoulder to shoulder with him. In his mind, I was just a Chinese cook in Dr. Weiner's kitchen. I looked over Dr. Weiner's shoulder to where Miller stood near a window. I had endured his slights and insults for years, and I was suddenly consumed with the urge to punch him like Bruce Lee would do in his kung-fu movies. Even though Miller was much bigger than I was, I imagined myself leaping up and kicking him in the jaw so hard that his whole body would fly through the glass window and land outside with a loud thud.

But I didn't want to be like the Red Guards in China, who assaulted and dishonored their teachers. Restraining my fury, I instead forced a slight smile.

Professor Miller's constant discriminatory rebuffs only made me more determined to succeed. Late one night, our research team had been working for hours, and we were ready to call it a night. It was the dead of winter, the temperature outside had been falling, and forecasters were warning of nasty, freezing rain. We were worried about getting home before the road conditions became dangerous. But I continued tweaking the electrical current around the cylinder and readjusting the laser light, with no results. Just before shutting down the entire apparatus, I decided to give it one last try by boosting the current just beyond its limit.

"Be careful, Ming," warned John, my lab partner. "If you turn it up too high, the coil could melt and then we'll have to spend months rebuilding the whole machine."

I nodded, nervous that I might ruin our entire project, but then increased the heat anyway. I just didn't want to give up, as I hoped that maybe under hotter conditions, the atoms would fly a bit more quickly and our odds of atomic coupling might increase. Under the higher electrical current, I smelled the coil start to sizzle. My stomach fluttered and my breath was shallow. I knew I couldn't keep the machine running this hot for very long because in a matter of minutes, the cylinder's coils could melt.

By this point, I had done everything I could think of and had reached the limit of my capabilities. I felt helpless, and I longed for assistance from a power greater than myself. I hadn't had much exposure to religion and spirituality except for the world literature I read back in China. The concept of faith was still very foreign to me, but at that moment I thought that if there was indeed a God in the universe, this would certainly be the time for Him to show up.

Peering into the chamber window, I whispered, "God, if you do exist, please come help us!"

I took a deep breath, and as I looked through the glass again, I saw something I had never seen before. There in the middle of the gas chamber, a bright yellow dot was glowing.

"There it is!" I shouted. As John rushed over to look, I ran out of the lab and straight into Dr. Weiner's office to deliver the news. He was just about to go home, but he dropped his bag on the ground and hurried ahead of me back to the lab. He leaned over and saw the bright yellow dot in the middle of the chamber, our first successful atomic marriage. He then fell to his knees, lay down on the floor with his arms and legs spread out to each side, and sang loudly.

I laughed at the sight of my esteemed professor lying on the floor being as joyful as a kid on Christmas. At long last, a sodium dimer was formed and was glowing with atomic happiness . . . and so were we. After two years of effort, we had finally gotten the atomic collider to work. Not only had we seen it with our own eyes, but the detector on top of the machine also confirmed the results. I was filled with a sense of awe, not just that the experiment had finally succeeded, but also that I felt as if something supernatural had occurred. But I was a scientist, and there was no room in the scientific mindset for the supernatural. Yet I couldn't deny the overwhelming sense that perhaps God did exist, that He did hear my simple prayer, and that He showed up in the bright glow of that yellow dot. I began to imagine that this God might be real and powerful and infinite, extending from the grandeur of the universe to the infinitesimal specks of subatomic particles.

On my way home, I was grateful for the empty roads. I was driving an old car I had bought with my roommates, a white 1973 AMC Matador so massive that we nicknamed her "M1" after the giant U.S. military combat vehicle. M1 was temperamental and stalled out every ten minutes when she was driven. But that night, I didn't care when M1 choked, shook, and sputtered. In fact, she seemed to be celebrating with me! I was utterly ecstatic, whooping and hollering at the frosted windshield, singing in the icy rain. M1 and I careened joyfully from side to side across the slick streets and swerved our way home.

The next day, our team recorded the details of the molecular miracle and redesigned the machine to work safely at a higher level of electrical current. Now that we had produced a state-of-the-art collider, I spent the rest of my time in the doctoral program elevating the experiment to a more sophisticated level. We still needed to determine the best speed for the atomic coupling. If the atoms were traveling too slowly with respect to each other, they wouldn't get close enough to bond; but if they went too fast, on the other hand, they would fly right past each other. Eventually, I fine-tuned a novel technique to measure the ideal speed and direction for forming new atomic couples using the Doppler Effect, a physics principle that links the speed of a moving object and the color of light perceived by it. I was the first author on a series of original articles published by Weiner's lab team in the authoritative physics journal, *Physical Review A*. Our work was cited by scientists like Yuan T. Lee, Steven Chu, and William D. Phillips, who all won Nobel Prizes for chemistry and physics with atomic beam experiments which were similar to ours, but more refined. Each of my *Physical Review A* papers became a chapter in my thesis. I finished my doctorate in about four-and-a-half years, but I stayed on for another year in a postdoctoral fellowship to continue our team's work.

Toward the end of my graduate program, I began pondering what to do next. Watching Shu prepare for medical school had rekindled my childhood dream of being a doctor. I remembered being a teenager, standing in the circle of medical students in Hangzhou, watching my father leading rounds at the hospital. I was so filled with pride and hope back then, and the years in America had helped me find the freedom and confidence I had been longing for. Maybe now I could finally pursue this beloved dream I always had, but once thought was lost forever.

And like the sodium atom pairs in my team's experiment, I had bonded with someone and planned to settle down. Shu and I were married before she left for medical school in West Virginia. I may have been an excellent molecular matchmaker, but what worked in the lab didn't work the same way in life. Shu and I eventually discovered that our marriage was not very stable. For years we lived, studied, and worked in separate states. The distance would eventually be our undoing, as our career paths launched us into very different orbits.

Chapter 9

The White House

"Mr. Ming Wang? This is the executive office of the President of the United States," said a voice through the telephone. "We'd like to talk about arranging for you to visit the White House to meet the President."

I wasn't sure I was hearing him correctly. It was the spring of 1984, a few weeks before President Ronald Reagan was to go to China for an official six-day visit. His staff member told me that the President wanted to meet a select group of Chinese students before his trip.

"How many students can I invite?" I asked.

"Up to seven," replied the coordinator.

"Will we actually meet the President?"

"It's possible, but we cannot tell you for sure at this time."

For security reasons, there was no guarantee we would actually meet President Reagan, but eight of us would at least get an up close and personal glimpse into the most iconic building in the country, the White House. My mind traveled back more than a decade to the moment when I stood on the banks of West Lake in Hangzhou to welcome President Richard Nixon. And now, I just might meet another American president. My head was spinning, as I could hardly believe this was really happening.

A year prior, during my second year at the University of Maryland, I had joined the Chinese Student and Scholar Association, a group that met about once a quarter to plan activities. Our primary objectives were welcoming incoming Chinese students and hosting a Chinese New Year celebration each year. The student exchange from overseas continued to flourish, and we wanted to support the new arrivals in their transition to life here in America. I would never forget how clueless and unprepared I felt when I first arrived on the College Park campus with Jason and Ji-hong, so I was eager to help others transition more easily .

Jason, Ji-hong, and I would take our M1 to pick up arriving students from the airport and shuttle them around town. We also helped them find and haul used furniture for their apartments, and run any necessary errands. After a year of dedicated involvement, the Chinese Student and Scholar Association voted me president of the University of Maryland chapter of the association, and I told them I had great plans for our organization.

Up to that point, our group had been rather insular, but I had a vision of reaching out and welcoming our American friends into the Chinese community as well. One of my earliest projects as president of the association was producing and hosting a Chinese film festival. The Chinese embassy in D.C. allowed me to borrow a large number of movie reels, which I took back to the theater at the student union on the College Park campus. The films featured archetypal aspects of Chinese culture, including the Peking Opera, ancient dynasties, and epic moments in history, as well as the difficult stories of the Cultural Revolution depicted by China's fifth-generation filmmakers. The American movies I had seen back in China had transported me to a previously unknown world. By showing great Chinese films, I wanted to offer the Americans a portal, so they too could experience the unknown world of China.

The film festival featured movies twice a month. American students and faculty made up about half of the audience at every showing. I was thrilled that the movies were having an impact. After watching these films, our American friends and colleagues said things like, "I've never seen such colorful costumes," or "I had no idea there were so many different ethnic minorities in China." More understanding between us meant that friendships could blossom more easily. The movie theater became our meeting ground, and these stories helped us communicate with each other. These newly forged connections were exactly what I had set out to foster. Not only did I want Americans to understand more about China, but also I wanted my Chinese classmates to extend themselves beyond their comfort zones as well, and embrace the culture of America. I also wanted to learn more about this great country, in hopes of one day becoming its citizen myself.

In February of 1984, we hosted a Chinese New Year celebration that was open to the public. About four hundred people congregated in a high school auditorium in Silver Spring, Maryland. The room was strewn with bright red ribbons and banners. Actors and actresses walked around wearing traditional Chinese garb, and many of the American guests were specially dressed for the occasion as well. Women wore the traditional *chipao*, a form-fitting, ankle-length gown made of embroidered silk. Men wore *Tang* suits with rounded collars. The sight made my heart swell, as I felt I had found my calling— to create a cultural heart-to-heart link between my birthplace and the country I now called home. That night I played the erhu onstage, but not the melancholy sounds of blind Ah Bing that I had played during the Cultural Revolution when I struggled to survive. This time, upbeat folk tunes whose rhythms celebrated the new year and a new era of freedom in my life emanated from my instrument.

As word spread to other campus chapters across the country of how successful our association was in facilitating these cultural connections, I was asked to serve as the national president of the Chinese Student and Scholar Association. It wasn't long after assuming that post that I received the invitation to visit the White House to meet President Reagan as a representative of Chinese students and scholars here in America.

I extended this special invitation to seven other Chinese Student and Scholar leaders from nearby universities. On the day of the event, the M1 chugged her way through the streets of D.C., and I parked just a few blocks from Pennsylvania Avenue. The closest I had ever been to the White House before that moment was standing well outside the guarded gates like any other tourist, but now I was honored and excited to be going inside. The grand and gleaming white building struck me as a perfect symbol of America's open, civilized, and fair democracy, a blazing contrast to the oppressive darkness I had known in years past.

Our group went through security at the entrance to the West Wing, and a staff member came to greet us in the lobby.

"A presidential appearance might be possible," he said, "but I can't guarantee anything. Vice President Bush will meet with you first."

I admired both of these leaders. George H. W. Bush was well known in China, since he had spent more than a year as the head of the U.S. Liaison Office in Beijing in 1974. I also knew that Ronald Reagan had been an actor before he became president. His move from Hollywood to the White House amazed me. I was astounded that such an opportunity to go from actor to president could exist in any country. But I also appreciated President Reagan's accomplishments, how he restored confidence in the American dream and promoted freedom at home and abroad.

We were ushered into the Roosevelt Room, a large conference room across a corridor from the Oval Office. The eight of us remained quiet in such an esteemed place. We sat on thick, high-backed chairs around a long, shiny table set with green tea in Chinese porcelain cups. I was positioned in the middle of one side of the table, with my compatriots on either side of me. We faced the doors and looked up in anticipation whenever they opened.

The staff member who had greeted us in the lobby poked his head in the door. "We still don't yet know if the President will show up."

The next time the door opened, Vice President George H. W. Bush walked in with a few associates. He sat directly across from me on the other side of the table and proceeded to tell us how much he and his wife, Barbara, had enjoyed living in Beijing.

"I really appreciated being able to ride bikes everywhere," he said. "If I did that here, I would get run off the road."

I smiled at the image of George and Barbara Bush riding bikes in China. I was certain he had ridden a much better bike than the rundown one I pedaled to the paper-wrapping factory when I was a teenager.

"We appreciate your support of Chinese student programs," I said. By that time, some ten thousand students from China had arrived to study at universities across the United States. I asked the Vice President if he knew how many American students were in China, and what subjects they were studying.

"You know, I'm not sure. But we'll find out," he said.

After nearly half an hour of relaxed, amicable conversation with Vice President Bush, the doors suddenly swung wide open. An influx of nearly fifty people swooshed into the room so fast that a breeze swept over us. The first to come in was a group of reporters with flash cameras, who made their way to the perimeter of the room. Standing tall in the middle of the next group to enter was President Reagan himself. He walked right up to us, leaned in and shook each of our hands.

"We are delighted to be going to China," he said. "China and the U.S. have been building a very strong relationship in recent years. I have great hopes for what we can accomplish together."

In that moment, I felt like I was living in one of the movies I had screened at the film festival on campus. I was just a poor kid from Hangzhou who almost didn't make it to college. And now here I was, face to face with the President of the United States in a West Wing conference room. Amazing!

President Reagan talked about the history of educational collaboration between the two countries. He described the Boxer Rebellion near the end of the nineteenth century, and how America had asked the Chinese government to use the money that it otherwise would have paid the U.S. for helping to put down the rebellion, to instead send students overseas to study in America. That resulted in the first wave of Chinese exchange students who came to the U.S. in the beginning of the twentieth century.

After he talked with us for a few minutes, President Reagan said, "I'll be happy to meet each of you for photos."

As head of the U.S. Chinese Student and Scholar delegation, I was the first to be escorted across the hall to a smaller room, where President Reagan was waiting with a photographer and other members of his staff. He welcomed me and shook my hand again. I held this leader in great esteem, so I was surprised by how warm and friendly he was. He asked me how I was doing, where I was from, and what I was studying in graduate school. He was down-to-earth, and we had a wonderful conversation. Talking to him felt like being with my own grandfather.

We had our picture taken in front of an oblong mirror on the wall, my young face beaming as bright as the mirror's flowery gold frame. While it may have been hard for me to believe, the truth was that I wasn't on a movie set, and Reagan was no longer an actor. The eight of us who met Vice President Bush and President Reagan that day were completely ecstatic when we left. The photo of the President and me arrived in the mail at my home not long afterward, signed with the President's own hand. Little did I know at the time that this event, along with many more to come, would inspire my interest in making a difference in social and political issues in America.

I have treasured that photograph with President Reagan ever since that day, and so does my family back in China, where world leaders are esteemed as kings. I sent copies of the photo to Hangzhou, one of which my family framed and hung on the wall, right near the front door where visitors would surely see it. One of my uncles showed his copy of the photo to his manager at work, and was soon promoted for apparently being so well connected. Though I lived so far away, I continued to fulfill the promise I made to my family when I first came to America—to bring great honor to the Wang family name. At the same time, I was indebted to those who had given me the chance to shine, both in China and here in the States.

Chapter 10

A Dream Renewed

D r. Norman Anderson walked into his office where I had been waiting for some time, patiently perched on a couch just inside the door. He glanced at me, stopped only briefly to shake my hand, and then walked across the spacious room to a big, oak desk by the far wall. With his back to me, he began shuffling some papers.

"What brings you here, Mr. . . . er . . . Wang?" he asked, not looking up from the file in his hands.

"I want to find out how to apply for medical school," I said. "I was hoping you would advise me on the application process."

I followed him across the room, expecting him to ask me to sit down in one of the chairs near his desk. But he didn't. We stood for the entire length of our interview, which turned out to be not very long at all anyway.

It was the spring of 1986. I had scheduled a meeting with Dr. Anderson, the assistant dean of admissions for the Johns Hopkins University School of Medicine in Baltimore, to find out the prerequisites for medical school. Dr. Anderson was tall and imposing, and wore a white lab coat that would barely close around his massive frame, the buttons bulging from the strain.

He lifted his head and looked squarely at me. "So, where are you from?"

"I'm from China," I replied.

The look on his face implied he had already assessed my ethnic origin. I told him I had come to Maryland to study laser atomic physics. I handed him a copy of my résumé, but he gave it only a cursory glance.

"I have no idea what kind of education you received in China, and now you want to go to medical school here in the U.S.," he said in a haughty and dismissive tone. "Do you understand how difficult it is even for American students to get into medical school in this country?"

I stared at him, completely taken aback.

"Johns Hopkins is one of the best medical schools in the U.S." he continued. "You're wasting your time here."

My face felt hot. I couldn't believe what I was hearing. Dr. Anderson hadn't even looked at my résumé, nor inquired about anything I had done, yet he had already questioned my academic preparation and abilities. Had he simply judged me with a look? Was my ethnicity and the color of my skin all he needed to know?

I contained my anger and remained polite.

"You really don't believe I can do this?" I asked.

"That's correct. Given where you came from, you're not being realistic about what it takes to get into medical school in this country." He closed my file and handed back to me and headed for the door. "You'll see yourself out?"

He left me standing there by his desk.

I walked out of the building with slow, heavy steps. I felt so insulted that my stomach churned as I thought about Professor Miller and his repeated slights about my ethnicity. I recalled the empty lecture hall on my first day of recitation classes, and again felt the sting of not being trusted because I was from a foreign country. However, despite those initial troubling moments, my experience in America had been overwhelmingly positive … until now.

For the first five years, I'd had the freedom to live and study without the kind of fear and constraints I experienced during the Cultural Revolution. I thought I had finally found the land of freedom and opportunity. I thought I now lived in a free society. But the prejudice I felt in Dr. Anderson's office felt eerily similar to what I encountered back in China as a child in the stinking ninth class. Maybe America wasn't a whole lot better than China after all.

Though I did understand that Dr. Anderson's behavior was not representative of the majority of Americans, I was still amazed how one person's behavior can affect the perception of a whole culture. At that moment, I came to the realization that each of us not only is responsible for our own behavior, but also needs to know that as a member of the community our own action could affect the perception by others of our whole community as well.

For weeks, I was listless and depressed. Maybe medical school just wasn't meant to be because, although I could change many things about myself, ethnicity wasn't one of them. If Dr. Anderson was right, perhaps I should just give up on the idea of being a doctor altogether, no matter how long I had held on to that dream. Maybe I should be satisfied with the doctorate in laser physics—which I knew was a notable achievement in itself—and seek the promising career in the research and development of laser technology. After the long distance that I had come in life's path, perhaps I should have been satisfied with what I had already accomplished. This option would certainly be a more comfortable route since at least there would be likely no more disappointments, and perhaps no more discrimination.

But whenever I thought of giving up, I would hear my father's voice saying, "Don't give up. Go for it." Throughout my life, I had been driven to succeed, especially whenever I encountered something dark and oppressive. I wanted to fight, to get as far away as I could from the ghosts that I have encountered in my life—the black dot, the threat of deportation, the corpses in coffins, and now the racial discrimination—and move toward higher ground.

One thing Dr. Anderson said was true; it was indeed very difficult to get into medical school, even for Americans who had advantages like language, culture, and pre-med preparation. Getting into medical school would be exponentially harder for me as a foreign student without such preparation.

But I knew that abandoning my dream would be confirming Dr. Anderson's prejudice that minority students just don't have what it takes to succeed in medical school. I was disgusted at the thought that I might prove him right.

As I emerged from the fog of despair, I began to see clearly what I had to do next. The prejudice only spurred me on to work even that much harder to prove that prejudice is wrong. I poured all the anger I felt toward Dr. Anderson into preparing for the medical-school entrance exam. Ten years earlier I had fought against all odds to win a fiercely competitive spot in taking the first college entrance exam after the Cultural Revolution had ended. But back then, I was only concerned with my own future. This time, I felt I was fighting not just for myself, but also on behalf of all minorities who had endured prejudice and discrimination. I was going to get into medical school and show the likes of Professor Miller and Dr. Anderson that they were completely wrong in condemning a person based solely on the color of his or her skin.

Unfortunately, I felt rather alone in this pursuit of honor. With Shu at medical school in another state, I lived more like a bachelor than a married man. The distance was a tremendous strain, and our bond was continually disintegrating. I was thankful when my mother later joined me in Maryland during the summer of 1986. She and my father felt strongly that the family needed to live closer to each other, even though my brother and I were both grown-ups and were starting professions of our own. Thanks to drastic economic improvements throughout China during the 1980s, my parents' income had risen rapidly and they could finally afford the airfare to travel across the globe. They each came to the U.S. on visiting scholar visas and worked as researchers to support themselves. My brother was studying at the Hangzhou Medical College—an affiliate of the Zhejiang Medical University—where both my parents had worked. He would later join us in the U.S. when he finished his MD in 1990.

Mom arrived two years ahead of Dad. She conducted research in infectious diseases at the University of Maryland in College Park. She stayed at my apartment and cooked me dinner each night, while I immersed myself in studying to apply to medical school while continuing my doctoral research in laser physics. I had flashbacks of the times Mom would bolster me during the trying times back in Hangzhou when I was cramming for the impossible college entrance exam. Yet again, she would be there for me during another very challenging time of my life.

I had about six months to prepare for the Medical College Admission Test (MCAT) that fall. I'd taken ample chemistry and physics courses, but nothing in the biological sciences, which would make up half the MCAT. There wasn't time for several semesters of biology courses, so I enrolled in an accelerated summer program and did my best to study the necessary materials.

Besides the pre-med courses, I also had to learn how to perform well on an exam that tested one's logical thinking, reading comprehension, and essay writing. My English had improved greatly by then, but it was still my second language. I came across a Kaplan test preparation center, not far from Dupont Circle in Washington, D.C. To pay for the prep course, I picked up night and weekend shifts at the Best Western whenever I wasn't doing research in the lab; and three long evenings a week, I studied and practiced for the MCAT at the Kaplan Center.

I studied very hard and threw every bit of my energy and every moment that I could find into the study. During the daytime, I immersed myself in my PhD research in laser spectroscopy in the lab; in the evenings and weekends, I poured all of my time into studying for the MCAT while also at the same time holding on two side jobs so I could pay for it. I remember how hard that I had to study at the end of the Cultural Revolution to overcome an almost insurmountable barrier to survive. Now I had to study just as hard so I could not only realize my life-long dream of becoming a doctor but also prove people like Drs. Miller and Anderson wrong who discriminated others based on ethnicity or race. After months of intensive preparation, I took the MCAT on campus that August. I spent nearly five hours in a room with other medical school hopefuls, pouring over question after question, praying that I would get enough right answers. A month later, I got a call from the pre-med advising office at the University of Maryland, telling me that I could pick up my scores.

The early fall day glowed with golden leaves and warm sunlight. I ran all the way across campus to the pre-med advisors' office. For the past few weeks, I had tried not to think about the test results because every time I did, I would seize up with anxiety. But today was the day, the moment of truth. My childhood dream would either live or die.

An advisor handed me an envelope, but I didn't open it right away. I went back outside and stretched out on the grassy lawn, the envelope resting on my chest. I had no way of knowing how I had done, as the test wasn't designed to be completed, nor to be answered perfectly. It had six categories, each with a top score of fifteen. The national average per category was around seven per subject. If I scored as high as ten, I was confident I would get into a medical school, and if I scored eleven or twelve, I could get into one of the top schools. Scoring thirteen or fourteen was very rare. And a perfect fifteen in any subject was nearly inconceivable.

"What's it going to be?" I asked the big blue sky. Following in my family's footsteps had been my dream since I was a kid with my little kit full of ointments and bandages, and although the dream was dashed in China, I felt I now finally had a real chance of the dream becoming a reality.

I took a deep breath and opened the envelope. My hands shook, just as they did when I opened the letter from the Ministry of Education back in China a decade ago. There on a sheet of paper were my scores and my ranking compared to test takers across the nation. I gaped at the piece of paper in my hands.

My reading comprehension score was average—a seven—but I scored perfect fifteens in each of the science subjects, and was ranked in the 99.999th percentile. I was in shock! How was this even possible? I sprung up from the lawn and dashed back to the advisors' office to show them my scores. None of them had ever seen perfect MCAT scores like that in all the science subjects.

Apparently, neither had Kaplan. Rosalie Kaplan Sporn, niece of the organization's founder, Stanley Kaplan, called to congratulate me.

"You've set a record," she said. "We've never had any of our students score perfect fifteens across the board like that. Would you consider teaching for us?"

Rosalie managed the Washington-area Kaplan Centers, and the instructors she hired were always those who had done well on the MCAT. She offered me an hourly rate nearly six times the minimum wage. My days at the Best Western and Burger King were over! Besides the extra money, I was excited because I loved teaching. I worked hard to improve the materials so my Kaplan students could score higher on their MCATs. Unlike previous tutoring sessions I had held that did not attract many students when I arrived at America years ago, my Kaplan sessions were now always packed with people who had chosen me from among the other instructors.

I taught off and on at Kaplan throughout my ten years in medical school and clinical training.

I had been advised to apply to up to thirty medical schools, but that would have meant thousands of dollars in application fees. I didn't have that kind of money, so I only applied to a handful of top institutions, including Harvard Medical School and Johns Hopkins University School of Medicine. Acceptance letters from these two schools arrived in January of 1987.

Not long after that, I received an unexpected phone call.

"Is this Ming Wang?" the caller asked. "Have you received our admissions package for Johns Hopkins? We've extended to you the highest scholarship in our school's history. We're anxious to know if you'll be accepting our offer."

The voice sounded familiar. "I'm still considering it," I said, "but I've been accepted to Harvard as well."

"I understand. Both are very good schools," he said. "You might find that some schools treat you differently, but just remember that here at Johns Hopkins, we greatly respect talent and academic achievements. We hope you'll consider joining us."

When I finally recognized the voice on the other line, I was amazed that he was the same person who had discriminated against me due to my ethnicity only a few short months ago . . . Dr. Norman Anderson. He hadn't believed that a minority student could succeed in getting into medical school. I felt the urge to point out that I was the same student he had brushed off a few months ago, that his prejudice against ethnicity or skin color was just wrong, and that it hadn't stopped me but rather energized me to study for the MCAT to prove him wrong. I thought that information could possibly help him, but I didn't say anything because I come from a culture that respects and values its elders. I couldn't speak against a teacher, not even one like him.

And I chose Harvard.

* * *

Thinking back, I was happy I didn't let one person's bad behavior deter me from the great opportunity that America had to offer to me. In fact, I realized that it wasn't America that was broken, but rather Dr. Anderson himself, and America deserved better. Besides my love for America, my hard work and accomplishments were also due to my own drive and my need to prove that we should never let narrow-minded people like Drs. Miller and Anderson stop us from achieving our dreams. I wanted to do my part to help defend the most prized foundation of this great country—the concept that all men and women are created . . . and shall be treated . . . equally.

While I'd like to say my choice of schools was due to my desire to have sweet revenge against Anderson, it was actually just a smart decision. Harvard was not only the top medical school in the country, but my admission also included acceptance into a highly competitive joint MD program with the Massachusetts Institute of Technology (MIT), called Health Sciences and Technology (HST). As an HST student, my training would encompass not only medicine at Harvard, but also biological sciences and engineering at MIT.

By the early 1980s, ophthalmologists were studying how lasers could drastically improve the precision and effectiveness of eye surgeries. The same tool that was used in microscopic electronics—like computer chips and atomic colliders that I experimented with for my PhD thesis—could now be used effectively for clean, precise incisions on the intricate and delicate eye. Since I was entering medical school as a laser physicist, I realized I had a unique opportunity to contribute to the advancement of how this new biotechnology was applied to the treatment of eye diseases. Using a laser instead of a scalpel in eye surgery was still a very new concept at the time, and I wanted to be part of the impending innovation.

Several months earlier I had traveled to Boston for admissions interviews at Harvard. After my final interview, I found myself walking around the medical school on a cold night. I dug my hands deeper into my coat pockets, and strolled along the walkways in front of the imposing buildings that framed the long, rectangular lawn called "the quad." The moon was full and bright, and the white marble structures were lit up against the dark backdrop. I remembered being a little kid walking through the woods of Hangzhou at night with my dad, in awe of the moon. And I remembered how only ten years earlier, I was penniless and was denied any opportunity to attend college, and now here I stood on the brink of acceptance into the most prestigious medical school in the world. How is it that I was able to overcome such tremendous odds to get to this point?

At the time, I believed that I made it through the extreme circumstances of China's Cultural Revolution and challenges that I faced when arriving in America as a penniless student due mainly to my parents' help, my own innate tenacity, and this great country of America, which gave me the freedom to choose and to reignite my lifelong dream to pursue medicine. People like Miller and Anderson are few and far between, and the vast majority of Americans are loving, fair, and supportive toward people from all over the world, and toward all cultures and ethnicities. China and my family had given me cultural roots and had helped shape my character, and America—my adopted country—gave me a positive outlook and valuable opportunities.

But later I realized that above everything else perhaps something more important, and much deeper, was to be credited for my accomplishments. Yes, I had worked diligently and had been given many opportunities, but on several occasions the results struck me as truly amazing. I thought back to my prayer for help over the atomic collider in the lab, when I had done everything I could think of and couldn't continue any longer. That moment, as I prayed and watched the bright yellow dot magically start to glow, was my first experience with the power of spirituality. This divine encounter opened the door to a place of wonder and sparked questions about what existed beyond the material realm. I had begun to believe that maybe there was indeed something beyond myself; a more powerful force was at hand.

I stood in front of the quad's stately main building, gazing up at the enormous Greek columns and the words "Harvard Medical School" prominently inscribed on a horizontal panel at above them. Beyond all logic, I sensed this force might be guiding my life for a reason I couldn't yet comprehend. I had lived my life unrooted in faith of any kind, driven by the need to escape constant darkness and ghosts. Now, given all that had happened in my life—much of it beyond my own expectation and capability—I realized that perhaps my life might indeed have a purpose. But if so, what was it?

Though I would never forget the harsh words Miller and Anderson had spoken, their prejudice would no longer remain my only inspiration to work hard. Yes, I would still fight to prove their discrimination unethical, but if God did exist and had a purpose for my life, then the stakes must be much higher than just my own personal gain or benefit. To discover this deeper sense of meaning and my life's purpose became the ultimate inspiration that moved me forward.

Chapter 11

A Higher Power

The room was barren and cold. Rows of steel tables reflected the glare from overhead lights. Air hissed through circulation vents to reduce the smell. I had known this day was inevitable, and there was no way I could escape it. We stood in small groups around the tables, quiet since it felt like a sacred moment, yet also nervous about what would come next. On the steel tables, draped in white sheets, were bodies that had been donated to science. Except for the body parts in jars at the medical college back in Hangzhou, I had never before been this close to a dead person. Now not only was I close to one, but I also held a scalpel in my hand, ready to cut into it. My hands shook. I closed my eyes for a moment and took a deep breath.

It was September of 1987, and I had just moved into Vanderbilt Hall at Harvard Medical School. I loved being in Boston. Newspaper stands sold papers from around the world in a variety of languages. Harvard Square in nearby Cambridge brimmed with ideas, history, books, and poetry. The abundance of literature from around the world stood in stark contrast to how deprived we had been of reading materials in China during the Cultural Revolution. I thought about the clandestine book of Tang Dynasty poetry my dad and I had kept hidden in our bookcase in China a decade earlier, when knowledge and education were stripped from me. But now I lived in the hub of education and intellectual drive in this country. It had indeed been an incredible journey so far!

In the mornings, those of us in Harvard and MIT's Health Science and Technology (HST) program went to medical school classes at Harvard; and in the afternoons, we were shuttled to the MIT campus on the north side of the Charles River for corresponding courses in biomedical engineering. For example, in the mornings we would study the cardiovascular system at Harvard Medical School to learn its anatomy and physiology for the MD program. Then in the afternoons, we would learn the cardiovascular system at MIT from a bioengineering perspective, that is, how the heart is like a battery, with arteries as resistors and veins as capacitors. As a student in the HST program, I was fascinated with going beyond mere anatomical descriptions and delving into the mechanics of the human body to see how engineering principles could be applied to the understanding of human body and development of new medical treatments.

I had entered medical school with a unique background as a laser physicist, intent on eventually practicing ophthalmology and using lasers to improve the treatment of eye diseases. During my early years at Harvard, leading medical researchers in the U.S. and Europe were among the first to use excimer lasers for vision correction surgeries on human eyes. The excimer laser was so named because it was the product of "excited dimers," similar to the sodium dimers that I studied in the laser atomic physics program in graduate school in Maryland. The excited dimers produced ultraviolet light, and at that wavelength, the laser could remove a tiny amount of tissue without damaging surrounding tissues. I had been intrigued by the application of this emerging laser technology in physics and engineering well before I started medical school, but I soon came to see the poignantly human side of the field.

One day during my first semester, I attended a lecture at which several blind patients had been invited to talk about their experiences. One woman sitting with the professor at the front of the lecture hall particularly grabbed my attention. She was a fifty-something Italian-American from the North End of Boston, with jet-black hair and a commanding attractiveness, except for her eyes. Her eyes were malformed and shrunken, the result of a genetic disease that had left her blind since birth.

"What do red and blue mean to you?" the professor asked her.

She hesitated for a moment. "Red to me is something warm and fluffy," she said, "and blue ... umm ... cold and slippery."

I was amazed at how this woman described colors as tactile sensations. Though she couldn't see the world around her, she could feel it. It suddenly dawned on me that she was actually missing out on a vast, significant aspect of the human experience. Her genetic condition deprived her of sight, but her blindness deprived her of so much more. She could have enjoyed a full and rich life, but what she described was lonesome and bleak. Her upbringing had been traumatic; being blind not only ensnared her in darkness, but it kept her indoors, isolated from the freedom that other children in her community were able to experience. As an adult she lived alone, unmarried, and without children. To ease her loneliness, she had embraced music and was an avid guitar player. I thought about blind Ah Bing, the Chinese composer of the mournful erhu music I had played as a teenager in my desperate attempt to escape deportation. This woman also used music as an outlet the way he did—to express grief and the pain of isolation, as the world around her remained interminably dark.

Her genetic condition was permanent and her blindness irreversible. I began to wonder how many people with such a grim diagnosis might one day receive their sight back with breakthrough medical procedures, particularly utilizing laser technologies. What if I could be part of that life-transforming process of restoring sight in such blind patients? As I imagined these possibilities, my ideas about the science of sight evolved from the use of advanced technology into the emotional and human costs of blindness. After that morning's lecture, ophthalmology began to feel like much more than just a career; it felt like a calling.

Throughout my studies at Harvard and MIT, I spent several evenings a week in a research lab as both a medical student and a postdoctoral fellow. I wanted to delve deeply into the molecular base of genetic diseases like the one that had struck the woman blind whom I had met at the lecture. I chose to conduct research under molecular geneticist, George Church, PhD, a world-class scientist with a background in physical chemistry. Dr. Church was very tall and sported a thick, bushy beard. He was dating Professor Ting Wu, a Chinese-American woman who would later become his wife, so he appreciated my cultural background.

I first met Dr. Church at his eighth-floor office in a building just off the quad. The walls were lined with diagrams of human gene sequences, colorful patterns of G, A, T, and C, the letters that represent the four nucleotides in DNA. For all the complexity of a human organism, there was a dazzling simplicity in the array of these four letters. His office reminded me of Tian-ma's walls in his bedroom back in Hangzhou, all lined with drawings and poetic verses. Here I was encountering poetry of another sort, no less beautiful in its expression of humanity.

The year I entered Harvard was a fascinating time for molecular biology. The Human Genome Project was just getting underway, and Dr. Church had been one of its initiators. In just a few years, more than a thousand researchers from sixteen institutions and six countries would join in a global effort to sequence the entire array of three billion base pairs of human DNA. Every scientist involved, including Dr. Church and myself, hoped to understand more deeply how genetics contribute to human disease, and then use the discoveries to develop more effective treatments.

Sequencing the entire human genome, though a crucial and massive undertaking, would only be "the first step in a 10,000 mile journey," as the Chinese saying goes. Once the patterns of Gs, As, Ts, and Cs were sequenced, scientists would then have to interpret what the sequence actually meant. Reading this blueprint of life but not knowing its interpretation was like walking into a library, opening a massive chronicle and seeing nothing but scrambled letters. In order to interpret the meanings, we have to learn the grammar behind the letters, namely: what were the functions of the genes and how genes were turned on or off? Why did some people with genes for certain diseases develop the condition, while others do not?

During our first meeting, I told Dr. Church about my previous studies in chemistry and physics, and how I hoped to better understand disease at the molecular level.

"I can tell that you're genuinely interested in the technical aspects of medicine," he told me. "I'm very pleased to work with a fellow physical chemist."

Dr. Church and I began a unique and ambitious project. As the Human Genome Project progressed, larger and larger segments of DNA were sequenced and more genes were discovered. The next major challenge was to develop better technology to study the functions of these genes and how they were regulated. The mere presence or absence of certain genes and mutations did not necessarily lead to disease. More often it was the activation or repression of such genes that caused diseases such as cancer. Since large, complex proteins are the molecules that regulated gene activity, Dr. Church and I wanted to develop a new technology to study the DNA-protein interaction and the regulation of gene expression, and we wanted to do it inside a living cell.

Up to that point, most studies had examined the interaction of proteins and genes *in vitro*, that is, in an external environment like a test tube or a petri dish. We wanted to develop a technique to explore the interaction of DNA and protein *in vivo*, that is, inside a living cell. We used the *E. coli* bacteria as our model genome system. If we were successful, then the methodology that we developed could possibly be applied to the human genome once it was sequenced within the next decade, which would have a tremendous impact on medicine.

Outside of Dr. Church's lab, I experienced the miracle of biology and genetics in my own personal life as well. One day in the spring of 1988, not long after Dr. Church and I had started our project, Shu called me from West Virginia to tell me that she was pregnant.

"I'm going to be a father!" I told my classmates excitedly.

Shu and I were both thrilled that we had a little one on the way, but the excitement was consumed by anxiety. We were both in medical school and we lived six hundred miles apart. During the first two years of our marriage, we only saw each other for a total of two weeks, usually on school breaks and holidays. We were neck-deep in classes, research, and rotations. We could barely nurture our marriage, so how were we going to care for a newborn?

Our son Dennis was born on December 5, 1988. At his birth, the obstetrician let me cut the cord that connected him to his mother. It was such an awe-inspiring experience to play a part in bringing new life into the world. I'd had enough training to evaluate his Apgar score, the measure of a newborn's health, and I rated him 9.5 out of 10. Maybe I had paternal bias, but he did come out kicking, crying, and completely healthy . . . and with so much hair! I'd never before seen an infant with a head of hair like that!

Shu took a month off school, and I spent two weeks with her and Dennis. We scrambled to figure out a plan to care for our new baby. Once we returned to our respective medical schools, my parents were able to provide much-needed help since my father had finally arrived from China earlier that year, so he and my mother were living with me. Dennis was shuttled between our place in Boston and Shu's parents' home in Maryland until Shu and I finished school. In the end, Dennis's grandparents were more like parents to him than Shu and I were. I would later regret not taking a bigger role in Dennis's upbringing during those early years, but at the time I didn't know what else to do. Medical school was an all-consuming endeavor, and success or failure would determine the course of our careers . . . and our lives.

* * *

Becoming a parent is a rite of passage in many people's lives. About a year before Dennis was born, I encountered another rite of passage, one that all medical students experience. Before I ever welcomed new life, I was face to face with death. Like doctors in training have done for hundreds of years, I encountered my first cadaver in the gross anatomy lab. Walking into this cold, clinical setting reminded me of being in the anatomy lab at my parents' medical college in Hangzhou long ago, with the glass jars of floating body parts, the coffins behind the bookcases, and the vivid nightmares of dead people in search of their missing organs. This time there was no escaping the dead bodies. I couldn't run away like I had done in my nightmares as a teenager. Standing over that steel table rattled me to the core.

But not as much as having to make that first incision.

My lab partners and I were assigned a female cadaver. I kept reassuring myself, "This isn't a human being anymore. It's just a body." Mortality stared up at me from her lifeless face. At the end of the semester, her body had been cut into hundreds of pieces and put in boxes labeled by bones, muscles, or ligaments. This woman had donated her body for our education. While I was tremendously grateful to her, I couldn't help but wonder: was this it, the end of our lives?! What was the purpose of life itself? Or was there one at all to begin with?

Many doctors point to cadaver dissections as the starting point to becoming desensitized to illness and death, but the opposite happened to me. I actually became increasingly sensitive to life, growing more and more curious about the origin of life, the complexity of the human body, and the determination of whether there was any meaning to it all. I had previously held the singular conviction that science alone was the key to understanding life. It taught that life had occurred and developed by random chance, which meant there couldn't be any inherent meaning or purpose behind life itself. But the deeper that I delved into the wonders and intricacies of living things, the more I began to question everything I had once believed.

My dad used to say, "Master mathematics, physics, and chemistry, and you can go anywhere in the world you want to go." I had come to medical school with a unique amount of experience in physics and mathematics, so while other students were memorizing the facts, the human anatomy and physiology, I approached medicine from a different point of view, i.e., from the prospective of a mathematician, running numbers and calculating probabilities. The more I learned about the complexities of human organs, such as eyes, the more puzzled I became when the numbers just didn't add up. I learned that there are twice as many neurons in the human brain as there are stars in the Milky Way galaxy. The human eye was another masterwork of engineering, with billions of photoreceptors and neural connections. My mathematical calculations suggested that it would take trillions of trillions of years for organs that complex to evolve randomly, but the universe was presumed to have existed for less than fourteen billion years.

I was thus nagged by the sheer improbability that life could form at random. But most scientists make no room for the possibility of God. The profession demands allegiance to positivism, the philosophy that only what can be tested actually exists. Scientists will argue that, in spite of its inherent complexity, the eye could still have evolved at random, even in such a short period of time. But I was shocked to discover that it actually took more "faith" for me to believe in random formation of the eye as such than to believe that perhaps some other force was at work. Life just appeared to be arranged far too well to not have been designed for an intended purpose.

During my studies, I did an off-site rotation in which I shadowed a pediatric ophthalmologist named Dr. Stanley Hand, Jr. Our young patients in the local children's hospital had congenital eye disorders, like cataracts and glaucoma. I told Dr. Hand about the research I was doing with Dr. Church, and how fascinated I was by the complexity of DNA replication and genetic disease. Dr. Hand and I talked about how many times the three billion base pairs of DNA in cells had to split and replicate during an embryo's formation. As an embryo's cells become tissues, organs, and limbs, there are so many opportunities for errors, even the slightest of which could result in significant congenital defects.

"It's amazing that anyone could come out of the womb normal and healthy," I said as we walked through the corridor toward another patient's room. "How is it even statistically possible that gestation is so orderly and complete?"

At first, Dr. Hand gave me only scientific explanations for my constant inquiries. I continued to pepper him with questions, not just about biology and medicine, but about the underlying meaning of it all. Eventually he realized that I was searching for answers that wouldn't be found in any textbook. I was on a quest for something bigger and deeper than science.

"If human existence is accidental, then what's the purpose?" I asked. "If the most complex living organisms on the planet are the result of random chance, how can life hold any meaning?"

"I don't believe that life is meaningless at all," he finally said, "because I'm a Christian."

Up to this point, no one had introduced himself or herself to me as a Christian, and I was intrigued to find out what that meant. I had read about Christianity in the great literature of the West while I was in college back in China, but I hadn't yet explored the tenets of the faith. All I knew at the time was that perhaps God did exist and possibly He was guiding my life. This sense of calling had continued to grow slowly and had crystallized throughout my years at Harvard. Perhaps Dr. Hand could finally help me find the answers I was seeking.

One afternoon, Dr. Hand took me to lunch in the hospital cafeteria.

"Do you see that car outside?" he asked, pointing through a nearby window to the parking lot outside.

I nodded.

"What is the difference between a car and a human brain?" he asked.

"The human brain is infinitely more complex," I said.

"Do you think a random collection of scrap metal could assemble itself into a car?"

"Of course not!"

He leaned in, looking at me intently. "Then how about the human brain?"

I was speechless. If a complicated machine like a car couldn't create itself, how could I believe that an intricate organ like the human brain could? Even though the brain consisted of living tissue, both materials were made up of the same molecular pieces. At the level of atomic particles, there was no fundamental difference.

"So, what's the answer to all of this?" I asked. I had been baffled by the limitations of science, and I was ready to find more legitimate answers to the pressing questions about the nature and meaning of life.

Dr. Hand gave me a Bible, and in the weeks and months that followed, I read it intently. It wasn't clear at first whether or not I would find what I was searching for on its pages, but I was open to the possibility that it might hold answers that science hadn't provided. The idea that life wasn't fortuitous, that there was a Creator with a purpose for humanity, gave me great relief from all my confusion. The immortality and eternity of such a Being filled the void that science could not.

I kept in touch with Dr. Hand for a while, but we eventually lost contact. Years later we met again at a Christian Ophthalmology Society meeting, and I told him how much he had impacted my life, and how my journey of faith had begun with the wisdom he had shared with me.

Meanwhile, my experiments on *E. coli* DNA in Dr. Church's lab only increased my conviction that there must be a cosmic, supernatural designer behind the complexity I witnessed under the microscope. As far as we knew, no one else was researching protein and DNA interaction inside a living cell. We soon discovered the fundamental difficulty that blocked the success of any such project, that is, the moment we lyse a cell, or break it open to inspect its contents, the interacting protein and DNA molecules are torn apart in the process. How could we then study the way these two components bind together inside a living cell if they came apart every time they were exposed? It seemed to be a scientific dead end, a logical impossibility. By then, however, my time with Dr. Hand had expanded my perspective to include the possibility of a solution beyond logic, and I was inspired not to give up just because I faced a scientific improbability. I trusted in a wisdom behind the cell's design that was beyond what scientists presently understood.

We persisted in our experiment and looked at the problem from several different perspectives. Eventually, we realized that perhaps one creative way to assess how protein and DNA interacted in a living cell was to look at a third component, namely methylase, an enzyme that patrolled DNA to protect and stabilize its structural integrity.

We theorized that since the methylase enzyme constantly went back and forth over the whole DNA molecule, if any part of the DNA was not methylated, then that meant that perhaps there were proteins bound to that DNA region that were blocking the methylase's access. We performed a series of experiments that searched the entire *E. coli* genome, and found out that there were indeed several dozen regions of DNA untouched by the methylase enzyme, suggesting that these could be the sites of protein-binding. I calculated that the probability of this result occurring by chance was one in 1,000.

We wanted to double-check our theory that these unmethylated regions of DNA indeed represent regions bound by proteins, and thus are inaccessible to methylase. To do so, we used cells in which we knew that one of the biding proteins itself was absent, and we found that indeed the corresponding DNA region was now methylated, suggesting that the methylase enzyme now had unimpeded access to that DNA sequence since no protein factor bound there. It was another one-in-1,000 possibility that what we observed could happen by chance.

Before long, the cumulative results of the experiments had pushed the statistical probability that what we observed could occur by chance to one in a million. We then reached the third and final stage of this groundbreaking project. If all our theories were correct so far, then there was one last test that would definitely confirm it. If we grew the cells in an environment that forced a protein to bind to a DNA region, then the methylase enzyme should no longer be able to access that DNA region. We conducted that final experiment and indeed confirmed that finding, yielding yet another one-in-1,000 chance that the observation could occur out of random! Therefore, the three stages of testing all confirmed that using methylase was an ingenious way to assess DNA-protein binding in a living cell. The final estimation of the cumulative probability that what we observed occurred by chance was one in 1,000,000,000, infinitesimally small.

This chemical trinity of methylase, protein, and DNA was a true marvel of nature, an ultraprecise biological system whose parts interact in perfect synchrony. It was so beautiful in its complexity, so perfect in its coordination that I was now convinced this did not happen randomly at all, but rather by divine design. Dr. Hand was right; there had to be a Creator behind such intricate, complete, perfect designs that brought life to species from bacteria to human beings.

Dr. Church and I had thus succeeded at developing a new method of studying DNA-protein interaction inside a living cell, a scientific achievement that I treasure to this day. Our discovery had wide-ranging implications for medical treatments, since researchers could use this methodology to study how genes were turned on and off in a living cell and how that led to disease. The paper we wrote about this new method was published in *Nature*, the most prestigious science journal in the world. Dr. Church and I were impressed at the publication's impact—we received requests for copies of the paper from scientists in eighty nations. We were invited to present our findings at conferences around the world, and we applied for a U.S. patent through Harvard University. The research we did in Dr. Church's lab was the beginning of many successful biomedical explorations I have undertaken throughout my career, each of which have not only excited me about the marvels of science, but more importantly, have revealed to me more and more of the glory of the Creator.

* * *

On June 6, 1991, my time at Harvard came to an end. That morning, nearly twenty thousand students, family members, professors, and alumni congregated in Harvard Yard. The university president gave the commencement address and conferred degrees upon students from both the undergraduate and graduate schools. Students were seated according to their schools, forming rows and rows of black and red graduation caps and gowns. The medical-student section was rowdy and fun. We blew up surgical gloves into five-fingered balloons, and when our school was announced, we tossed them into the air and watched them bounce throughout the audience. Adjacent to us were the law-school graduate students, a much quieter and tamer bunch than we were. Among the law students was someone who, back then, was known as ... Barry Obama.

That afternoon, the Harvard Medical school graduates came together for our own private ceremony, under a canopy that stretched across the quad. My parents and brother sat in a row next to Shu and her family, and our son Dennis bounced happily from lap to lap. I listened as names were called from the stage, gazing across the quad and remembering the late night stroll that had followed my admissions interviews. During the Cultural Revolution in China, I had been condemned to the bottom rung of society with no hope of a future, and now I was about to receive my Doctor of Medicine degree from one of the most prestigious universities on the planet. Such a wondrous improbability hinted yet again that my life had a spiritual purpose, and now I knew that purpose would be found in the field of ophthalmology.

"Ming Wang, MD, *magna cum laude*," announced the dean, "and winner of the best graduation thesis in biomedical sciences of the Harvard Medical School and MIT Class of 1991."

The entire crowd erupted in applause.

I walked onto the stage with Dennis, holding his small hand. The dean handed me the diploma, but I only held it for a moment before Dennis grabbed it and carried it offstage. Years later, Dennis boasted that this moment was his claim to fame because he had received a degree from Harvard too! My father stood ready to take a picture, beaming from the other side of the camera. I knew how proud he was, since he had led our family through the tumult of the Cultural Revolution and had watched his son's life nearly be destroyed. I would never forget how much he and my mom had done for me, and that the culmination of their efforts allowed me to graduate from the top medical school in the world.

Our commencement speaker, Harvard University president Derek Bok, had said earlier that morning, "Is it enough for Harvard to attract the brightest students if we do not excel in making them caring, active, enlightened citizens and civic leaders? ... Surely we must teach our students to appreciate the Biblical admonition, 'To whom much has been given, from him much will be required. Luke 12:48 (NKJV).'"

His words resonated deeply with me. I had been given much more than I could have ever imagined possible, and my hope was to find a way to give back more than I had received. I knelt down next to Dennis and smiled broadly, as my dad counted to three and snapped another photo.

Chapter 12

My Adopted Country

"**I**'m an American now!" I shouted, the phone pressed to my ear. I felt like I was floating in the spring air. After living in the United States for ten years, I had just been sworn in as an official U.S. citizen.

My parents were on the other line, congratulating me from back in Boston. Mom worked in the department of molecular and cellular biology at Harvard, and Dad was a visiting scholar in the Department of Pathology at Beth Israel Deaconess Medical Center. My brother, Ming-yu, came to the U.S. in 1990 for a graduate program in genetics and microbiology at the University of Massachusetts in Boston. During my last few years at Harvard, my parents, brother, and I shared a two-bedroom apartment on Worthington Street near the medical school. For the first time in nearly a decade, our entire family was living in the same home, more than seven thousand miles from Hangzhou.

Following medical school, I moved to West Orange, New Jersey for a yearlong internship in transitional medicine at St. Barnabas Medical Center. During the first few months I was in West Orange, Shu, Dennis, and I lived together for the first time in our entire five years of marriage. We had been living completely separate lives, both of us consumed with school and work, but we hoped that now we could finally be a family. Unfortunately, by that summer we realized it was too late and our marriage had disintegrated irreparably. We filed for divorce that fall. Dennis, who was only three years old, was once again in his grandparents' care. I felt a deep sense of failure at the collapse of my young family. Perhaps Shu and I had gotten married much too young, or perhaps we were naive to think we could make it work while living so far apart. Regardless of the reasons, I felt terrible despair about not being able to create a family life for Dennis like the one I had enjoyed as a young boy. Years later, I would look back with profound regret at how much of his young life I had missed. To escape the painful emotions I felt about my failed relationships, I poured myself even further into my work.

Given how fragile my own young family was, I was thankful to have my parents and brother with me. Moving from China to America had been a drastic change in geography and culture for all of us. But I also noticed that a profound inner change had been taking place in me over the course of many years. Becoming an American wasn't just a move across the ocean or an event facilitated by a bureaucratic process. It was a gradual inner transformation over a decade of life here in the United States.

My first inkling of this metamorphosis occurred when I returned to Maryland after my first trip back to China in 1984. After two-and-a-half years of graduate school at the University of Maryland, passing my qualifying exams and defending my doctoral thesis proposal, there had been a natural break that seemed perfect for me to visit my family back in Hangzhou. Working at the part-time jobs allowed me to save up enough money for a round-trip plane ticket and for the eight big-ticket items I was allowed to import without paying customs.

Mom and Dad got married right after graduation from Zhejiang Medical University, Hangzhou. (1958)

My little brother Ming-yu is born. (1968)

At age one I learned to rock my high chair back and forth to move it around so I could explore the world. (1961)

With my parents and Ming-yu right before Mom was separated from us for two years to face forced labor and re-education in a remote area of the country. Three of us wore badges of Chairman Mao. (1970)

Playing erhu with Ming-yu, who was unaware that my constant practicing was an attempt to avoid the devastating deportation. (1974)

Learning to dance was another skill I hoped would end the seemingly inevitable fate of deportation and a life of poverty and hard labor. (1974)

Denied an education and earning 10 cents a day as a factory book wrapper during the Cultural Revolution, I rode my bicycle to work everyday. (1976)

In front of the University of Science and Technology of China (USTC) as a freshman. (1978)

The Three Musketeers (Jason, me, and Ji-hong) arrived in
America, nearly penniless yet formally dressed. (1982)

The Three Musketeers and our first
American car—a 1973 AMC Matador—
which we named "M1" due to her massive
size. (1982)

The yellow dot! The sodium dimers
finally formed in the center of the laser
atomic collider, beaming with atomic
happiness. (1985)

With my lasers and atomic collider,
conducting experiments for my PhD thesis
at Weiner's Lab, University of Maryland at
College Park. (1986)

With my PhD thesis advisor, Professor John Weiner, beside
our laser atomic collider. (1986)

With Professor George Church,
Department of Genetics, Harvard
Medical-school. (1987)

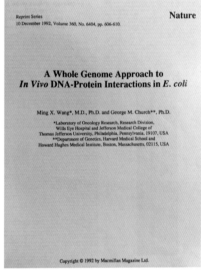

Reprint Series
10 December 1992, Volume 360, No. 6404, pp. 606-610.

Nature

A Whole Genome Approach to
In Vivo DNA-Protein Interactions in *E. coli*

Ming X. Wang*, M.D., Ph.D. and George M. Church**, Ph.D.

*Laboratory of Oncology Research, Research Division,
Wills Eye Hospital and Jefferson Medical College of
Thomas Jefferson University, Philadelphia, Pennsylvania, 19107, USA
**Department of Genetics, Harvard Medical School and
Howard Hughes Medical Institute, Boston, Massachusetts, 02115, USA

The *Nature* paper I wrote with Professor
George Church about the development
of a new method to study DNA-protein
interaction in a living cell. (1992)

On the MIT campus, as a student in
the Harvard-MIT Health Science and
Technology (HST) MD program. (1987)

As the president of the U.S. Chinese Student and
Scholar Association, I was honored to meet with
President Ronald Reagan at the White House. (1984)

To Wang Mingxu
With best wishes,   Ronald Reagan

A private photo-op with President Ronald Reagan
at the White House. (1984)

In front of the Chinese
Embassy in Washington, DC,
protesting the atrocities at
Tiananmen Square. (June,
1989)

With Senator Bill Frist, MD.
(2006)

My mother, Dennis, and Shu in Boston. (1990)

At the Harvard commencement ceremony, Dennis grabbed my MD diploma before I even had a chance to look at it myself. (1991)

Graduating with my MD degree (magna cum laude) from Harvard & MIT, and the first-place award for my MD graduation thesis. (1991)

With my parents and Ming-yu at my graduation from Harvard & MIT. (1991)

VNIVERSITAS HARVARDIANA

CANTABRIGIAE IN REPVBLICA MASSACHVSETTENSIVM

PRAESES et Socii Collegii Harvardiani consentientibus honorandis ac reverendis Inspectoribus in comitiis sollemnibus

MING XU WANG
ad gradum Medicinae Doctoris
magna cum laude et thesi propria

admiserunt eique dederunt et concesserunt omnia insignia et iura quae ad hunc gradum spectant.

In cuius rei testimonium litteris Academiae sigillo munitis die vi Iunii anno Domini MDCCCCLXXXXI Collegique Harvardiani CCCLV auctoritate rite commissa nomina subscripserunt.

My Harvard Medical-school diploma.
(MD, magna cum laude, 1991)

HARVARD MEDICAL SCHOOL

DR. HAROLD LAMPORT BIOMEDICAL RESEARCH PRIZE

presented to

Ming Xu Wang

for the best thesis reporting
original research in the biomedical sciences

My first place award from Harvard for my
MD graduation thesis. (1991)

HARVARD
UNIVERSITY

MASSACHUSETTS
INSTITUTE
OF TECHNOLOGY

DIVISION OF HEALTH SCIENCES AND TECHNOLOGY

The Dean of the Harvard Faculty of Medicine, the Provost of the Massachusetts Institute of Technology, and the Co-Directors of the Division of Health Sciences and Technology hereby attest that

Ming Xu Wang

has successfully completed the requirements for the Division's doctoral curriculum in Medicine, in recognition whereof they hereby set their hands and seals at Cambridge, Massachusetts this 5th day of June, 1991

Graduation diploma for Harvard & MIT joint MD
program. (1991)

My eight ophthalmology textbooks. (2015)

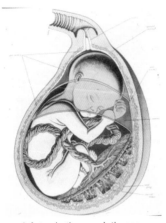

A fetus in the amniotic sac,
showing the amniotic membrane.
(1996)

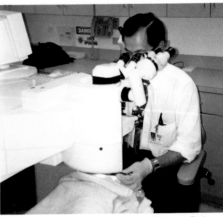

During my corneal fellowship at Bascom Palmer
Eye Institute, I conducted amniotic membrane
transplantation experiments on rabbits involving
lasers. (1996)

My U.S. patent for the amniotic membrane
contact lens. (1999)

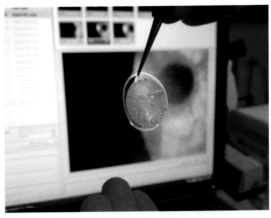

The world's first amniotic membrane contact lens, based
on my 1999 U.S. patent..

We prayed, just before we removed the patch from
Francisco's eye, after over two years of surgeries,
including an unprecedented quadruple surgery.
(2001)

Seventeen-year-old blind Mexican patient,
Francisco, sees himself for the first time in
seven years! (2001)

The top panel was the last time Francisco
used Braille; the lower panel was the first
time in seven years he was able to see to
write (in Spanish). (2001)

Twenty-four years after I completed high-school in
China but without a diploma, North Carolina's Chapel
Hill High-school awarded me this honorary diploma, a
gift from Francisco. (2001)

Wang Foundation for Sight Restoration
From Darkness to Sight

Mission
The Wang Foundation for Sight Restoration is a 501(c) (3) charitable organization that helps blind patients from all over the world (from over 55 countries to date) in their quest for sight.

History
The foundation doctors performed the world's first laser-artificial cornea implantation, a new technology developed to restore vision in terminally corneal blind patients. They also published the world's first scientific paper that demonstrated the reduction of corneal scar and apoptosis after amniotic membrane graft.

Your help
Although these surgeries are performed free of charge by our doctors, we need your help in aiding travel, lodging and hospital expenses so that these patients' world will no longer remain in darkness. All proceeds from the Eye Ball will go to help give these blind patients the chance to see again.

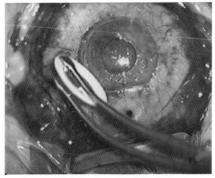

The world's first laser artificial cornea implantation on Wang Foundation's first patient, Bobby Joel Case. (2004)

Our 501(c)(3) non-profit charity has helped patients from over 40 states and 55 countries, with all surgeries performed free-of-charge. (2015)

With Bobby Joel Case and his mother Anna at the first EyeBall. (2005)

With China's first bladeless all-laser LASIK patient, the first in a country of 1.4 billion people. (2005)

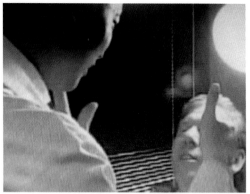

Brad, blind for 13 years, saw me for the first time and asked me, "Is this your face? Yeah, I can see your face over there!" (2007)

"Yeah, that's me!" Brad saw himself for the first time in 13 years. (2007)

"I can see you now!" Brad saw his wife Jackie for the very first time! (2007)

With Jackie and Brad, the world's first combined saliva gland transposition and laser artificial cornea implantation patient. (2007)

Kajal, a four-year-old orphan, was blinded by her stepmother,
who poured acid into her eyes while she was sleeping in order to
make money by turning Kajal into a "blind child singer." (2006)

With Kajal and her caretaker, Grace,
before Kajal's surgery. (2006)

Kajal sang a song at the foundation's annual
EyeBall gala. (2007)

Kajal and I did the·first dance at the
EyeBall. (2007)

With Gwen, Elisa, my parents, my brother, and Parish. (1995)

With Dennis and my parents on the Stanford University campus. (2005)

With my godparents, June Rudolph and Misha Bartnovsky. (1998)

With Dolly Parton, composing, playing, and recording erhu for her country song, "The Cruel War," for her album *Those Were the Days*. (2005)

On a mission trip to Moldova,
Lynn Hendrich met Maria, an orphan who
was shy and withdrawn because she had
been blind since birth. (2012)

Examining Maria for the first time. She
made a long trip around the globe to our
sight foundation, with the hope of having a
chance to see again. (2013)

Moments before Maria's extremely difficult
sight restoration surgery. (2013)

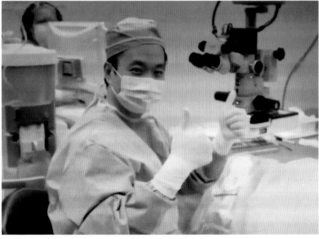

"We got it!" God successfully pulled us through Maria's nearly
impossible surgery. (2013)

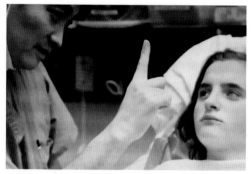

"How many fingers?" "Unu!" Maria can see! (2013)

"I am so pretty!" the 15-year-old, formerly blind orphan from Moldova exclaimed (in Romanian) when she saw herself for the very first time! (2013)

Maria has gone from a blind orphan, at the brink of human trafficking and prostitution, to a happy teenager who can now see and lives with the Hendriches in Franklin, TN. (2013)

With Anle and Maria. (2015)

Competing in a pro-am ballroom dance competition with my teacher, Shalene Archer. (2007)

A family photo (left to right): Xiao-hua, Lili, Peggy, Ming-yu, Alisa, Dennis, Dad, Yong-yong, me, Mom, and Anle. (Thanksgiving, 2014)

Receiving an honorary doctorate degree from Trevecca Nazarene University, with Richard, Tony, Anle, Jim, Tony, Christin, Megan, and David. (2015)

Nashvillian of the Year Award, and the team of Wang Vision 3 D Cataract & LASIK Center: Front row: Drs. Ebrahim, Zimmerman, Connolly, Wang, and Rock. Second row: Shannon, Beth, Heather, Leona, Anle, Ana, Tammy and Clare. Third row: Cameron, Skyler, Chloe, James, Suzanne and Dr. Zhao. Back row: Crystal, Amanda, Ashley, Kayla, Erica, Haley, Eric, Scott, and Dr. Jiang.

My family picked me up from the airport in Shanghai. My little brother was a short, adolescent thirteen-year-old when I first left China but at sixteen, he had become a man and was as tall as our mother. I didn't even recognize him! We took a train from Shanghai back to Hangzhou, and other than my brother's growth spurt, not much else had changed. My hometown was still very poor despite the country's recent economic reforms, so even with lifelong careers as doctors, my parents could never have afforded the appliances I had purchased for them from the States. I bought my parents their first refrigerator, color television, washing machine, clothes dryer, home stereo, modern bicycle, and Canon camera. Before coming to America, I could never have imagined being able to afford such extravagant things.

I also had a lot of small gifts for my friends, former classmates, and the many teachers who had helped me through the traumatic years of the Cultural Revolution. To save money and space in my luggage, I brought back about forty travel-size bottles of shampoo, which was a uniquely American product and a novelty item in China at that time. The little bottles with labels in English were a big hit with my elders and friends.

During the two weeks I was in China, my teachers and former classmates asked me many questions about my life in America. They were wide-eyed about this wondrous faraway place. I recognized how differently I ranked in China versus in the States. In America, I was at the bottom of the totem pole—a poor student, a minimum wage, night shift worker at Burger King and Best Western, cleaning up grease. I was poor in the eyes of the wealthy American society, but in China I was rich. They noticed I had gained weight from all the fast food I had been eating. In China, where so many people still had limited access to meat and nourishing food, my weight was yet another sign of prosperity to them.

Whenever people asked what I was doing in Maryland, I would say, "I'm studying on a beautiful university campus with pure air and roads so clean you can lie down on them. I live in a luxury apartment with only two roommates, rather than thirteen like at USTC. I buy clothes for cheap and watch movies for a dollar." But I didn't mention to anyone how hard I had to work, nor about the prejudices I faced. My neighbors and family expected me to do well, so I only shared the most glamorous aspects of life in the States. China, the country of my birth, no longer felt like a harsh place that nearly stripped me of a life I longed for, but instead I felt reconnected with my ethnic origins and grateful for the realization that it was my Eastern upbringing, family values, and work ethic that had helped me overcome life's challenges so I could succeed in America.

When I went back to Maryland, I realized that something else in me had shifted. My roots were in China, but I had become very comfortable in America and had aligned myself with the interests of my adopted country. I felt like a citizen of both countries and an intermediary between them. But my two homes had different values, histories and cultures, so I had an identity crisis. Was I American ... or was I Chinese?

I remained in this liminal zone between cultures for several more years, during which my appreciation for America increased and my English continually improved. Eventually I found myself even thinking in English. Before that time, I would think in Chinese and then translate the thoughts into English before I would speak, but over time English became more natural to me. Not only did I start thinking in English; I also started thinking like an American. I embraced wholeheartedly American values like freedom and democracy.

I encountered perhaps my strongest feeling of allegiance to America in June of 1989.

At the end of my second year at Harvard, the Tiananmen Square protests of Chinese students in Beijing had reached fever pitch. For several weeks, students had been peacefully demonstrating in city centers around China, calling for democratic reforms. I was returning to my dorm room on the evening of June 4, with the events weighing heavily on my mind. The day before, the students had been given an ultimatum to clear Tiananmen Square or they would be forced out by government troops. It had been hard for me to focus on my studies that day. When I got home I turned on the news, and as I listened to CBS's Dan Rather reporting on the scene, my heart fell to the floor.

I grabbed the phone and dialed quickly.

"They're killing people!" I hollered, my voice strained and trembling. On the other end of the line was a compatriot from the Chinese Student and Scholar Association back at the University of Maryland.

On the news report, I could hear gunshots and could see the dead and wounded being carted away. Hundreds were presumed to have been killed. It was unthinkable to me that any country could do this to its own people.

"There's going to be a protest in D.C.," my friend said. "We are asking Congress to protect the Chinese students here in the U.S. Can you join us?"

"I'll see you on Capitol Hill."

One morning a few weeks later, I joined a group of my fellow Chinese American students for a rally on the steps of the Capitol building to protest the cruelty of the Chinese government in Tiananmen Square. Following the rally, we were granted an audience with congressional leaders, including Nancy Pelosi, who was then a junior congresswoman from San Francisco. We told her and other representatives that the Chinese students studying in the U.S. who had supported the demonstrations could be in grave danger if they were forced to return to China when their student visas expired.

I had never been politically active in my life prior to this moment. Though I had been the president of the U.S. Chinese

Student and Scholar Association and had met an American president in the White House, I had never appealed for congressional action for any political purpose, so actively participating in democracy was a major turning point in my young life. I had come from a one-party dictatorial political system that, as the events on June fourth had made clear, tolerated no opposition. To be allowed to walk the halls of Capitol Hill and speak freely to the men and women who represented everyday Americans was empowering. I had experienced profound psychological trauma as a teenager from political oppression during China's Cultural Revolution, so now that I had tasted the freedom of democracy as a young adult in America, there was no turning back.

I had truly become an American.

Since this inner transformation occurred over a period of many years, the naturalization process itself was simply a formality. After I completed the required paperwork and passed the background checks, I received notification that I could come in for my interview with an officer from U.S. Customs and Immigration. I was tested on my basic knowledge of English, history, and government. By far, this was the least stressful test I had taken in my entire life, yet at the same time, it was replete with meaning all the same. The last step would be to return for a ceremony to take the Oath of Allegiance.

In the spring of 1992, the day of the official ceremony had finally arrived. I parked my car in downtown Newark and walked toward the Peter W. Rodino, Jr. Federal Building on Broad Street. The winter had been harsh, but now the air felt light and full of the excitement of a new beginning. I walked through the front doors and took an elevator upstairs to a bland, gray office where I joined twenty other foreigners, some speaking Spanish, others dressed in brightly colored saris, a few wearing turbans, all of us ready to pledge faithful allegiance to the United States of America.

We stood in front of a large American flag, its red, white, and blue colors draped around a tall pole, topped by the emblem of an eagle. A federal judge led us through the official Oath of Allegiance to the United States. We held up our right hands, repeating our solemn promise to renounce all previous loyalties to foreign states, and to support and defend the U.S. Constitution and the nation's laws.

Standing before that vibrant flag, I realized how blessed I was. What other country in the world embraced so many people from foreign lands and allowed them to make that country their home? I had gone from a communist country that had nearly destroyed my future to a free and open nation that enabled me to go to graduate schools with the brightest minds in the world. Thanks to America, my childhood dream of becoming a doctor—like my father and grandfather before me—had finally come true. The U.S. was also the origin of my spiritual nascence and the incubator of my continued quest for faith. My experiences in this country, and the people of faith that I had encountered, had initiated my first awareness of God and the emerging purpose for my life.

I had brought from China a disciplined work ethic, and a character that had been enriched by its cultural roots and shaped by suffering. In the United States, I had received freedom, an education, and a promising career. I felt tremendously indebted to both countries, and particularly to America; so to have the chance to finally become an American meant to me that I now had the duty to serve and to defend this great country, and to help protect the most important foundational concepts of American society, namely that all men and women are created equal, one Nation under God.

"When I'm finished with my medical training," I told myself, "I will do something worthwhile to express my gratitude to my newly adopted country. I will loyally serve this nation and its people for the rest of my life."

The United States was now my home and my country. My parents and brother eventually naturalized as well. Until their retirement in 2006, my parents continued to dedicate their lives to improving the quality of life of patients here in America suffering from diseases. Like the field of medicine, giving back to our adopted country became a family tradition, which continues to this day.

I also longed to find someone here in America, with whom I could build a future. Though my first marriage was not successful, I would not let that deter me from continuing to grow my family, specifically a family built on love and Christian faith.

Chapter 13

Gwen

When the elevator doors opened and I saw her standing there, I stood a little taller and tried to look relaxed. She and another resident were laughing as they walked in. I had seen her only a few times before, usually from a distance. She was striking and tall, with thick golden-brown hair and big green eyes. Besides her beauty, I was also impressed by her lively demeanor, as she was smiling and joking every time I saw her.

Who was this dazzling young woman? I just had to find out.

I had moved to Philadelphia, Pennsylvania in July of 1992 for a fellowship in ocular genetics research with Wills Eye Hospital, the first eye-care facility in the United States. After the year-long fellowship, I would complete my three year residency in ophthalmology at the same facility. My goal was to combine my training in lasers with a top-quality training in ophthalmology. I was fortunate to be recruited as a resident at Wills Eye, one of the top eye institutions in the world.

In a laboratory on the fourth floor of the six-story building, I worked under Dr. Larry Donoso, the director of clinical research and a professor of ophthalmology. Our work focused on pinpointing the DNA mutation that caused ocular melanoma and retinoblastoma. Dr. Donoso was in his early fifties, a very kind and charming man from Utah who served as a mentor to many young doctors in training. One day I asked Dr. Donoso if he knew who the young woman was.

"Her name is Gwen," he said. "She's a third-year resident. She worked in my lab several years ago when she was a student at Jefferson Medical College next door."

"What's she like?" I asked.

"She's smart and capable," he responded. "She finished experiments very efficiently and was always eager to do more."

Naturally Dr. Donoso talked about her work but I wanted to know more about her personality.

"Is she always so happy?" I asked.

"Yes, she is," he said. "Why do you want to know?"

I shrugged. "Just curious."

Dr. Donoso grinned at me. "She is always smiling and joyful," he continued. "She treats everyone with kindness. Her good nature sometimes seems too good to be true."

But it was all true. When I looked into those large green eyes, they seemed like a lake of clear water, so pure and honest. I had a few opportunities to chat with her—in the cafeteria, along hospital corridors and outside lecture halls after presentations. She was a ray of sunshine, and I was mesmerized by her. By the time I finished my fellowship and joined the ranks of the other residents, she had finished her residency herself and had left for Tampa, Florida for a fellowship in cornea.

A year later, I was going about my life as usual when one day I received a letter in my hospital mailbox. There, on top of the return address, was Gwen's name.

"I've just returned from a mission trip to China," she wrote, "and I have pictures I want to share with you."

We hadn't interacted much while she was at Wills, but I was excited to hear from her, this girl I had so admired. We met up for a meal in Chinatown in the center of Philadelphia, and she shared that she completed her fellowship in Tampa, traveled overseas and was now back home in Philadelphia looking for a job. She showed me photos she had taken during the two months she spent in China's Hunan Province, where she had worked alongside other Christians providing assistance in local hospitals.

"I loved the food!" she said. "I want to eat Chinese cuisine all the time now, and I really want to learn to speak Chinese. It's such a beautiful language."

"I would be happy to teach you Chinese," I replied enthusiastically. We both smiled.

Even though I wasn't sure that Gwen had contacted me out of any romantic inclination, my curiosity about her was nonetheless piqued. I had been single for more than a year by then, so despite my hectic schedule as a resident, I found the time to meet with her quite frequently at different restaurants in Philadelphia's Chinatown. Over the next few months, we became very good friends. I wanted to find out why she was so joyful and upbeat all the time, and I soon realized that her Christian faith had a lot to do with it. She came from a devoted Christian family and knew the Scriptures very well. She had graduated from Wheaton College, a prominent evangelical school, and was smart and well read, so although she wanted me to teach her about the Chinese language and culture, there was much I could learn from her about the Christian faith.

It had been a few years since Dr. Hand had introduced me to Christianity, and I was still seeking so many answers to questions about life and spirituality. I studied the Bible by myself, and I had started attending the First Presbyterian Church on Walnut Street, a gothic building that had stood in Philadelphia's Center City for more than two hundred years. I hadn't become a Christian yet, but I was curious and open to the faith. I wanted to know more about God and to explore this sense of calling in my life. At the same time, I hoped that embracing the faith would help me grow closer to my newly adopted country with its strong Christian heritage.

One Sunday at the church on Walnut Street, the pastor gave a sermon about suffering and its hidden blessings. Suffering was something I had known all too well and intimately. From my place in the wooden pews, I looked up at the streams of light pouring through the stained-glass windows in shades of blue and green. The colors that streaked above me were a vibrant contrast to the bleak shades of gray that had hung over us in China during the Cultural Revolution. As I reflected on the years I was immersed in terror and darkness back then, I wondered why I had endured so much suffering. Why was I forced to bear so many unending nightmares? Was there a reason for it all?

"Suffering serves to draw us closer to God," the pastor said. "Through the painful seasons of life, our hearts are softened toward others, and we grow in compassion."

I realized that although God had allowed me to suffer, He had also sustained me. The hardship I had endured instilled in me a deep sense of gratitude for the opportunities that had followed. What I had overcome had not depleted me. On the contrary, my cup was now overflowing and I wanted to give to others from that abundance.

Gwen and I didn't attend the same church, but she often took me to Christian medical society meetings where physicians of faith came together for Bible studies, lectures, and fellowship. These doctors from various specialties were exceptionally loving, kind, and happy, just like Gwen was, and they led such upstanding lives. I found in this group of medical professionals a remarkable balance between their respect for science and their profound faith in Jesus Christ. The environment allowed me to ask complex questions and receive insights from people I admired and trusted.

Not long after Gwen and I had reconnected, we attended a Saturday seminar with the Christian medical society on the University of Pennsylvania campus. A pastor named Dr. Simms spoke with eloquence to an audience of about a hundred doctors who had gathered for the daylong event. Dr. Simms related raw and honest emotion, including the intense anger and frustration he felt when his wife endured a debilitating stroke that left her helpless and entirely dependent on his care. Like the sermon on suffering I had heard from my pastor at church, I felt reassured and encouraged by such humanity and honesty from another person of faith.

"Jesus was a man who faced many sorrows, and was acquainted with grief," Dr. Simms said. "In Him we see God, who takes on flesh and suffers alongside us and for us, and by His wounds we are healed."

In the person of Jesus Christ, God had a name, a face, a personality, and a purpose for humanity. The God of the Christian faith was real and accessible. After the day was over, I felt a deep sense of calling and was ready to commit my life to Him.

"How do I become a Christian?" I asked Gwen.

"Once you've received Christ, you get baptized," she said.

"Do you think we could ask Reverend Simms to baptize me now?"

It was getting late, and the last of the other attendees had filed out, so we were finally alone with Dr. Simms. When Gwen relayed to him my wish to be baptized, he went straight for a cup of water.

The three of us huddled together in the lecture hall. I lowered my chin as Dr. Simms poured a small amount of water over the crown of my head. I could feel a trickle flow over my ears and down my neck. Though the water was room temperature, I felt a chill pass through me. How appropriate that a university lecture hall—the focal point of so many of my struggles to excel—would be the place where God's spirit united with my own.

Dr. Simms placed his hand on my head and prayed.

Like becoming an American, becoming a Christian had been for me an extensive process of internal transformation over many years, culminating in a ceremony that took only a few minutes. I felt a deep peace. While the baptism did not take place in a traditional church, there was still a profound sacredness to the moment. I knew that God was with me, that He had been guiding me through all the hardships and struggles in China and America, and that He would continue to do so . . . but I had so much more still to learn.

* * *

Gwen and I spent more and more time together. We had so much in common—we were both ophthalmologists and were both interested in corneal diseases and treatments—so when we would get together, we constantly discussed the cornea. She had already completed her corneal fellowship, so she had a lot to teach me. She also loved the Chinese culture and language, so I enjoyed being her dedicated Chinese teacher. I loved the adorable, mischievous smile that appeared on her face when she would make a mistake in the pronunciation of a word. We both loved fine art and classical music as well. We often dined at a small, artsy restaurant on South Street in the southern part of the town, called Victor's Café, at which all the waiters were opera singers. In the middle of dinner, one of the waiters would stop serving, climb up a set of stairs and break into a beautiful aria. Both Gwen and I loved it! Gwen was also excited about learning ballroom dancing, so I took her to dance studios every weekend, and we thoroughly enjoyed dancing together. Despite the fact that we had grown up in vastly different cultures that were also the farthest apart geographically, Gwen and I found to our delight that we were so much alike, shared so many common interests, had the same values regarding family and work, and we both love reading the Bible and we both had a deep appreciation of life itself. When we were together, time flew by quickly, and we would look forward to the next time we could meet, even before we parted.

A few weeks before Thanksgiving, Gwen invited me to dinner at her parents' house. Both Gwen and her younger sister still lived at home. Her mother introduced me to her father as "Gwen's Chinese friend." Her parents were retired physicians, both specialists in obstetrics and gynecology. Gwen's mother was polite, if not overly warm, but her father was a science buff so he took a liking to me right away. He was curious and high-spirited, and asked me all kinds of questions about the eye.

"What drew you to ophthalmology?" he asked as he passed me a heavy bowl of potatoes.

"I studied lasers back in Maryland, and I believe they can work wonders in improving eyesight," I said.

"How so?"

"We can use lasers to reshape the cornea so patients never have to wear glasses or contacts again," I explained. "Once the devices are approved by the FDA, people's lives will never be the same again."

The original approach to laser eye surgery was photorefractive keratectomy, or PRK, which reshaped the outer layer of the cornea to correct vision. A new procedure called laser-assisted in-situ keratomileusis, or LASIK, had first been performed in Greece in 1990, and then in the U.S. around the time I started my residency at Wills Eye in 1993. Eye surgeons would first use a blade to create a flap on the surface of the cornea, and then a laser would reshape the tissue underneath to better focus light on the retina to improve sight. LASIK resulted in less discomfort and quicker recovery than PRK.

"We call the new approach 'flap and zap,'" I joked.

Gwen's father was fascinated by our science conversation, and as I left that night, he told me, "Come back anytime, Ming. You are always welcome in our home."

I did return quite frequently, especially given my growing interest in Gwen. While her dad was keen on asking me questions about laser physics and ophthalmology, I wanted to ask him about my newfound Christian faith. Gwen's family had been devoted Christians their entire lives. And as an obstetrician, her father had delivered a lot of babies, so I was especially curious to know his take on the latest ethical issues facing scientists who engaged in stem cell and fetal tissue research.

Over dinner one evening, I told him about a time during medical school at Harvard when I was on an ophthalmology rotation in the trauma unit at Massachusetts General Hospital. I had helped treat a man who had been badly burned by a phosphorus explosion in the factory where he worked. His face had been seared, and the front parts of his corneas were completely stripped away. During the months he was in the hospital, I took care of him and watched his eyes heal, but the resulting thick, white scars on his corneas left him completely blind, barely able to perceive light. The scar tissue and blood vessels that grew over his eyes also meant that surgery to restore his sight would be too difficult to perform. I asked the attending physician what could be done to help this man, but he responded that scarring was unfortunately the natural way we all heal. The immune system seems to overdo its job in the adult wound-healing process, which results in scars. I was deeply frustrated that modern medicine could do so little, and that this man in our care would leave the hospital completely blind.

Around the time I encountered the injured man, I began reading about fetal regeneration. In the womb, injured fetuses healed with practically no scarring, so why was there so much scarring with adult body healing? I reasoned that since the womb provided a safe and sterile fluid environment, perhaps the unborn child could afford to take a lot more time to heal. The healing process in the womb was less rushed and more orderly, resulting in layer-by-layer regeneration with no scarring. Adult bodies, in contrast, are exposed to a dry and dirty environment, so the wound has to be closed as quickly as possible to reduce bleeding and the risk of infection. The price that we pay as adults for such quick healing is disorganized scarring, called fibrosis.

For years medical researchers had been studying fetal tissue and stem cells—the undifferentiated cells of a newly conceived embryo—in an attempt to bring the healing properties of the womb into clinical treatments for adults. During the early 1990s, scientists hadn't yet reached the point where they could manipulate the stem cells, but once they did, it would result in significant advances in medical treatments for a wide range of human diseases. On the other hand, it was bound to erupt into tremendous amount of controversy since extracting a stem cell to use for a treatment would destroy the embryo.

I felt torn by both sides of the issue. Fetal tissue and stem cell research held so much promise for treating traumatic injuries and diseases related to aging, like Alzheimer's, Parkinson's, diabetes, glaucoma, and macular degeneration. Nevertheless, I couldn't justify harming an unborn baby for any reason. But if we didn't continue such research, what hope could we offer our injured and aging patients? What else would I be able to do to prevent scarring and the resulting blindness for the patients who came to me after eye injuries?

I shared my inner turmoil with Gwen's dad. "How on earth can we study fetal tissue to benefit adult patients *without* harming the fetus?"

"I don't know how to resolve that dilemma right now," he admitted, "but I'm confident we'll find ways to pursue research without getting into troublesome moral and ethical areas. Don't give up on your pursuit, Ming. Keep the faith, and I'm sure in time God will grant you wisdom."

As a new Christian, I was deeply grateful to have this man as my mentor. Like Gwen, he was upbeat and cheerful and always smiling. Rather than pitting faith against science in hopeless polarity, he had a remarkable way of balancing the two and being patient through the conflict. He nurtured both my growing faith and my scientific curiosity, and he confirmed my conviction that we should be able to embrace and advance scientific breakthroughs while remaining consistent with our Christian values. We should never harm an unborn child for the benefit of sick or injured adults, but perhaps God would show us a way to access the healing power of the womb without the moral quandary. I had been deeply impacted by watching that injured man go blind due to scarring, and I would continue seeking a solution for many years to come.

* * *

In no time at all, I felt like I was part of Gwen's family, and I spent both Thanksgiving and Christmas Eve at their home. After we finished Christmas Eve dinner, Gwen's father asked, "Ming, why don't you just stay over?"

"I'd love to!"

In the dozen years I had lived in the States, I had never before experienced a traditional American Christmas. My heart was full of joy knowing I would spend my first one with an American family who loved me.

They made up a bed for me on the living-room sofa. The next morning, the stockings hanging from the mantle were brimming with gifts, and beneath the tree were presents wrapped in brightly colored paper with curled ribbons and bows on top.

Gwen handed me a gift and when I unwrapped it, I found a bright red sweater inside. I pulled it over my head, feeling cherished by this family, as if I were one of their own.

On New Year's Eve, I accompanied Gwen and her family to Longwood Gardens to see the trees decorated for the holidays. I wore the red sweater the family had given me for Christmas.

"Get together for a photo!" Her father motioned to Gwen and me.

Gwen and I moved toward each other, and I put my arm around her shoulder. As she leaned into me, my heart fluttered. I hadn't yet seriously considered that we would become more than just friends, but in that moment I felt an unmistakable spark. Maybe I could be more than just her Chinese teacher?

After the photo was taken, we moved apart, looking at each other a bit nervously. She seemed to have felt it too. I glanced at her parents, who suddenly had quizzical expressions on their faces. Did they notice what had just happened between us? I couldn't quite tell, but if they did, there was no mention of it for the rest of that day.

Not long afterward, there was an unmistakable change in Gwen's parents' demeanor toward me. They became more polite and detached. As for me, now that my interest in Gwen had grown, I wanted to see her more often and spend as much time as possible at her family's house. But her mother, who was never warm toward me to begin with, became absolutely icy and told me that the family was too busy with other things, so I was no longer welcomed. She thought it best that Gwen and I spend less time together, not more. In an instant, in one click of the camera, I had gone from being loved to being rejected.

I was very confused and upset. I kept wondering what had happened to cause them to not like me any longer.

In spite of her mother's opposition, Gwen and I started dating in the beginning of 1995. She had never had a boyfriend and wanted to be with me constantly, but she was concerned about upsetting her parents.

"My mother says we are just too different and we shouldn't be together," Gwen explained. "She told me the Bible says that people who are very different should not be together because we are not to be unequally yoked."

This was the first time I had heard the word "yoked."

"What does she mean by saying we're very different?" I asked. Gwen wouldn't answer. Perhaps it was because I was such a new

Christian? Maybe her mother just needed time to get to know me and see how I lived out the Christian faith. I was hopeful and confident that I could change her mind.

My own parents, on the other hand, had taken an instant liking to Gwen. When she visited them in Boston, they embraced her and took her to their labs at Harvard to show her their research projects, and my father patiently explained his project about Chinese herbal medicine and its beneficial effects on the cardiovascular system. Though Gwen wasn't Chinese, she was well educated and family-oriented, which are important attributes to Chinese parents. Gwen also loved me deeply and had made a concentrated effort to learn the Chinese language and culture, so my parents were very pleased with her.

I only wish that Gwen's parents had shown me the same acceptance. I started working diligently to earn their favor. I even went as far as throwing a special Chinese New Year party just for them. I wanted to show them that I loved their daughter and that I was a good, responsible, and caring man. I also wanted to demonstrate my fascination with both America and my birth country. I decorated my high-rise apartment with red lanterns, ribbons and figurines of young boys setting off fireworks, and I planned to perform for them and a few friends on my piano.

After my party began, my friends kept asking me to play the piano as I had promised, but my eyes were glued to the door. I didn't want to start playing until Gwen and her parents arrived. A full two hours passed with no sign of them, and I was ready to give up. Then I finally heard a knock.

I opened the door to see Gwen dressed in a beautiful jade green *chipao*, the traditional Chinese evening gown that I had bought for her during a trip to San Francisco. The color matched her eyes. She smiled happily at me, and her father was as friendly and warm to me as he had been when we first met. He apologized for being late, glancing tentatively at Gwen's mother, who stood there suppressing a scowl. She was clearly in charge.

I was nonetheless overjoyed that they had finally come! I took them around the room, introducing them to my friends, and explaining that 1995 was the Year of the Pig on the Chinese lunar calendar. I shared the meaning behind each of the decorations, and told them I would be serving a traditional Chinese soup right after the piano performance.

As soon as I finished my first piece, Gwen's mother stood up abruptly, eager to leave. They hadn't even had a bowl of my special Chinese soup yet! Gwen pleaded with her mother to stay and enjoy the rest of the evening, but she simply flashed a fake smile and headed for the door.

Defying social etiquette, I left my other guests in the apartment all by themselves while I accompanied Gwen and her parents on the twenty-six-floor elevator ride down to the lobby. I glanced at Gwen and was reminded of one of the first times I had seen her, in an elevator not too different from this one. She was still so beautiful, vivacious, and cheerful. However, regardless of how close Gwen and I had become since the beginning, her parents' behavior toward me made Gwen seem still so distant and inaccessible. I felt so frustrated since I still did not know why I went from being loved to being rejected. We talked on the descent—Gwen ebullient over the party, her father happy and interested—as her mother remained cold and silent.

The next time Gwen saw me, she apologized for what had happened. With tears in her eyes, she reluctantly explained the truth behind her mother's complete rejection of me. The problem wasn't that I was a new Christian; it was that I was Chinese, not Anglo-Saxon. That was all that mattered to her mother.

I realized what a big mistake my Chinese New Year party had actually been, as it had only worsened the situation! Despite my good intentions, the party only emphasized my cultural and ethnic origin ... and our cultural differences.

I was stunned. They had loved me when Gwen and I were just friends, so why was my ethnicity an issue now that we were dating? Christianity seemed to be a faith that embraces people no matter what their race or national origin is, so how could these Christians not accept me into their family solely because I wasn't white?

By that time, I had been in the United States for twelve years. I had embraced this country, had become a citizen, and although China was my country of origin, I was now an American and had worked diligently to serve my adopted country. In the early years after arriving in the U.S., I had faced discrimination and prejudice from people like Drs. Miller and Anderson, men who never took the time to know me beyond my ethnicity. In contrast, Gwen's family did take that time, and they grew to like and care for me as well. But somehow I had crossed a line; I was acceptable as their daughter's friend, but not as a potential son-in-law, and there was nothing that I could do about it! The blow was devastating. I came to the realization that racial discrimination tends to exist on the deepest and most personal level. Even though one can accept another person as a friend, or sometimes even as a very good friend, one still may not actually be willing to accept another person wholeheartedly into one's own family through marriage.

Gwen's mother did everything she could to talk Gwen out of seeing me. "Can you imagine having a mixed-race child?" her mother asked her. "I don't think you would be happy."

"You know I don't agree with her," Gwen said to me. "I love you, and I love everything about the fact that you are a Chinese-American. I don't think your ethnicity is a problem at all."

The problem, if not my ethnicity, was how devoted Gwen was to obeying her parents' wishes. She was thirty-one years old but her parents still ruled over all aspects of her life, from what time she came home at night to where she worked. Since I was still completing my residency in Philadelphia, her mother's strategy was to push her to take a job as far away from the city as she could.

"It's crazy for you to leave Philadelphia," I said. "Your family, your schooling, your residency, your physician contacts, and your patients are all here ... and I'm here! You have every reason to stay."

"She doesn't want me working in Philadelphia, or in Pennsylvania, or in any neighboring state for that matter. This is what we're up against, Ming."

We were sitting in one of our favorite Chinese restaurants. I contemplated for a moment how the green of her eyes rivaled the jade dragon that hung on the wall behind her. The carved dragon was pursuing a jewel just out of its reach. I felt trapped in the same perpetual pursuit, with no assurance I could hang onto this gem that was only an arm's length away. How could this family who had embraced me so endearingly, who had encouraged my Christian journey, now turn and say that I was not good enough to be part of their family just because of my ethnicity?

Three months later, Gwen made the announcement I had both expected and dreaded.

"I'm taking a job in Ohio. I'm leaving in two months."

"At least Ohio is a neighboring state," I said, trying to be lighthearted. But I looked at her with incredible sadness. "You know you hate the cold. You're going to freeze there. It's even colder there than it is here in Philadelphia!"

Gwen loved warmth. She would practically freeze whenever the weather dipped below fifty degrees. She had been so much happier in sunny Florida during her fellowship. We both knew she would be miserable. She couldn't respond, so we sat in silence for several minutes until Gwen sighed deeply.

"Dad misses his time with you," she finally mumbled awkwardly.

"I miss him too."

Gwen left for Ohio in August of 1995. I went to see her as often as I could, but during my visits, I could sense her mother's control all the way from Philadelphia. Gwen never allowed me into her apartment, not even the lobby of the building.

The following summer, after I had completed my residency at Wills Eye, I left for a corneal fellowship of my own at Bascom Palmer Eye Institute in Miami. Gwen was envious of my retreat to warmer weather, and I hoped that my living in perpetual sunshine might finally draw her to me. We continued our long-distance relationship, enduring her mother's standoff while holding onto the belief that as long as we love each other the geographic and cultural distances would eventually be bridged.

Chapter 14

The Two Letters

I left my apartment early in the morning and drove south along A1A in Miami Beach, with the sapphire and emerald waves of the Atlantic Ocean on my left, and bright, colorful Art Deco buildings on my right. The road was lined with palm trees whose leaves were still in the quiet of the dawn. The colors of the sunrise were spilling over the horizon and across the water. Miami Beach was breathtaking, and the area was alive with an abundance of fun things to do. Unfortunately, I had very little time to enjoy it because after I finished seeing patients all day, much of my evening was taken up with a certain company of rabbits.

While I was more than willing to travel the more than 1,200-mile trip to visit Gwen, who was busy building an ophthalmology practice near Cleveland, Ohio, she preferred to escape the cold and come my way so she could enjoy sunny Florida. Every time she arrived in Miami, we would hit the beach, soaking up the warmth from the rays above and the sand beneath. Despite her mother's continued resistance, Gwen seemed to become even more committed to our relationship, so I felt confident that it was just a matter of time until we would win over her parents so we could finally be together.

In between Gwen's visits, I was immersed in research to find a way to prevent scarring and the resulting blindness after corneal injuries. Seven years after my encounter with the patient at Massachusetts General Hospital who had been blinded by scarring after a corneal trauma, I could finally delve into the question that had plagued me ever since, as I was now doing a corneal fellowship and had more time to devote to the study of corneal trauma and injuries. I still hoped to figure out how stem cells and fetal tissue could be tapped to improve the healing process in a human cornea after injury, but *without* harming the fetus. For years, a solution evaded me and I had nearly given up trying to reconcile this conflict between stem cell and fetal tissue research and the sacredness of life. But I felt empowered and transformed by my newfound Christian faith, and supported and encouraged by Gwen. I also kept in mind what Gwen's dad had told me early on at a dinner—if we are patient, God will grant us wisdom in time.

After that conversation, I kept a piece of paper in my pocket on which I had written out the Bible verse, James 1:4, which says: "Let perseverance finish its work so that we may be mature and complete, lacking nothing." My life's journey had taught me over and over again that nothing worthwhile came quickly or easily. Just because the solution to the conflict between scientific research and Christian faith was elusive, that didn't mean the solution didn't exist. I needed to persevere and trust that God would show the way in His perfect time.

At Bascom Palmer, I had chosen Professor Scheffer Tseng—a world-renowned specialist in ocular surface disease and reconstruction—as my research advisor. I shared my qualms, conflicts, and confusion with Professor Tseng, as I had done with Gwen's father.

"I don't see how we can avoid this research, since fetal tissue has magical scarless healing properties," I said. "But I don't want to hurt the fetus. I've been wrestling with this question for years. How can we benefit our adult patients without harming unborn children?"

He shared with me that his lab had actually reintroduced the use of the amniotic membrane very recently.

"The amniotic sac has the same biochemical properties as fetal tissue, so we're exploring whether the membrane that lines the sac holds the same healing power outside the womb."

Professor Tseng's words truly excited me. I began to read about the amniotic membrane's use in medical treatments. The amniotic membrane is part of the tough, transparent amniotic sac where a baby grows in the womb. At the turn of the twentieth century, doctors had started using the amniotic membranes from placentae to reduce scarring in procedures like stomach surgery. In the 1950s, doctors again experimented with the membrane to reduce fibrosis in general surgery. The application hadn't come into widespread use because of inherent limitations in the bioengineering of amnion tissue during those years.

Nearly a century after the first experiments with amniotic membranes, Professor Tseng was applying the idea to ophthalmology. I felt an immense swell of excitement at the possibility that perhaps the time had finally come for a solution to the problem that had puzzled me for so many years. I was grateful to God that my life's path had led me to Dr. Tseng's lab in South Florida, so many years and hundreds of miles away from my earliest questions at Harvard Medical School.

Dr. Tseng and I collected amniotic sacs donated by mothers who had delivered their babies via Caesarean section, which was the only way to keep the amniotic sac intact and usable after birth. We began testing the amniotic membrane on lab rabbits to see if we could recreate the fetal environment, the membrane's rapid regeneration and scarless healing properties. Following laser treatments on each of a rabbit's eyes, I covered one eye with the amniotic membrane for a week and left the other uncovered, in order for the experiment to be controlled and the results compared.

After several weeks of observing the rabbit's corneas, I then invited Professor Tseng and Bascom Palmer's cornea specialists—including Professors Richard Foster, William Culberson, Andrew Huang, Carol Karp, Eduado Alfonso, Khalil Hanna, and Stephen Pflugfelter—to inspect the corneal scarring and note their impressions of the results.

"No one knows which eye was treated with the amniotic membrane," I told them. "Just take a close look and grade the amount of corneal scarring in each eye."

This double-blind study confirmed what I had witnessed myself—that is, that the eye that was covered by the amniotic membrane had 75 percent less amount of scarring than the eye that was left uncovered. I was elated that the healing power of the womb was, in fact, still present in the amniotic sac tissue, and since the placenta was simply discarded after birth, the use of this tissue presented absolutely no harm to the baby.

I was very curious about the molecular mechanism by which the amniotic membrane reduced scarring. When I took a closer look, I discovered that the eye treated with the membrane had less inflammation. By covering the cornea within twenty-four hours of the laser treatment, the membrane inhibited the natural, exaggerated wound healing response. Less inflammation meant less cell death, which ultimately resulted in less scarring. We published the first paper in scientific literature that demonstrated laboratory success in reducing corneal scarring and cell death with amniotic membrane transplantation, and we explained how the treatment helped restore sight.

Our work had been a dramatic leap forward in the quest to capture the healing power of the womb, but when we explored how to apply our findings to the clinical setting for patients, we hit a significant roadblock. We had been working with sedated rabbits in a highly controlled laboratory setting, but in a real-life trauma situation, it would be very difficult to suture a membrane onto a patient's painfully damaged cornea. Additionally, injured eye tissue would be vulnerable to perforation from suturing, which could expose the eye to dangerous infection and blindness. Furthermore, the technique to perform the minuscule sutures necessary to attach the amniotic membrane also required highly specialized surgeons who might not be on hand when needed. The amniotic membranes also had to be available at all times so patients could be treated within twenty-four hours of their injuries.

We needed to come up with a much better way to apply the amniotic membrane to a freshly injured eye in a safer, more effective and more timely manner.

We were so close to the long-awaited ethical solution to using fetal tissue to treat corneal scarring, but now we faced this new challenge. I felt frustrated by this break in our momentum, but I was still convinced that we could advance medical breakthroughs while staying consistent to the principles of faith. Having come this far, I couldn't be daunted by the obstacles. I repeated to myself the words Gwen's father had said, and I trusted that God would help us find a way to make the healing properties of the womb widely available to patients with eye injuries. I just needed the right idea, and it did come in time thanks in part to the help of my brother, Ming-yu.

In July of 1997, Ming-yu flew down to Miami from Boston to help me move to Nashville, Tennessee, where I had accepted a new job at Vanderbilt University. We hitched a U-Haul trailer to the back of my car, packed with everything I owned in the world. Gwen couldn't get away for the long drive to my new job, but she was planning on a visit shortly after I settled in. I appreciated having my brother along for the trip, as I had taken care of him throughout his childhood, and now he had arrived to help me.

Ming-yu slammed the trailer door shut, yanked on the padlock to be sure it was closed securely, slid into the passenger seat, and I pulled the car onto the I-95 North out of Miami.

"How's your amnion research project going?" he asked me as he leaned forward to turn up the air conditioning.

"The amniotic membrane transplants were successful on the rabbits, but for actual patients, we still need to find a better way to deliver the membranes to injured eyes, hopefully without having to suture them to the corneas, since suturing poses too many risks and often cannot be done immediately."

I gripped the steering wheel and maneuvered through traffic, the white lines on the interstate whizzing quickly past us. As I considered the benefits of the amniotic membrane, I wondered how I would find the solution I was seeking. I told Ming-yu I had been pondering this issue, praying to God for a creative solution, and trusting that God would again grant me wisdom.

I glanced over and saw Ming-yu pull out a bottle of eye lubricant to moisten his contact lenses.

At that moment, an idea came to me.

"That's it!" I shouted.

"That's what?" asked Ming-yu. His head was tilted back as he squeezed a few drops into each eye.

"Contact lenses!" I said with a rush of excitement.

It seemed so straightforward that I couldn't believe I hadn't thought of it sooner. People had been putting contact lenses into their eyes for decades. We could fuse the amniotic membrane to the underside of a contact lens, package them in bottles, and store them in emergency rooms around the world. Anyone with basic medical training could insert a contact lens onto a patient's injured eye. I realized that Ming-yu's question and my reaffirmation of my trust in God had brought about the inspiration of this simple and beautiful idea, and the answer to my long quest for a solution that aligned faith and science.

I laughed out loud, and then reached across the front seat and threw a playful punch at my brother's shoulder.

"Thanks, Ming-yu!"

"I didn't really say anything, but you're welcome."

As soon as I landed in Nashville, a friend and I sent paperwork to the U.S. Patent and Trademark Office for two patents on the amniotic membrane contact lens, one for chemical injuries and another for laser corneal treatments. The patent process could take a year or two, so in the meantime I continued my research using the traditional method of suturing the membranes onto patients' corneas. The amniotic membrane transplant would play a crucial role in the reconstructive eye surgeries I performed in the coming years.

* * *

During my fellowship at Bascom Palmer Eye Institute, I had been fully trained in cornea and laser refractive surgery. Throughout the late 1990s, the FDA rolled out a number of approvals on LASIK, which ushered in a new era in refractive surgery. Bascom Palmer bought its first laser in preparation for the first LASIK procedure at the institute. I used my expertise in laser physics to help the engineers set up the laser and calibrate it for surgery. After recruiting the first group of patients, I performed one of the first LASIK surgeries at Bascom Palmer, becoming part of history at the institute.

After nearly twenty years of laser physics and medical training, I was now working in and contributing to my chosen medical field, just as my father, mother, and the long line of doctors in our family had done. I felt deep gratitude that I was continuing this honored family tradition of healing.

I arrived in Nashville, Tennessee as the newly appointed director of the Vanderbilt Laser Sight Center. My job was to build the center from the ground up. During my tenure at Vanderbilt, I performed the first LASIK procedure in the school's history. For about five years, I served as a consultant to the FDA Ophthalmic Device Panel for the first LASIK approval in the U.S. and worked for the FDA on approvals for a wide range of innovative refractive surgery technologies. I later started my own practice and became the first surgeon in the state to perform bladeless all-laser LASIK, then laser cataract surgery, and most recently the laser KAMRA procedure.

Before I moved to Nashville, I didn't know much about the city besides its reputation for country music, but as I settled into my new life, I grew to really like the area. The scenery around Middle Tennessee reminded me of my hometown of Hangzhou, with its rolling hills, deep valleys, rivers, and lakes. When I first arrived, Nashville was still a small city centered almost entirely on West End, which turned into Broadway on its descent into a kitschy, neon downtown full of honky-tonks and souvenir shops. But I loved that there also seemed to be churches on almost every corner. Between my work at Vanderbilt and my life in this Christian community, I saw not only opportunities for professional development, but also for personal and spiritual growth. Now I just needed to convince Gwen to move to Nashville.

By 1997, Gwen and I were into the third year of our relationship. I was certain she would love the warm weather and Christian community in Nashville. She could find a job as an ophthalmologist, perhaps in my own department at Vanderbilt, and we could finally be together without the control of her parents.

While I was trying to convince Gwen to move, she was having major discussions with her parents. She didn't mention all the details, but I could tell the arguments were intense. No matter how much our relationship solidified, one thing would never change—I could never stop being Chinese—and as long as I wasn't Caucasian, her mother's attitude toward us wouldn't budge. Despite her mother's continued objections, Gwen and I wanted to get married, and we continued to move slowly but surely in that direction.

In October of 1998, a little more than a year after my move to Nashville, Gwen and I decided to get engaged. We went ring shopping while we were both in Chicago for an ophthalmology meeting. The one we both loved the most had a beautiful round diamond weighing a little over a carat, set in white gold. Unfortunately it was way beyond what I could afford at the time, as I had just started my first job, and was paying heavily on student loans.

We stood there staring down at the rows and rows of diamond rings, sparkling against the darkness of the black velvet-lined glass cases.

"I'll buy it first, and you can pay me back later!" Gwen suggested.

I looked at her, partly shocked and partly amused. "What? Are you sure? Why don't I just save up for it? You still haven't even announced this to your mother anyway."

"I know you're just starting out, but I've been working for several years now so I can do this."

"It's not very manly of me, you know."

But Gwen was eager. She obviously wanted this marriage as much as I did. I was moved by her gesture, and I felt convinced that she was as committed to our being together as I was. Gwen bought the ring, and I promised I would pay her back as soon as I could. We were both thrilled to be so close to an official engagement. I reflected back on seeing her years ago in the elevator at Wills Eye Hospital, meeting up with her after her trip to China, and keeping our long distance relationship alive from distant corners of the country. After nearly five long years filled with love and pain, joy and stress, it looked like we were finally going to make it!

Following the trip to Chicago, I wanted to give Gwen some space to discuss the impending engagement with her mother. I knew the ordeal put a strain on her, and even though we had already bought the ring, she still wouldn't fully commit until her mother had given us her blessing.

I didn't see Gwen again until November, a month later. We met in Columbus, Ohio for a dance performance that I'd told her she just couldn't miss. At the Columbus airport, we stood there holding each other closely before I headed back to Nashville. I was about to be late for my flight, but she didn't want me to leave. Her face was streaming with tears, cutting streaks through her makeup and causing her mascara to run down her cheeks. I couldn't understand why she was so emotional, but she looked beautiful—albeit comical—with her messed up makeup. I stopped to take her photo before I rushed to catch my flight.

It turned out to be the last photo I would ever take of her.

After that visit, she stopped talking to me and wouldn't return my calls. I wanted to go up to Ohio and find out what was wrong, but I waited. I wanted to give her time, but I was also afraid to know the truth. After weeks of silence, Gwen finally reached out and confirmed what I had feared all along.

One day in January of 1999, I received a bulky letter in the mail. When I opened it, I found a long, crumpled letter written in Gwen's handwriting, page after page smeared with tear stains. She wrote that she couldn't marry me after all—not without her family's blessing—and her mother simply would not give her consent. After nearly five years, she didn't want to keep my life on hold anymore, nor cause any further hurt for me or for us.

It was over.

The very first letter I had received from Gwen back in Philadelphia when she returned from China in 1994 had been so full of promise...and her last letter dashed all hope.

Five years gone, just like that. Five years of enduring her parents' objections to our relationship, all because I was an ethnic minority and not Caucasian. I felt so defeated. Throughout those years, Gwen and I had arrived at several moments where we were ready to give in to her parents and give up on our relationship. But our love was stronger than the challenges, and we had fought against her parental objection and persisted through them all. After we bought the ring, I thought we had finally figured things out. Gwen seemed resolved to marry me in spite of her mother's hostility toward me.

We had come so close, so close! The expectations that had been mounting, the hope of finally being together, came crashing down. I was awash in grief.

A few days later, I received a very different type of letter. This one was from the U.S. Patent and Trademark Office, notifying me that I had been awarded the first of two patents for my amniotic membrane contact lens invention. A process that had been conceived more than a decade ago in medical school, for the good of all my future patients, was finally coming to fruition. I approached Vanderbilt University about starting EyeVU—a joint-venture biotechnology company— to create prototypes of the lenses, with the hope of an eventual commercial launch.

The two letters—from the patent office and from Gwen— rested on my desk for months, representing two extremes of emotion from elation to despair. Between the two letters hovered the memory of my dinner conversations with Gwen's father, who had given me so much encouragement to keep moving forward with both science and faith. God had finally granted me the wisdom I needed, but it was bittersweet because I longed to be at Gwen's family table again, sitting across from her father as his son-in-law, sharing the good news about how we had persevered until we found the solution to our moral dilemma with fetal tissue research, and now we were enjoying victory with the amniotic membrane contact lens patent.

But now that would never happen. I would never be able to tell Gwen's father that he had been right all along.

I didn't write Gwen back, and I never called, no matter how much I missed her. I knew her mother wouldn't ever change her mind. At first I couldn't understand how Christians could discriminate against others like that. Christianity was supposed to be a religion rooted in love, so such blatant prejudice seemed downright *ungodly*. But when my relationship with Gwen failed, I came to a painful realization that the faith itself—and how people live out that faith—can sometimes be two entirely different things. Just because Gwen's mother was controlling and unloving didn't invalidate the Christian faith that the rest of her family and I shared. Learning to separate the faith itself from the behavior of some believers was a slow and painful process, but it also inspired me to live out my own Christian life more honestly, to be more open, and to embrace people different than me. I resolved that I would never treat anyone in such a discriminatory and unloving manner, no matter what a person's ethnic background was.

While my relationship with Gwen didn't culminate in marriage as I had hoped, the sense of failure was as poignant and arduous as it was at the end of my first marriage. Though the reasons for the failure of those two relationships were very different, my coping mechanism was the same—I retreated into the refuge of work. My research and clinical practice were more measurable and controllable, and less disappointing than the messiness of relationships.

While my romantic relationships seemed to always end in heartbreak, my work on the other hand had lasting and positive effect on people's lives. It was through my patients that I would find my true calling and a certain selfless drive that ultimately would lead to love. One specific patient, a Mexican teenager named Francisco, altered the course of my career and he gave me a gift that I thought I would never be able to receive.

Part Four

Giving Back

Chapter 15

The Sight Foundation

"He's been blind since he was ten," said the woman on the other end of the line. "A chemical burn severely damaged both of his eyes. It's really tragic. He's already had surgeries at several major medical centers, all of which have failed, and doctors have said there's nothing more they can do. But I've heard of your groundbreaking work and thought you might be able to help."

It was the summer of 1999 when I received that call from Carole Klein, a former nun who taught visually impaired students at a high school in Chapel Hill, North Carolina. She told me about one of her blind students, Francisco Salazar, a seventeen-year-old from Mexico whose mother, Clementina, had brought him to the States in search of a miracle to restore his eyesight. After multiple failed surgeries, numerous doctors had told them that Francisco's eyes were beyond repair, but Clementina refused to give up hope.

Carole related to me what had happened to Francisco. Seven years ago in his hometown near Monterrey, Mexico, Francisco and a cousin were walking past a drainage ditch near a factory, when they came across a shiny glass bottle that stood out like a gem among trash. When Francisco pulled the stopper from the mouth of the bottle, sulfuric acid streamed out. When the acid hit the water in the ditch, it exploded into a gas cloud that seared both of Francisco's eyes. He was blinded instantly.

Several months later, an ophthalmologist in Mexico City performed a corneal transplant on Francisco's left eye, but its restored sight lasted only two days, and the cornea soon clouded over. His right eye was deemed too damaged to be repaired. Now permanently blind, Francisco retreated into himself over the next several years, no longer the fun-loving, outgoing boy he once was. Clementina, a woman of deep faith, was determined to save her young son's eyesight. So in the spring of 1998, she and Francisco came to the U.S. to seek medical help. They joined relatives in Chapel Hill, North Carolina, carrying about as much luggage and cash as I did when I first arrived in the U.S. in 1982. Hearing their story took me back to my earliest days in America, when I was trying to find my way in a foreign land. Deep down, I could relate to Francisco's struggle, and I was moved by his mother's love and resolve.

In North Carolina, Clementina met Carole Klein, who was so taken with Francisco's tragic situation that she began helping his mother search for possible restorative medical care for him. A local surgeon who examined Francisco said that the injury from the chemical burns was too severe to proceed with any restorative surgery. He directed them to a surgeon at Duke University, but that too turned out to be a dead end, as he too felt Francisco's eyes were damaged beyond repair. There was no chance for the left eye, and since the right eye was so badly damaged, if he received a corneal transplant in that eye, it would soon scar over with an aggressive regrowth of dense blood vessels and become blind, just like his left eye had done back in Mexico City.

"What he needs is a rare and special microsurgery," advised the surgeon from Duke. "But only three doctors in the country perform this procedure. We recommend the one in Nashville."

That's when Carole called me. "You are our last hope," she said.

I told her I would do my best to help. I was anxious to meet this young man, so I asked them to come to Nashville as soon as possible.

They arrived a week later. I examined Francisco's eyes and discovered that his left eye, which had already received the failed corneal transplant, had already shrunk. It had no light perception and was indeed irreparable. So our only hope was to try to restore sight in his right eye, which could only see light due to severe scarring and blood-vessel growth. The special microsurgery, which was what the Duke doctor was referring to, would involve a complex stem cell transplantation. However, it would be extremely risky in Francisco's case because if it failed, the right eye would shrink just as the left eye had, and Francisco would be plunged into total darkness for the rest of his life. As Carole translated, I explained to Francisco and his mother the difficulty of this special microsurgery, the limited benefits, and the risks. After praying together, Francisco and Clementina decided to proceed.

I resolved to do my very best as an eye surgeon to help Francisco.

As he sat across from me, I told him honestly, "Your sight restoration process will be a very long and difficult journey, like walking all the way from Nashville to New York City on foot. But I'm going with you every step of the way."

By this point in my life, I was quite acquainted with long, hard journeys, so I knew I would honor the promise I made to Francisco.

On August 11, 1999, three weeks after his initial eye exam with me, Francisco returned for the first stage of surgery on his right eye. I removed the scarring and blood vessels that had formed over his right cornea, and sutured an amniotic membrane in place to prevent his eye from scarring again as the tissues were healing.

Francisco was then to return to Nashville a few months later for a corneal transplant and stem-cell graft from adult donor tissue, but before we had a chance to perform the surgery, things went horribly awry. The chemical injury had damaged his right eye so badly that the cornea actually perforated, producing tiny yet dangerous fluid leaks. Consequently, we had to perform two emergency corneal transplants in his right eye within a matter of months just to salvage the eyeball itself. As we anticipated, vascular scar tissue quickly grew over the eye again in the same disorderly scarring process that had repeatedly blinded countless number of patients with such severe corneal injuries.

At this point, the only way we would have any chance of restoring sight in Francisco's right eye was to perform a complex corneal stem cell transplantation surgery, a procedure which was only being performed in a few centers in the country. The stem cells are found in a ring of tissue that surrounds the cornea, and they are the key to the eye's ability to heal. The chemical burn in Francisco's right eye was so severe that it had destroyed all of Francisco's own corneal stem cells, which was why his eyes healed abnormally with such aggressive, repeated formation of scarring and blood vessels. Though the odds were against us, we were able to successfully perform the surgery, and for several months it seemed that his eye might actually heal and his vision finally be restored.

But by late November of 2000, Francisco's eye was rapidly deteriorating again. On Friday, November 24th, I told Carole and Clementina to bring him back to Nashville so we could attempt an unprecedented quadruple-step surgery that would include another corneal transplant, another corneal limbal stem cell transplant, a cataract removal, and an intraocular lens implantation. Francisco and his family arrived the following Friday, and we scheduled the procedure for the next Tuesday.

"Where will the donor tissue come from?" Carole asked.

As I considered her question, an eerie feeling crept over me.

"I don't know yet," I admitted. "Since the corneal transplant is scheduled on Tuesday, we'll get the fresh tissue on Monday, which means the person destined to donate his or her eyes to Francisco is still alive right now."

On Tuesday, as Francisco was prepped for surgery, I waited anxiously for the shipment of donor cornea. At 8:00 am, the air-freighted shipment finally arrived. When I looked at the return address, another chill went through me. The donor was a twelve-year-old boy from Chapel Hill, North Carolina, the very city from which Francisco had come. The moment was charged with a sharp duality of feelings. I was immensely grateful for young tissue to restore Francisco's sight, but also deeply saddened that his hope came through the tragic loss of someone else . . . from his own local community.

With the donor cornea tissue in hand, we could now finally begin this groundbreaking quadruple procedure. The surgery began well, but halfway through, something unexpected occurred. The assisting surgeon and nursing staff grew very quiet and tense as they witnessed an impending disaster unfold on the large monitor. As I attempted to remove the old corneal graft, the inner matter of Francisco's eye clung to it stubbornly, threatening to spill out. If this occurred, there would be no possibility of reconstructing the eye at all, and all hope for any sight in his right eye would be permanently lost.

I was sweating from the severity of the situation. I had to do everything I could to prevent this disaster from happening. My heart pounded as I moved quickly and decisively. Finally after an intense moment, during which I felt I wasn't even breathing, I was able to successfully reposition the content back into the eye that was threatening to come out.

I paused and took a deep breath of relief. At least the eyeball itself was saved, for now. I asked a nurse to wipe the beads of sweat from my forehead, and give me a sip of water. Francisco was still sleeping deeply under general anesthesia. Looking at his young face, images flashed through my mind of myself at the beginning of my own long journey out of the darkness of the Cultural Revolution. Over the decades of medical training and growing faith, I knew without a doubt that I had been called and was equipped to help blind kids just like Francisco. I had experienced my own darkness when I was his age, and now with everything in me, I wanted to pull him out of his darkness into the light.

With a bit of rest, and renewed determination and mental clarity, I resumed Francisco's surgery, starting with the risky process of trying to remove the old graft, while doing all I could to avoid repeating the problems experienced in the last attempt. I tugged delicately and slowly at the old graft, elevating and gently pulling it, like the ancient Chinese micro-sculptors did when they would carve a line of poem in Chinese characters onto the side of a strand of hair. After what felt like an eternity, the old graft was finally separated and removed from the underlying tissue. I then removed the cataract, implanted an intraocular lens, sutured the new cornea into place, and transplanted adult stem cells around the new cornea. After four long hours, the unprecedented and intense quadruple-step surgery was finally completed, and Francisco's eyeball was saved. I dropped my shoulders and exhaled.

The following morning, Francisco returned to my clinic with Carole and Clementina to find out the results of his surgery. Both Carole and Clementina were unusually quiet and looked as if they had been carrying the weight of the whole seven-year journey on their shoulders for longer than their strength could bear. I felt anxious, not knowing whether my best efforts had been enough to save this teenager's sight.

Before I removed the bandage from Francisco's eye, we gathered in a circle and held hands—a Dominican former nun, a Mexican mother and son, and a Chinese-American doctor— and we prayed.

"Dear God, we know you have the power to heal this young boy who has lived in darkness these last seven years," I said softly. I had done my utmost, and I had no idea if God would allow Francisco to see again, but I trusted Him. "Thank you, God, for bringing us this far. Thank you for Francisco and his courage. Thank you for all that Carole and Clementina have done for him. God, please help us to accept whatever your will is for this outcome. Amen."

I reached forward and peeled back the tape to remove Francisco's bandage.

He opened his right eye slowly, blinked and looked around in bewilderment. Then a broad smile appeared across his face.

"Can you see?" I asked.

He nodded. "Who do you recognize in the room?" I added.

Francisco looked around. He didn't recognize me or Carole, since he had only known our voices over the past several years. Only one person in the entire room of a dozen people had been part of Francisco's life before he became blind seven years earlier.

"My mother," he said.

I turned toward Clementina, who was standing in a far corner. She burst into tears, made her way to Francisco and embraced him tightly.

Carole jumped up and down, her hands raised up toward the ceiling, and thanked God over and over.

I let out a huge sigh and said my own prayer of thanks. We had made it!

Francisco could now see!

After years of many failed surgeries, this final and critical microsurgery was the one that was finally successful! In the ensuing several months, Francisco's vision in his right eye improved to 20/40. He threw away his Braille books and replaced them with regular school books. He could now go on to live more independently than ever before.

After seven years of being locked in darkness, Francisco came into light. He got his life back, he was overjoyed with happiness!

While I helped restore Francisco's sight, he also gave me something very precious in return. Back in Chapel Hill with his newfound sight, Francisco read about my life story online, about the hardship and danger of the Cultural Revolution that had threatened to destroy me when I was around his age. Francisco then shared with his high school principal how my education had been cut short at age 14, how I faced deportation, poverty, and hard labor, how I later fought hard to get into college after years of no education, and in all the chaos, how I never actually received my high school diploma back in China.

"Dr. Wang helped me wake up from my long sleep of darkness," Francisco told the principal. "In return, can we give him the one thing he deserves but has never received, a high school diploma?"

So in 2000, twenty-three years after finishing high school in China, I finally received my diploma, an honorary graduation certificate from Chapel Hill High School in North Carolina.

It now hangs on the wall in my office, right beside my undergraduate and graduate degrees. More than a piece of paper, these certificates represent to me the blessings that I have experienced against so many odds. From college in China to medical training in America, influences from both the East and the West have made me who I am today. I have realized that life is truly a circle of give and take, and of helping and allowing yourself to be helped by others.

On a wall in the Wang Vision Institute hangs another special memento from Francisco, a plaque with a thank-you note in Braille at the top (the last time he ever used Braille) and below it, a thank you note in Spanish (the first time he had written since before his accident seven years ago).

Out of my gratitude for all the opportunities this country has offered me, I waived my surgeon fees for all of Francisco's surgeries, and out of his gratitude for sight, Francisco helped me complete a missing link in my own education. His gift was and still is special to me, and every time I look at it, I think of the wooden plaques that grateful patients had given my grandfather back in China some seventy years ago, and I'm proud to know that I've followed in his footsteps down this very rewarding path of helping the needy.

* * *

I experienced a revelation through caring for Francisco. I found that nothing excited me more than witnessing a patient emerge from darkness into sight. This ability to change people's lives was both a heavy responsibility and an immense blessing that I got to enjoy nearly every day I went to work.

After Francisco, I had many other cases like his, but insurance companies weren't willing to pay for these experimental sight restoration surgeries. Not everyone had a special person like Carole in their lives, who had gone above and beyond to raise money for Francisco's care. Even though I waived all my fees as the surgeon, there were still other expenses involved, such as lab testing, donor tissue, surgical facility and travel and lodging cost.

After five successful years at Vanderbilt, I took a step back and looked at the bigger picture. It became increasingly clear to me that God had a purpose behind the suffering of my early years in China, and the incredible trajectory of my career since then. After twenty-five years of education, training, and clinical practice, I was now in a position and had a unique set of skills that could make a significant difference in other people's lives, people who had been told there was nothing more that could be done to restore their sight.

I wanted to donate my medical care to more patients like Francisco, but working at a large university meant that I didn't have much say in the matter. I wasn't the owner of the business—I was merely an employee—so I couldn't waive charges to deserving patients at will. As long as I worked for a larger institution, I was constrained in how much charity care I could offer. However, if I started my own private practice, then it would be a different story.

So on April 1, 2002, I left the university and opened my own business—Wang Vision Institute (WVI)—in the Palmer Plaza on West End Avenue, near downtown Nashville. Our practice focuses on highly customized laser vision correction, cataract surgery, and complex sight restoration procedures, always using the most innovative technologies available. In 2002, WVI became the first center in Tennessee to offer bladeless all-laser LASIK, which improved the accuracy and precision of LASIK to an unprecedented level. WVI has since been the site of many other groundbreaking eye surgeries, including the world's first 3D LASIK procedure and laser-assisted artificial cornea implantation, the country's first laser Intacs procedure for advanced keratoconus, and Tennessee's first 3D laser cataract surgery, 3D Laser KAMRA procedure, and 3D Forever Young Lens surgery. Besides my paper in the world-renowned journal *Nature*, I have also published eight textbooks regarding the corneal and lens surgeries and hold several U.S. patents for inventions of new biotechnologies to restore sight. My work was recognized with an Achievement Award from the American Academy of Ophthalmology and a Lifetime Achievement Award from the Association of Chinese American Physicians.

Starting a private practice wasn't just about more freedom—it was a calling. My discovery of faith through hardship reinforced the notion that everything I had been given held the larger purpose of helping those most in need. With my dual specialties in laser physics and ophthalmology, I feel blessed to have had a unique opportunity to conduct research to develop novel laser eye treatments for even the most dire cases.

As my practice grew, people started contacting us from nearly every state in the U.S. and from countries around the world. I have performed more than 55,000 procedures, including over 4,000 on fellow doctors, which earned me the distinction of being the "doctor's doctor." Since many of the critically injured patients I saw had been to other surgeons who told them that they would never be able to see again, I became these patients' last resort, something I didn't take lightly. But many of them did not have insurance, nor the finances to pay for advanced care. The success of my private practice allowed me the freedom to provide such care, but I couldn't do it alone. I needed an organization and a team to help me realize my vision of offering free sight restoration surgeries to those who needed them the most, but couldn't afford them.

So in 2003, one year after I started my private practice, I created the Wang Foundation for Sight Restoration, a 501(c)(3) nonprofit organization. The foundation enabled me to organize a group of doctors who could each devote a small portion of their time to caring for charity patients. This care would represent a commitment of only five percent or less of a participating physician's overall clinic time. Nearly thirty doctors signed on to help, many of them inspired by their faith and intrigued by the technology available for these complex sight restoration cases. In addition to the volunteer doctors, medical companies donated supplies, and a board of directors of the foundation consisting of community philanthropic leaders helped to ensure adequate funding for our activities.

The first Wang Foundation for Sight Restoration patient was Joel Case from Crossville, Tennessee. Joel was in his early forties and had been blind since he was young. A rubella infection in utero had scarred both of his corneas so badly that they were cloudy white, which meant that from birth onward he would look at the world as if through wax paper. In his earliest years, Joel could see the big "E" on the sight chart, but by the time he was eight years old, he could only perceive light and shadows. His mother, Anna, had taken him all over the United States to major hospitals, and Joel underwent several transplant surgeries on both of his eyes, but with no success. Joel's doctors told him that he would never be able to see again. Though he had been deprived of sight his entire life, he lived independently and worked alongside his father in the family vending business.

Joel first came to see me in 1997. His eyes were covered in white scar tissue, ribboned with tiny blood vessels. He had already suffered a retinal detachment in his right eye, so his only hope for restored vision rested on treating his left eye. Over the next several years, I performed three major surgeries on that eye, including a corneal transplant and two amniotic membrane transplants, but Joel's immune system rejected the transplanted corneas. I held onto hope, however, because I had been witnessing medical treatments advance enormously in recent years. By 2003, an artificial cornea had been invented, and I was anxious to see if the new technology could benefit Joel.

In early 2004, eight years after I started taking care of Joel, he came in for a checkup and made an exciting announcement.

"I've found the love of my life," he said. Joel introduced me to Beth Ann Dahl, a darling young lady. "I love her, and I'm going to marry her."

I realized that Joel had actually never seen Beth Ann. I was moved by their love for each other, particularly that of Joel for Beth Ann, since his feelings could not have been based on any physical attraction having never seen her. I was happy Joel had found someone with whom he could share his life. Their wedding would be eight months later, in September of 2004. I began to think how marvelous it would be if we could restore Joel's sight before his wedding day. I wanted Beth Ann's groom to see her walk down the aisle, beaming in her beautiful wedding dress. Was that possible now that we had artificial cornea technology?

I was thrilled to tell Joel that after years of testing, the U.S. FDA had finally approved AlphaCor, a new artificial cornea implant designed especially for patients whose eyes had rejected traditional corneal transplants ... patients just like Joel. Artificial body parts reduced the chance that the body's immune system would reject them, which was the number one issue with organ transplantation and was precisely why all Joel's previous corneal transplants had failed. The artificial implant was clear and flexible, and resembled a small contact lens. Joel would become our foundation's first patient, and the first in the state of Tennessee to receive this new artificial cornea. If the surgery was successful, Joel might be able to finally see the world around him, and most important of all, he'd see his bride, Beth Ann, at their wedding!

We discussed the surgical plan, which was to create a pocket in his cornea and embed the artificial cornea. Next we would wait three months for his eye to heal around the implant, and then remove the outer flap of the corneal pocket so Joel could see through the new cornea. Joel and Beth Ann were both thrilled and decided to proceed with the artificial cornea surgery.

Unfortunately, I was unable to complete the surgery because, during the surgery after I removed the scar tissue, I could see through the microscope that his cornea was too thin and misshapen to withstand any blade dissection in order to create the pocket for the artificial cornea. The irregular and unevenly thin cornea meant that I had to completely abandon the blade pocket dissection. I didn't dare cut any further, for fear of perforating his eye and causing him to possibly lose the only eye that he had left.

After the aborted surgery, I met with Joel, Beth Ann, and Anna to explain the situation.

"I'm so sorry, but I couldn't proceed with the surgery as I had planned because Joel's cornea is just too thin and irregular, so it would have been unsafe to move forward with blade dissection to create the pocket for the artificial cornea," I said.

We were all very disappointed, but none more than Joel, who realized that even though the new artificial cornea technology was available now he still would not be able to benefit from it and hence still wouldn't be able to see after more than forty years.

"I have another idea," I said, "but it might be a long shot."

I explained to Joel and his family, who were now very intrigued, that I had the only bladeless laser eye surgery device in Tennessee, a femtosecond laser, which has an ultrashort pulse and replaces the microkeratome, a surgical blade typically used to cut into the cornea. I believed the femtosecond laser would be much more precise in the pocket creation and would allow me to much more safely control the level of cutting than is possible with a blade.

While the idea sounded wonderful, there was a catch—no one had ever used the femtosecond laser for the purposes of creating a corneal pocket and implanting an artificial cornea!

So if we did choose to use this powerful new laser instead of a blade, Joel would become the world's first patient to undergo a laser-assisted artificial cornea implantation. The thought of being able to utilize a laser in such an innovative manner to possibly bring Joel's sight back brought me an immense feeling of gratitude and hope. Back at the University of Science and Technology of China and the University of Maryland, I would have never guessed that my years of training in lasers would one day be so useful in medicine. I now understood why God had allowed so much hardship and learning in my life throughout my early years. I believe He wanted me to not only build character, resilience, and resourcefulness, but also to learn both parts of the knowledge to treat patients like Joel successfully, namely both technology and medicine. I also realized that treating these patients, for whom all traditional technologies had failed, was God's calling for my life. I could now possibly help Joel and other terminally blind patients by combining medicine with the laser technology that I had spent decades learning.

I explained to the Case family the high risk involved with this laser artificial cornea surgery as it had never been done before, so even though Joel was excited about the idea, I asked him to go home and think about it carefully. Throughout that weekend, I thought a lot myself about Joel and the procedure. His left eye was his only hope, but because of the thinness and deformity of his cornea that we have just discovered, the surgical risk was now even greater than I had originally anticipated. If anything went wrong—with either the new laser or the surgery itself—Joel could lose his already very limited light-perception vision in that eye, which was all what he had left. The surgery could only go one of two ways—it would either be a success, and Joel then might possibly be able to see after forty years, and see Beth Ann on their wedding day, or it would be a failure, and then Joel would be thrust into pitch darkness for the rest of his life.

The magnitude of that responsibility weighed heavily on me. But just as I had done at other crucial times in my life when my own capabilities did not seem to be sufficient, I sought God's guidance and strength.

"God, what should I do? Should I allow Joel to take this risk?" I prayed repeatedly throughout that weekend.

By Monday a peace had come over me, and I sensed that God had answered my prayer. I felt confident that laser artificial cornea surgery was the right thing to do. Joel returned and decided to proceed with the surgery, fully understanding the risks involved. The historic femtosecond laser part of the artificial cornea procedure went beautifully. Joel was then immediately transferred to St. Thomas Hospital for the implantation of the artificial cornea, which also went well.

So the first two steps of the world's first laser-assisted artificial corneal implantation were a complete success. Three months later, Joel returned for the final step of the surgery—the removal of the corneal pocket's outer flap, which would hopefully allow him to now see through his new artificial cornea.

The day after the surgery, Joel, Beth Ann, and Anna returned to my office for Joel's post-op visit. Just as we had done with Francisco, we stood in a circle and held hands to pray before removing Joel's bandage. I felt that my inner strength alone was insufficient to cope with the consequences of the surgery's outcome, so I asked God again to help us all accept His will, whatever it would be. I submitted my will to God and I was at peace.

I slowly peeled off Joel's bandage, feeling both nervous and excited. I had been treating Joel for more than eight years by then, but I knew that his own journey out of darkness had lasted more than four decades, and now the moment of truth was here.

Joel opened his left eye tentatively, then looked around, blinking rapidly. Suddenly a smile burst across his face as he cup his hand over his eyebrow and gazed out the window.

He could see! I anxiously pushed Beth Ann toward him. He turned and saw his future wife . . . for the very first time.

"Ah, you have brown hair!" he squealed. "And you're beautiful." They hugged and both cried with joy.

As Joel looked around the room, he was deeply moved when he finally recognized his mother. Anna walked over and put her arms around him. Since losing his sight, he hadn't seen her in more than thirty years. She had aged in all the years he was shrouded in darkness, but love transcends time, now Joel was thrilled that he could once again look at his mother's face and see the love in her eyes.

Joel and Beth Ann were married four months later. Unfortunately, I was out of the country on their big day, but they sent me photos. Joel gazed at his new wife lovingly in every one of them. I felt blessed that God had given me the very special honor of helping bring sight to Joel just in time for him to fully enjoy such an important event in his life.

But as I continued to look through the wedding photos, I felt a tightness develop in my chest. Although my patients were experiencing joy and happiness, those emotions eluded me at that time because my short-lived marriage to my second wife, Suyuan Liu, had failed.

I met Suyuan while she was pursuing a master's degree in communications at a university in San Antonio, Texas. Suyuan was extremely beautiful and intelligent. She shared my ethnic background, as well as many of my interests and passions, including dancing. As soon as she completed her graduate program, she moved to Nashville. We were engaged shortly after that, and we got married in 2001. But our marriage lasted only two years.

I couldn't believe I was facing another divorce. I had come from such a solid, devoted family and I was able to help my patients enjoy their family lives more fully, so I couldn't understand why I wasn't able to create a loving, stable family life for myself. I was a hard worker, an honest citizen, and a good Christian. What kind of weaknesses kept me from developing better personal relationships and building a family? It would take time for me to find an answer to that question, but not before my inner shortcomings would continue to render personal happiness an unobtainable goal.

Whenever I suffered setbacks in my personal life, I would escape by submerging myself more and more deeply into my work. I knew it wasn't the solution to my relationship issues, but it had always been my refuge in hard times. I justified it because I was driven to succeed, and I also greatly enjoyed the entire process of helping patients like Francisco and Joel. The lengthy and exciting task of bringing someone out of darkness inspired me. Ironically, as restoring the human experience for others became all-consuming, I allowed it to repeatedly rob me of what I consider one of the most important aspects of my own life. Sadly, the second failed marriage wouldn't be my last, and many years would pass before I would finally find strength and maturity in this area. As long as the foundation had patients to serve, I would have an outlet to which I could devote my time, while continuing my search for deeper love and meaning.

Chapter 16

A World's First

"Wear something cute tomorrow because your husband might be able to see you for the very first time!" I said to Jackie Barnes, whose husband Brad had truly never seen her. From the start of their marriage several years earlier, Jackie had tirelessly cared for her blind husband and sought the best medical treatments available in America, all to no avail. Now, after two years of treatments at the Wang Foundation for Sight Restoration, she was hopeful that the man she loved so dearly would finally be able to see, and see her for the very first time.

I first met Brad and Jackie Barnes in the fall of 2004. Brad was in his early forties and had been blinded a dozen years earlier in an industrial accident. Behind his dark glasses were eyes so severely damaged that his eyelids looked like they had been melted shut. Ten years ago, just fifteen days before his thirty-second birthday, Brad's life was altered in an instant as molten aluminum exploded from a container at the factory where he worked. Eleven hundred pounds of burning metal fluid, flowing at a blazing 1,550 degrees Fahrenheit blasted upward and splashed all over him, obliterating his protective goggles and severely scorching both of his eyes.

He was left with near total blindness and could barely perceive light. Over the ensuing decade, he had undergone many extensive surgeries at major medical centers including Harvard, the Mayo Clinic, and Washington University, but all with no success.

Brad spent his time working with the God Squad, a group of men who performed feats of strength as a way of sharing their faith with young people. Being blind didn't prevent Brad from smashing bricks, bending bars of metal, and tearing phone books in half. But it wasn't just his physical strength that kept him going; he also had the love and strong support of his devoted wife, Jackie. Despite his condition, Brad fell in love and got married four years ago in 2000. His wife was dedicated to his care, and her faith inspired her to continue seeking medical help for her husband.

Four years later, Brad's doctors at Washington University in St. Louis, Missouri referred him to the Wang Foundation for Sight Restoration. Word had spread about the work we were doing through the foundation, including the world's first laser artificial cornea surgery I had performed on Joel Case. Brad's doctors at Washington University had heard about the success of that surgery, which was why they referred Brad to us.

Despite our new laser technique, I feared that we still wouldn't actually be able to help Brad, given how extreme the nature of his injury was. Although I specialized in difficult sight restoration surgeries, Brad's case for me was at the farthest end of the spectrum. He had already been declared irreversibly blind, and his previous multiple failed surgeries made any subsequent procedure an impossibility.

His corneas were covered with flaps of skin and scar tissue so thick I couldn't see his eyeballs at all. Additionally, his conjunctiva—the tissue that covers the surface of the eye and inner eyelid—was acutely inflamed due to severe dryness, because Brad's tear glands had been completely destroyed in the accident. Without the tears normally secreted by these glands, there was no way the extremely dry eye would ever heal properly following any surgery. Additionally, Brad's right eye was too damaged for any surgery. So his left eye, which could only barely see light, was our only hope.

"The artificial cornea implant requires a moist and stable ocular environment to support it after surgery," I explained to Brad. "Unless we can somehow come up with a magical way for you to produce tears again, we're unfortunately not going to be able to do any reconstructive surgery for your eye, as it would never heal after the surgery."

Brad and Jackie had traveled a long way from St. Louis to Nashville, so the result of the consultation was very disappointing for all of us. What made the situation even worse was that Brad's dry eyes were also causing him to be in a lot of pain. He said it felt like glass was constantly cutting his left eye. So if we couldn't come up with a way to provide sustained lubrication to his left eye in order to substantially reduce his pain very soon, his only remaining left eye would have to be removed altogether, plunging him into irreversible total darkness for the rest of his life.

Since Brad's tear-secreting glands were all dead, we immediately began a treatment to keep his eyes as hydrated and comfortable as possible using medication, tear drainage duct blocks, and around-the-clock artificial tear instillation.

"We need to somehow find a way to make your tear glands secrete tears themselves again," I told them. "If we don't, not only will we not be able to do any reconstructive surgery, but the left eye itself may also have to be removed."

The winter of 2004 was especially cold in Nashville, with an ice storm that blocked the roads for days. But my heart felt even colder, and hopeless. Once again, the impending threat of total darkness over one of my patients deeply affected me. I was familiar with that darkness, one I felt as a teenager and almost didn't escape. I reflected on what it was that had helped me pull out of that darkness and survive.

"Never give up." My father's voice once again rang in my ears. I realized I had survived the darkest days in my life through my own determination and through the constant support of others.

I did not want to give up on Brad. I would never give up.

For months, I spent many nights poring over scientific literature to find out if anything had ever been done in the past for a dry-eye situation as severe as Brad's, but I found nothing. I then called many colleagues from around the world including my mentor, Dr. Tseng, to ask for advice and help, but to no avail. I still did not want to give up, so I kept searching and praying to God to help me sustain hope, and to allow my efforts to eventually point me in the right direction.

In the spring of 2005, Brad called me one day with the exciting news that he himself might have found the answer we were looking for! He had found an ear, nose and throat (ENT) specialist at Washington University in St. Louis, the facility that had originally referred him to me. The pioneering ENT physician, Dr. Randal Paniello, had performed the world's first procedure in which a saliva gland was taken from a patient's jaw and re-routed to the temple area to lubricate the eye. Saliva has a similar chemical composition as tears, so if we could transplant Brad's left saliva gland to lubricate his left eye, we might just have a chance to perform restoration surgery to bring back his sight!

I was fascinated by this idea. I called Dr. Paniello and asked him if he could evaluate Brad. Dr. Paniello agreed and called me after the evaluation to tell me that a saliva gland transposition on Brad would be very difficult, but he was willing to give it a try. The surgery was new, and there was no guarantee of success, but Brad had nearly nothing left to lose.

In March of 2005, Dr. Paniello performed the novel surgery. The thirteen-hour procedure was a success, and Brad became the second person in the world to undergo this saliva gland surgery. The funny thing about this procedure is that the saliva gland will still react to olfactory stimulation, rather than debris or dryness in the eye. So if Brad walked into McDonald's, the French fries just might make his eye water!

When I saw Brad at his next appointment in Nashville, his left temple was swollen to the size of a golf ball. It would take some time for the swelling to recede and for the gland to produce moisture. If it didn't work, we wouldn't be able to proceed to the eye reconstruction surgery. We all waited nervously to see if the gland surgery was successful. Finally, after waiting for nearly a year, the gland reduced in size and started producing saliva again, which alleviated the pain in Brad's eye significantly.

So by the summer of 2006, the stage was set for the reconstructive-surgery portion of the world's first combined saliva gland transposition and artificial cornea implantation surgery. My plan was to use the femtosecond laser to create the pocket in his left eye for the implant, just as I had done for Joel Case. Creating the corneal pocket and then putting in the implant is like burying a treasure. We would leave the implant in the pocket for a few months, and then remove the corneal flap to reveal the treasure that will hopefully give Brad back his sight. Our goal was to bring him from nearly total blindness to enough vision that he could function more independently and take care of himself at home.

In reality, being part of such a groundbreaking surgery like this really isn't result of confident masterminds meeting together to devise a plan. Such events tend to be the result of going step-by-step toward whatever options exist next to best help our patients. I really had no idea whether this combination surgical approach would work, and the stress of the uncertainty weighed on me from start to finish for that entire over-two-years-long process of helping Brad.

The first stage of the laser-assisted artificial cornea implantation surgery took four hours. Jackie was sitting patiently in the hospital waiting room when I came out of the operating room to give her the results. In the course of creating the corneal pocket and inserting the artificial cornea, I had located his pupil—which had been displaced during his accident—and I re-centered it.

"I rebuilt the front part of his eye, placed the artificial cornea into the pocket, and then sutured everything together," I explained to Jackie.

She jumped up and hugged me tightly. "This is so cool! Thank you!"

"This has been a long process, but we're off to a good start," I said.

After many months of healing, Brad returned on March 28, 2007 for the second stage of the surgery. I opened the outer flap of the corneal pocket, which would allow him to see through the artificial cornea.

The next morning, Brad was back at Wang Vision Institute for the moment of truth. In cases this extreme, it is impossible to predict the outcome. After two years of surgeries through our foundation, Brad and his family weren't the only ones anxious to know how it would all turn out. News teams in Nashville and St. Louis had documented the entire two-year process, and whole communities of people were on the edge of their seats to watch the results revealed live on television.

The presence of so many friends, colleagues, and news crews streaming results to thousands of people was nerve-wracking. My ritual is to pray with every patient who permits me to do so, but this time Brad himself was the initiator. He had brought his Bible, and he held it in his lap. He bowed his head to pray as Jackie and I stood on either side of him, each of us placing a hand on his shoulder.

I also said my own prayer to God in my heart. "God, I pray it is your plan to bring Brad out of darkness to see the world he has been missing for thirteen years. Will you please allow him to finally see his wife, Jackie, for the very first time? Amen."

Brad tapped his thumbs nervously on the cover of his Bible.

"Are you ready?" I asked. He nodded.

I carefully removed the patch, cleaned out Brad's left eye, and slowly pried open his swollen eyelids.

My entire office had shut down to witness this special moment. The staff joined Brad's supporters, who were crowded around the door of the exam room and down the hallway. The room was completely silent, and the entire crowd seemed to collectively hold its breath in anticipation.

As I examined Brad's left eye, it looked good but I couldn't yet tell if he would be able to see or not. I turned to face the team and gave them a thumbs-up to indicate that at least the surgery itself had gone well. As I began to talk to my staff, Brad's voice rang out unexpectedly behind me.

"I see a thumbs-up!" Brad exclaimed. "Yeah, I see it!"

The entire room gasped all at once.

"Yes!" Jackie shouted.

Amazed, I turned around to face Brad again.

"Hang on! Don't move!" Brad requested excitedly. His right hand reached forward slowly, and eventually touched my face. "Is this your face? Yeah, I can see your face over there."

We were all stunned.

But my face wasn't the one I really wanted Brad to see. I stepped back and nudged Jackie forward. This was the moment we had all waited over two years to witness. Would Brad be able to see his wife finally for the very first time?

Jackie moved her face closer to Brad's, looking at him intently. She seemed nervous.

"I can see you now!" Brad said, smiling broadly.

Brad and Jackie gazed at each other, their faces radiating happiness. Tears came to my eyes and I glanced around to see many others moved to tears as well.

I handed Brad a mirror so he could see his own face.

"Yeah, that's me!" he exclaimed, seeing himself for the first time in thirteen years.

Brad was so enamored of his newfound sight that even simple things fascinated him. "This is incredible! I can't even believe this!" Brad marveled at a piece of white tissue he had been holding in his hand...and everyone laughed with joy.

Few of us will ever personally know someone who has had sight restored after thirteen years of blindness. But even fewer will ever be present the very moment someone we know comes out of darkness and into sight. Everyone in the room with Brad felt privileged to be part of this powerful, once-in-a-lifetime opportunity. To me, such a moment is worth all these years of hard work, training and research, and all the sleepless nights that I have endured. Experiencing the joy that follows God's miracles over and over again is what continually refuels my commitment to this work.

And it is a gift that keeps on giving, as Brad's appreciation of his newfound sight wasn't restricted to that one day in my office. For several weeks, I received reports from Jackie and other friends of theirs of his fascination with the things he was seeing now, big and small.

"Brad is having so much fun looking at everything!" Jackie wrote in an email. "TV is fun for him; and he seems to see two-dimensional images better than in person. Cars are so cool because he says he feels like he's been propelled thirteen years into the future. Computers are cool too because they're no longer just black screens with amber writing on them."

I was taken aback by her words. Not only had Brad regained his sight, but he had essentially traveled through time, thirteen years in an instant! In Brad's mind, the world around him—the people, city structures and technology— had remained frozen in time since 1994. So to come out of darkness after such a long time was to discover a world that's not at all the same as the one he knew before. Brad's thirteen-year time travel then led me to reflect on my earlier patient, Joel Case, who had actually time-traveled even further, four entire decades!

Jackie's email continued. "He finds several new things to see every day. He loves looking at the sky, the clouds, the trees, green grass. It's like having a kid who's learning to walk or talk. I hate going to work now because I'm going to miss something."

Coming out of blindness is, in a way, like a new birth. The patient sees the world again for the first time in a long while. Thanks to the Wang Foundation and all of Brad's supporters, he is now rediscovering a life he had been missing for more than a dozen years, and the ability to actually see his beloved wife is what he considers his ultimate blessing.

"There is just no way to thank you for what you have done," Jackie wrote at the end of her email. "Not only have you changed Brad's life, through his testimony you have changed the lives of thousands. Now I'm crying again!"

Though taking care of charity patients is difficult and demanding on one's time, our foundation has shown that it can in fact be done and done well. I believe this model of care should be an important part of our healthcare system. I've been inspired to treat charity patients as a way of giving back to America, and many other Nashville doctors have joined me in this important cause as well. The model practiced by the Wang Foundation attests to the effectiveness of embedding charity patients into the flow of patients in private clinics, fully utilizing the technology and service available at such clinics. Our hope is that the success we have experienced with embedded charity care as such will spread to other medical specialties across the country, and will thus help reduce the nation's financial burden to care for the poor.

An example of this need is the fact that the second part of Brad's surgery almost didn't happen. After the completion of his saliva gland surgery, we realized that the costs involved with his and Jackie's travel and lodging, as well as hospital and operating room fees, was beyond their limited financial resources. Given how severe his damage was, even though I had waived all my surgeon's fees, the other aspects of his care were going to be expensive. Furthermore, insurance does not typically cover new, experimental sight restoration procedures such as laser-assisted artificial cornea implantations. Cases like Brad's were exactly the reason I had started the foundation in the first place, but now we needed to raise funds to cover the various costs beyond physician fees.

I came up with a plan to accomplish this goal. In the fall of 2005, I asked Brad and Jackie to be my special guests at the foundation's first annual fundraising gala—called the EyeBall—at which ballroom dancing would serve as a symbolic source of exquisite beauty that the gift of sight allows us to fully appreciate. At the event, Brad shared his story with the gala's attendees. In the end, it was the unique combination of modern technology, and the loving hearts and giving spirit of everyone involved, that ultimately gave Brad his sight back.

Chapter 17

The Dancing Doctor

An elderly couple had taken to the dance floor, and although the eight decades of life's joys and sorrows they had experienced were evident, their demeanor was lively and self-assured. The husband stood tall in his black coattails, leading his nimble wife with skill and sensitivity. She wore a light pink gown that flowed around her legs as the pair glided across the polished wood. They were doing the foxtrot with such light and airy ease that they seemed to be floating above the dance floor.

It was a Sunday afternoon during my first semester of medical school at Harvard, and I was at a community ballroom dancing event hosted by the MIT Ballroom Dance Club at Walker Memorial, a grand Beaux-Arts building on the Charles River. I watched in awe as these older dancers moved with grace. They made ballroom dancing appear to be perfectly ageless, and I longed to be part of this exquisite art form that transcended time.

The tranquility and elegance exuded by the dance couples was much different from the fear and panic that drove me to dance so many years ago.

When I was six years old and the Cultural Revolution in China had been going on for quite some time, I would watch my dad perform with his hospital's communist song-and-dance troupe. He was a spectacular dancer, stately and naturally graceful. He captivated audiences as he performed traditional Chinese minority dances in vibrantly colored costumes. Dad was recruited to perform at Chinese New Year parades and other festivals throughout the year. He was my first teacher in the art and discipline of dance, and I wanted to be just like him. I even joined my elementary school's dance troupe and performed quite frequently in public venues across Hangzhou.

When I was forced to drop out of school after the ninth grade at age 14, and took up dance more fervently in order to try to join the communist propaganda song-and-dance troupe so I could avoid the devastating fate of deportation and life sentence of poverty and hard labor. I would practice dancing for hours on end. I had no access to a studio, nor any recordings of the eight permitted model Chinese plays. In an open patch of land near my parents' medical college, I practiced the dances I had seen on stage and in movies. Since I had no recorded music, I sang tunes to myself while I danced. I constantly ran out of breath from trying to sing and dance at the same time, so I couldn't practice for very long before I would need to take a break. But because my life was on the line, I was driven to dance nonstop. Just like in the ballet *Giselle,* in which the young man was condemned to continue dancing until he collapsed and died, I danced constantly, consumed by the ever-present fear that I would be deported if I was not a good enough dancer to get into the communist song-and-dance troupe.

After I was finally able to pursue an education at the end of the Cultural Revolution, I didn't return to dancing as a hobby until after I arrived at Harvard Medical School in 1987.

Watching the elderly couple's timeless dance at the MIT event that day inspired me to resume my long-lost interest in dancing with renewed fervor. During my first year of medical school, I helped create the Harvard Ballroom Dance Club, which was made up of both undergraduate and graduate students from the U.S., Germany, Vietnam, China, and South America. Few of the students had any ballroom dancing experience prior to joining the club, but I had been through enough of the basics of dancing to help us get started.

We had to learn all 10 international-style ballroom dances, five standard and five Latin. The international standard ballroom dances—waltz, foxtrot, tango, Viennese waltz, and quickstep—demonstrated sublime beauty, elegance, style, and discipline. The international Latin dances—cha-cha, rumba, samba, paso doble, and jive—on the other hand, emphasized speed, rhythm, power, and passion. Together, the ten dances embody the full range of human emotion.

The Harvard Ballroom Dance Club practiced frequently, often with the MIT group. Our team of beginners was a sight to behold—stepping on each other's toes, bumping bellies, going every which way but in the right direction. Sometimes couples even got into argument or fight. Eventually we realized that our biggest problem was that the men on the team simply couldn't lead, and the ladies could not follow very well either. Dancers sometimes even argued with their partners because the men expected the women to know what they were thinking, and the ladies would retort, "How am I supposed to know what you want me to do before you actually do your part correctly yourself?"

We brought in a professional coach once a month, and we actually received our most valuable lesson in dance during one of those sessions.

"Gentlemen, you are the leaders," declared the teacher. Her name was Dawn. She was of medium height, svelte, and crowned with a blaze of red hair.

"So if the lady isn't following, then it's all her fault, right?" I asked.

The guys on the team laughed.

"No! In fact, if she's not following, it's most likely the gentleman's fault," Dawn replied.

"How come?" I retorted. "If I'm the leader, and she's not following properly, then it's only logical that it's her fault."

"Well, it could be your fault actually because you're supposed to communicate with her before you actually lead, in what we call the pre-lead phase."

"The pre-lead," she went on to explain, "is what occurs in the instant before the man actually leads. For example, if you want to make a back step, you don't just simply move back. You first need to stay in place, and expand your body outward with an intention towards the direction you want to move so your partner can feel that intention," Dawn explained. "Your partner will then have the time to read your intention and give you feedback as to what she wants to do herself. She might want to go in another direction. So you have to feel each other and form a compromised, unified plan to move together."

According to Dawn, the most beautiful part of ballroom dance isn't the movements that everyone sees. The magical part is the pre-lead moment before each movement, when the timing, musicality, and amplitude of impending movement are negotiated and then decided together, through the communication between the two partners.

Our team's initial response to this lesson was less than enthusiastic, mainly because we didn't really understand it. To us, there simply didn't seem to be enough time in that split second to accomplish so much. Also, the men didn't want to let go of our egos and compromise. We just wanted to lead without having to alter our original plan. Not willing to learn this pre-lead technique properly, we continued to step on toes and bump into our partners' bellies, often going nowhere.

A few months later, the Harvard Ballroom Dance Club team entered a small regional competition on MIT's campus that included many schools and more than 100 dancers. At the competition, the standard dance pairs were outfitted in tuxedo tails and flowy gowns, and the Latin dancers wore black shirts and pants and sexy, barely-there dresses. We danced our hearts out from dawn until dusk, but the Harvard team came in dead last because we simply weren't good! The male members of the team had been convinced that Harvard men can accomplish whatever they do, without compromising leadership. But when we came in last place in every dance category, we walked out of the gym slumped in defeat.

But this loss was a turning point for our team. The men realized that embracing the pre-lead technique—giving our partners the time to understand our intention and negotiate a joint plan as a couple before we actually move together—was the only way to have a partnership on the dance floor. The guys reluctantly let go of their pride and started practicing true partnership dancing.

We poured our Harvard work ethic into ballroom dancing as if it were a math or science class, and we practiced more frequently and with more devotion. Over the next four years, our team grew from the initial few students to more than fifty dancing pairs. Every semester our results in amateur ballroom competitions inched closer and closer toward the top. By my senior year, we took first place in the U.S. National Collegiate Championships—hosted by the U.S. Amateur Ballroom Dance Association—which was an unexpected victory for Harvard, known otherwise only for our academic achievements.

After graduating from Harvard, and throughout my years of clinical training, I continued to dance for fun, and occasionally I would even teach my colleagues and friends to dance ... but always for free. All I wanted was to encourage more people to enjoy ballroom dancing as I did. To me ballroom dancing was, and still is, a way to relieve the stress of daily life and demanding work by appreciating music, exercising, and learning to be sensitive to another human being, physically and emotionally. During my fellowship and residency at Wills Eye Hospital, I didn't have much time for dancing, but when I landed in Miami for my corneal fellowship at Bascom Palmer Eye Institute, I earnestly resumed my dance hobby.

At a dance party following my interviews at Bascom Palmer, I met a couple named Misha Bartnovsky and June Rudolph, who were both in their late fifties. Misha was a tall, elegant Jewish gentleman who was a fellow scientist. His wife, June, was a beautiful Japanese-American lady with a deep appreciation of art. We hit it off immediately; they invited me to join their table, and we danced and talked throughout the night. I visited them the next evening at their home in Delray Beach, and it became the start of a lifelong friendship. I was drawn to their joviality and love of life, and their cultural values resonated with my own emphasis on family and education.

During my year in Miami, I spent many weekends visiting Misha and June's home, where we would enjoy dancing, laughing and talking. My parents and brother were still in Boston, so I didn't know anyone else in town. Since my real parents were more than fifteen hundred miles away, Misha and June became my surrogate father and mother. Bascom Palmer's hospital cafeteria offered less-than-palatable meals, so I often went to June and Misha's house to enjoy delectable Japanese and American cooking. Misha was a master engineer and helped keep my used car running throughout my fellowship. We often took dance lessons together and discussed our love of dance. Even after my time in Miami, I went overseas with June and Misha on our annual pilgrimage to the capital of ballroom dancing—Winter Garden in Blackpool, England—home of the Blackpool Ballroom Dance Festival. June and Misha also helped me organize a ballroom dance event at the American Academy of Ophthalmology's annual meeting. Teaching dance to a group of ophthalmologists, who are not known for the dexterity of their feet, was a fun experience. June and Misha loved me as much as my own parents did, and I loved them too and eventually considered them my godparents.

At the end of my cornea fellowship in early 1997, ballroom dancing actually played a key role in my decision to accept the position as founding director of the Vanderbilt Laser Sight Center in Nashville. Dr. Harry Jacobson was the newly appointed vice chancellor for health affairs at the university. After my interview with him, he asked me, "Ming, what can we do to attract you to Vanderbilt?"

During my job search, his was the only laser eye surgery center at which I had been offered such a prestigious directorship, so I was already leaning toward accepting it. But our conversation that followed soon sealed the deal.

"I'm a ballroom dancer," I said. "Does Nashville have nice places to dance? Where can I go dancing tonight? I don't fly out until tomorrow morning."

As it turned out, Dr. Jacobson was also a ballroom dance enthusiast himself. He pulled out a pen and a piece of scrap paper and drew me a map to a studio in Belle Meade. I had a wonderful time dancing that evening, which made the decision to commit to the job at Vanderbilt even easier.

Ballroom dancing has served an even bigger purpose in my medical career since then. It has taught me how to better connect with my patients. Like the pre-lead—which requires sensitivity, awareness, and communication with your dance partner and try to make a joint decision together—these unique qualities, which I learned through ballroom dancing—have brought me closer to my patients and have allowed me to listen to them more and pay more attention to their needs. When insurance company restrictions and the costs involved with modern technology create barriers between doctors and their patients, this sensitivity allows me to overcome such barriers by listening to, caring for, and more fully connecting with my patients.

Before I perform an eye surgery, I always pray with my patients. Our prayer invites God into our team to lead us from the beginning of the journey, rather than asking Him for help only when we get into trouble. Praying also allows me to pause, slow down, focus, and emotionally connect with my patients before we begin. I learned much of that process from honing my partnership skills in ballroom dancing.

I continued dancing as soon as I was settled in Nashville. My teacher and partner, Shalene Archer, is a former U.S. professional ballroom champion, and I have taken lessons from her nearly every week since then. We have competed in competitions throughout the country in the Pro/Am division, which showcases professional-amateur pairs (she's the professional; I'm the amateur). Our dance career reached its peak in November of 2007 when we won fourth place in the U.S. Pro/Am International Ten-Dance Championships at the Ohio Star Ball in Columbus, Ohio. Years earlier, that same competition was the one I had invited Gwen to, and the last event we attended together before her final goodbye at the Columbus airport.

* * *

When the Wang Foundation for Sight Restoration was created in 2003, our founding board of directors included Gene Angle, a banker who served as board treasurer; Charles Grummon, a financial consultant; Mary Beth Thomas, an attorney who served as secretary; and Shirley Zeitlin, a real estate executive. Not long after we treated our foundation's first patient, Joel Case, we realized that we needed more board members, more awareness of our mission, and most of all, more funding to help cover the costs beyond physician fees. So we decided to host an annual fundraising event. We just needed to come up with a great theme.

Inspired by what I had experienced and learned through dance, I suggested that we have a gala featuring

ballroom dancing . . . and call it the "EyeBall." The idea
came to me as I was trying to find a way to create a ball
to signify the emotional aspect of the importance of vision.
Ophthalmologists tend to think of vision in terms of
numbers like 20/40, 20/60, 20/100. But vision is much more
than just numbers. It is an emotional experience that affects
the very core of a person. Seeing is a fundamental way of
living, both physically and spiritually. We visually witness
the world, find meaning, and discern truth. I felt that finding
a creative way to illuminate these deep human dimensions
of vision would have a powerful emotional impact for the
cause of sight restoration for the blind. I believed that the
elegance of ballroom dancing would lend itself perfectly as a
showcase of beauty and the importance of vision. When we
see something as breathtaking as ballroom dancing, we will
truly comprehend how emotionally devastating it would be
if we didn't have sight, and how important it is to help those
who have lost it.

Our first EyeBall was held on October 1, 2005 in the Pineapple
Room at Cheekwood Botanical Garden and Museum of Art in
Nashville. The theme of the event was "Sight and Sound," since it also
featured the Nashville Chamber Orchestra. The Pineapple Room
had polished concrete floors, crystal chandeliers, and an entire wall
of huge windows with a view of the outside veranda and gardens.
Beyond the veranda, hills and valleys rolled along the horizon.

Over two hundred people came to the 2005 EyeBall to
support the foundation, including congressional representatives,
university professors, business owners, members of the media,
and other people from the community. Once everyone had been
seated for dinner, we invited several foundation patients onto the
stage to share their experience of being blind. One woman had
gone blind because of a genetic disease. Born without an iris or
pupil, her eye couldn't regulate the amount of light it received, so
she gradually lost her sight during her young adulthood and was

completely blind by her thirties. She reminded me of the blind patient whom I met during my first year at Harvard and who inspired my journey to restore sight for others. A car accident took another patient's sight. The resulting pain and despair he experienced caused him to develop a destructive drinking problem with which he was still struggling to recover.

"It is a beautiful evening, isn't it? But I can't see it," he said.

Next, Brad and Jackie Barnes came on stage. At that point, Brad hadn't yet undergone his final restorative surgery. "I have never seen my wife's face," he told the audience. "I want to hear her laugh the way I hear her now, and I want to see her smile." Many eyes in the crowd glistened with emotion hearing Brad talk of such a simple yet overwhelming desire, something spouses throughout the room undoubtedly took for granted every single day.

Joel Case was the last to testify, and he shared his experience of coming out of darkness after his surgery, and how successful sight restoration surgery is a life altering event. He told the group how he had lived with blindness for forty years as a result of a rubella infection he contracted while still in his mother's womb, and how his foundation surgery had given him back his sight with which he saw his bride at their wedding the year before for the very first time.

After the patients had spoken, I walked out onto the stage.

"We rejoice with Joel Case for his miracle of sight restoration," I said, "and we long for others who still live in darkness to be able to experience this miracle of renewed sight. But do we really know what it's like to be blind? Those who truly appreciate sight are those who are blind, so I want all of us to experience for a moment what it is like to be blind and live in darkness."

The guests were asked to put on dark sunglasses that we had placed beneath their chairs, and then the house lights were turned off throughout the ballroom. "Dark Waltz," a haunting composition of plaintive strings and soprano vocals, started playing in the background.

Once the room was dark and the guests were wearing the sunglasses, I then said, "Ladies and gentlemen, now I would like to ask you to stand up, walk to the other side of the ballroom, and shake hands with someone over there."

A gasp instantly spread throughout the room. I could hear the sounds of people bumping into tables and chairs being knocked over. In the darkness, no one dared move far. I could sense their fear and apprehension at being asked to perform an otherwise routine task for those who can see.

As the audience stood frozen in the dark, fearful of making any move, a single candle held by board member Gene Angle was lit up on the stage. Guests looked toward the light with a sigh of relief.

"Like this one candle," I continued, "our sight restoration efforts begin with just one patient. One set of eyes. One surgery."

Gene then lit the candles of several board members and volunteers, who then went to each table and lit the candles there. The room slowly became aglow with soft, faint candlelight. The darkness continued to recede as the house lights were turned back on, one by one. The guests removed their sunglasses, smiling with relief and joy that they could once again see.

"That is how we start," I continued. "One light at a time, and then the light will spread. If we all take part, then the whole room will be lit up, then the city, the state, the country . . . and eventually the whole world."

When the program was over, I invited everyone onto the dance floor. A good friend and a professional dancer, Monika Olejnik, joined me. As we danced, I remembered the elderly couple I had seen do the foxtrot back in Boston nearly two decades earlier. My life's dancing endeavors had transformed from a way to avoid deportation to an appreciated art form to a meaningful way to bring people together for a purpose that transforms lives through restored sight. I felt as light as mist over water. At long last, I too was dancing agelessly.

Chapter 18

A Heart for Orphans

I was scrolling through hundreds of emails in my inbox one morning, when one in particular shocked me into full attention. I leaned toward my computer screen, and my jaw dropped as I read the message.

"The child was found wandering alone in a train station, dirty and hungry. She is only four. We were told she was intentionally blinded by acid and then abandoned."

It was the fall of 2006. That unexpected email marked the beginning of my journey with Kajal, a little Indian girl whose struggle to come out of darkness into which she was mercilessly thrown would have a big impact on the entire Nashville community.

Kajal's origins are shrouded in mystery. What we do know is that her stepmother had fought with her mother over custody. After her mother died, Kajal's stepmother intentionally blinded her by pouring a corrosive acid into her eyes while she slept one night. This horrific act was part of a plan to turn Kajal into a blind child singer who would inspire pity, and possibly donations, when she sang and begged in the streets. However, when her stepmother then discovered that Kajal lacked any talent in singing, she left the little girl to die in a train station near Calcutta. Kajal was rescued by a Christian mission group called the Society for Underprivileged People, who then transferred her to a shelter home in Allahabad, a city in northern India. Qamar Joy Zaidi and his wife, Grace, ran the shelter where Kajal lived with many other children who had been maimed, abused, and trafficked before being taken in by the organization.

In May of 2006, a Vanderbilt University student named Ashley Rogers had traveled from Nashville to India to volunteer at the shelter. Soon after she met Kajal, Ashley emailed her Grace Community Church family back in Nashville asking for help. A member of the church's prayer group, Jenna Ray, suggested that the shelter home contact the Wang Foundation for Sight Restoration.

Soon after I received that initial devastating email, the foundation launched what we called the "Kajal Project" to galvanize community support to bring her to the U.S., so we could determine if we would be able to restore her sight. As always, foundation doctors waived our medical and surgical fees, and donors from Nashville and beyond offered money and airline miles to fund Kajal and Grace's journey to the States. Several families offered to host the pair in their homes, including David and Jenna Ray, Blair and Karthi Masters, and Todd and Camilla Quillin.

One of the foundation's board members, a ninety-four-year-old gentleman named Wallace Rasmussen, contributed significantly to the Kajal Project. He also showed great compassion in the way he helped us welcome Kajal to Nashville. The evening I was due to pick up Kajal and Grace from the airport, Wallace came to Wang Vision Institute in his wheelchair, carrying a handmade music maker. Wallace was very sick—bedridden, on a respirator, and paralyzed from the waist down due to a stroke—but he was also an avid woodcraftsman and wanted to make a special gift for

Kajal. So he hauled himself out of his sickbed and wheeled himself into his woodshop, where he crafted a mechanical music-maker from dark red mahogany. On the flat surface was a brass cylinder that played the melody "Jesus Loves Me."

"You're picking up Kajal from the airport tonight," Wallace said, "and I can only imagine how stressed and afraid this poor child will be when she arrives in a foreign country. She can't see and she can't speak much English. Everything will be strange and frightening to her."

He handed me the music-maker. "Give this to Kajal when she arrives. Wind it up and put it against her face when she arrives. The vibrations of the music will comfort her," he explained.

I was deeply moved. I knew how hard it must have been for Wallace to get out of bed and make this gift. "Thank you, Wallace. This is really special. I know she will love it."

With special permission from Nashville airport authorities, I was allowed to go inside the airport and wait for our city's special guests at their arrival gate. Through the glass, I saw Kajal and Grace descend an open air staircase from the plane, and then I scanned the passengers emerging from the jet bridge until I saw the faces I had been anticipating. Grace held the hand of little Kajal, whose face was tense and her eyes were closed. She stayed very quiet and clung tightly to her caretaker. Grace looked down and placed a reassuring hand on Kajal's cropped hair.

I greeted Grace and bent down to whisper "hello" to Kajal. She smiled timidly, so I wound up the wooden music maker Wallace had made for her and placed it against her cheek as he had suggested. As Kajal felt the music, she lit up and the cutest smile appeared on her face.

As we walked toward baggage claim, I handed Kajal a lollipop. "Thank you, Dr. Wang," she said, a phrase she had learned especially for this moment. After our first meeting, we had a standing date each week for lunch at an Indian restaurant, and every time I saw her, I gave her a piece of peppermint candy.

I wanted to do all I could to bond with her before her surgery, by building consistency and a sense of familiarity using her other senses, since she couldn't see.

The next day, Grace and Kajal came in for the initial evaluation. The office was crowded with foundation board members, supporters and friends, who were all on hand to meet Kajal and present her with welcome gifts. Underneath all the excitement, however, I felt tremendous stress. For months, television and newspaper reports had chronicled Kajal's journey from India to America. It felt like the entire city of Nashville had come together to help and was now watching to see what would happen to this little girl. Normally, I try to remain emotionally detached from my patients because as an eye surgeon, when you're holding a blade and about to cut into someone's eyeball, a measure of objectivity is absolutely necessary. But my care for Kajal was totally different. I was deeply affected by the tragedy and darkness this four-year-old orphan had endured, which reminded me of my own darkness and struggle to survive when I was young , and I had put so much time and effort into the entire process leading up to this moment, so I was already emotionally invested. I had not even performed any surgery on Kajal yet, but I had already exceeded the usual demands of a doctor-patient relationship significantly.

Dr. Lisa Martén, a physician on a yearlong corneal fellowship with Wang Vision Institute, was the first to examine Kajal.

"Can you see the light?" Dr. Martén asked.

Grace translated for Kajal, who responded, "Yes."

"Can you see my hand?"

Kajal shook her head no. After taking digital photos of Kajal's eyes, Dr. Martén came to me looking very concerned.

"Her left eye is gone," Lisa whispered. She understood the level of stress I was feeling, and exactly how hard this news would be for me to hear. "There's no chance of saving that eye."

Kajal's left eye had lost inner matter and had shrunk from malnutrition, so its structure was destroyed. I felt like I had been punched in the gut because I had hoped I would have the chance to repair both eyes. I knew the damage was going to be severe given the nature of her injuries, so I reasoned that if surgery on one eye failed, we would have a second chance when we operated on the other eye. But with her left eye gone, our only hope now was in her right eye.

"As for her right eye," Lisa continued, "the injury is also very severe. She barely has light perception out of that eye, so maybe only one percent of that eye's vision remains."

My heart fell into my stomach. Kajal's vision was much worse than expected but more importantly, her injury had occurred at least a year earlier. Being blinded at such a young age posed problems beyond just the physical damage. The brain's ability to receive and process visual stimulation is constantly developing between birth and the age of eight. Kajal had already been in darkness for at least a year, so at four years old, the longer she went without visual stimulation, the less likely it was that she would ever recover any sight in her remaining eye.

But I held onto that slim bit of hope and refused to give up. We planned a series of surgeries for her right eye that would span a two-year period. A ruthless and abusive family member had stolen Kajal's sight but God willing, I would do whatever I could to give it back to her.

On Monday morning, May 14, 2007, I performed Kajal's first surgery. The goal of this procedure was to replace her scarred cornea with a clear one and prepare her eye for a more definitive, complex surgery involving stem cells.

However, I was completely unprepared for what I discovered.

During the surgery, I first carved out and removed the thick layer of cloudy white cornea and opened her eye cavity. Then I discovered that the inside of her eye looked like a bomb had exploded. Her eye was filled with a bloody gel and scar tissue that intertwined with a strange, shimmering substance.

"I've never seen that before," I said to the surgical team, in shock.

I had also never before encountered an eyeball quite that damaged, not even with Brad Barnes.

I was stunned when I realized that the atrocity against Kajal had been committed while she slept, with the full intention of damaging her eyes and blinding her. When Brad Barnes was blinded by a molten aluminum accident, at least he had some protective gear and the reflexes to shut his eyes and jump away from the source of injury. Despite how badly he'd been burned, the damage was still comparably superficial, so we were able to successfully treat him. But Kajal was utterly defenseless against her attacker, who chose to harm her while she was asleep, holding her down and prying her eyelids open long enough for the corrosive acid to destroy the deepest layers of both of her eyes. The acid had torn apart the colored iris and disintegrated the lens. The vitreous humor, the clear gel that fills the area between the lens and the retina, was bloodied.

I was encountering the worst-case scenario as a physician; I saw many things no surgeon should ever see, and found nothing I was hoping to find.

My shock gave way to a rising anger. I seethed at the thought of her stepmother's heinous act. How could anyone do such a thing to a young child? For the first time in my Christian journey, I was mad at God. I didn't understand how a loving God, one who cared for children—especially orphans—could have allowed such horror to be inflicted on one who was so innocent and helpless.

I cleaned up Kajal's eye and sutured on a clear, healthy cornea from donor tissue, which I covered with an amniotic membrane. She was then taken to recovery. After the long hours of surgery, I sat down and put my head in my hands. I was sweating from the difficulty of the surgery, but most exhausted was my spirit. I was not happy that God hadn't prevented this atrocity and that he had brought Kajal across the globe when He knew there wouldn't actually be much we could do to help her.

"God, if you love Kajal, why would you allow the absolute worst thing to happen to such a precious child?" I asked bitterly. "Why couldn't you have spared her even the least bit of vision, just a little bit, instead of letting her injuries go all the way to the last layer of the eye?"

I waited until Kajal had come out of general anesthesia to talk to Grace and the host families.

Kajal's right eye was patched with a thick, white bandage, but tears flowed beneath it as she awoke to the post-operative pain and discomfort. Grace cradled Kajal in her arms, gently swaying back and forth in the rocking chair.

"That was really tough," I admitted to Grace and Kajal's supporters, though I held back how deeply angry and upset I really was. "We did all we could. She may or may not regain any sight. We just have to see what God's plan is."

In July of 2007, I performed the second stage of surgery on Kajal to remove the amniotic membrane, transplant another new cornea, and graft stem cells that would help her new cornea heal. After the surgery, Kajal could make out shapes, shadows, and some color, which was about ten percent more sight than she had when she arrived. But I had hoped for more … so much more.

I didn't have peace with my faith or with God for a long time after that, but I didn't talk to anyone about how I was feeling. I kept it buried deep inside me. No one asked me how I felt anyway; I was the doctor—the one everyone was coming to with their own concerns and fears—so I couldn't be the one asking questions. I had not anticipated the stress and emotional burden of supporting everyone else's hopes while my own were crumbling. People turned to me with questions, but when I turned around, there was no one behind me to answer mine. "How could God allow this to happen to a vulnerable child?" I couldn't find an answer to this question, and I was haunted by it.

* * *

In the fall of 2007, the foundation hosted its third annual EyeBall fundraising gala at the Hilton Hotel in downtown Nashville. The theme that year was "Making Headlines in Black and White." Wallace Rasmussen was the chairman of the event, but he was too sick to attend. He would have been so tickled to see Kajal, our guest of honor, who was dressed in a billowy black dress with white polka dots and a white sash around her waist. Kajal had certainly been making headlines in Nashville, with her unspeakable tragedy, her courage, and the community's gallant efforts to help her.

At every EyeBall, patients who have been helped by the Wang Foundation for Sight Restoration share testimonials. Grace led Kajal onto the stage and thanked everyone for all they had done for Kajal. After that, many of the people who had supported or hosted Kajal went on stage and gathered around her and Grace. One by one, they told the audience how they had cared for Kajal and how she had impacted their lives in return. The parents and children in these host families talked about how much Kajal had meant to them, how she had burst into their comfortable lives here in America, and how she had given them a glimpse of another world where so many children suffer. Kajal had shown them how to be joyous and content even in the midst of blindness and uncertainty, and even after enduring such horrific abuse. One person after another shared that they originally thought they were helping Kajal, but in the end, she helped them so much more. They realized how much they had taken for granted, and all the things they should be grateful for living here in America.

Until that moment, I had been unable to let go of my anger at God for allowing so many bad things happen to Kajal, and for not allowing her vision to improve much, despite everything we had done. I felt Kajal deserved so much more. I profoundly wished that she had been able to recover much more of her eyesight like other foundation patients such as Francisco, Joel Case and Brad Barnes had. But as I listened to Kajal's supporters describe their appreciation for the opportunity they had to help her, the emotional connection they had formed with her, the joy she had brought to their lives, and the changes that they had seen in their own children who had now become so much more appreciative of what they have in America today. I looked down at Kajal, who was standing next to me waiting for her turn to speak. It occurred to me that Kajal was no longer the fearful, timid, quiet child that she once was when she arrived in the U.S. many months ago. She was now an entirely different little girl, full of life and joy, with a bubbly, enthusiastic personality.

Kajal was happy, and she was happy because she was loved.

For the first time in the months since Kajal's first surgery, I felt my anger towards God begin to abate, and gradually I felt my heart reconcile with Him. I had allowed myself to believe that Kajal's tragic circumstances were unredeemable, but as I considered her dramatic change and how deeply she had impacted the community, I realized the bigger plan in what God had done. Kajal had taught us that when we experience darkness, and it feels as though there is no light to be found anywhere we search for it, the light can come from within us. She radiated a luminescent joy that inspired everyone who encountered her, including Wallace Rasmussen, the host families, our entire surgical care team and office staff, and everyone in the world who had followed her story.

To be honest, I still didn't fully understand why God allowed such dreadful suffering, but I had at least accepted that there was a purpose in what Kajal had endured, just as I eventually accepted the suffering I had experienced during my younger years in China.

Once everyone had finished sharing their stories, I handed the microphone to Kajal and whispered softly into her ear, "Kajal, would you like to say something to everyone here tonight? We all love you so much!"

She had learned quite a bit of English since her arrival many months ago, so I assumed she would have something to say. But she was quiet for a moment, holding the microphone apprehensively in her hands. Then she broke into a big smile, with a tinge of mischief mixed in. Apparently Kajal had been preparing for this moment ... and she had a special surprise up her sleeve. Kajal had a secret.

I found out later that since Kajal had arrived in America, she had secretly wanted to learn to sing. From her four-year-old perspective, she believed the reason she had been abandoned at the train station in India after she was intentionally blinded was because she couldn't sing. She wanted to prove that she could indeed sing, and that she was therefore worth keeping. Kajal made friends with several of the host family children here in America ... and she learned to sing.

Kajal brought the microphone up to her lips and began to sing. "Yes, Jesus loves me. Yes, Jesus loves me. Yes, Jesus loves me. The Bible tells me so."

I recognized the song Kajal was singing. It was the song on the music box that Wallace had made for Kajal to welcome her to America.

As Kajal finished her song, the room erupted into a standing ovation fit for a symphony. As most of the faces around us streamed with tears, Kajal's face beamed with fulfillment. The band then kicked up a Tennessee waltz, and I led Kajal onto the dance floor for the first dance. She smiled as she danced and twirled in her adorable dress. She couldn't see them very clearly, but more than five hundred sets of eyes were aglow with tears and happiness at the sight of her.

Chapter 19

Dolly

"**D**olly Parton is here," announced one of the staff at Wang Vision Institute.

The queen of country music was waiting in my lobby! I smiled and went out to greet her. Other well-known members of Nashville's artist community have graced our exam rooms, including Nicole Kidman, Naomi Judd, Julianne Hough, Kenny Chesney, Jo Dee Messina, Charlie Daniels, and Ashley Judd to name just a few. I'm always honored when such luminaries seek us out for eye care or vision correction surgery. It is humbling to be entrusted with something as valuable as a person's vision—famous or not.

Dolly was petite, sprightly, and remarkably quick-witted. During her first visit, it became clear to me that she knew exactly what she needed, and she returned soon after for her LASIK procedure. A few months later she was back for what I assumed was a post-op visit.

"I'm actually not here for my eyes today," she said. "I'm here to play music with you, Dr. Wang."

"You're here to play music with *me*?" I asked, assuming she was joking.

"Oh, yes. I hear you play the Chinese violin, the erhu. I'm making a new album and I think it would be neat to experiment with your erhu on a country song."

I was surprised and delighted that this country music legend would want to play music with me, an amateur.

"You mean it?" I said. "Okay, let's do it!"

Dolly was working on an album called *Those Were the Days,* and she wanted me to play on the song "The Cruel War," an old folk tune dating back to the Civil War about a young girl who wants to accompany her sweetheart, Johnny, to the front lines of battle.

It was a hot and humid afternoon in July of 2005, I drove to Dolly's recording studio with my son, Dennis, who was spending his summer break with me in Nashville, and my friend and videographer, J.R. Davis. I was excited, but unsure of what to expect.

"Dad, do you think I could get an autograph from Dolly?" Dennis asked.

I laughed. "Sure! We'll ask her."

We got out of the car in front of Ocean Way Nashville, a beautiful studio housed in a century-old church in Nashville's Edgehill neighborhood. Dolly greeted us warmly and led us inside to Studio A, the main recording room. I was in awe of all the equipment, and I had never experienced anything like the thousands of little buttons and knobs I saw on the mixing console. It was worlds away from the laser lab I knew back in Maryland, with its own complex array of gadgets. Through a large rectangle of glass, I could see inside to the sanctuary-turned-studio, with its gleaming oak floors and soaring stained glass windows. Ocean Way Recording Studios embodied the essence of Music City, where sacred and secular worlds merge into a transcendent expression of human experience.

Dolly and I sat down at a long conference table with Tom Howard—who was arranging strings for the album—and we listened to a stripped-down demo of the song. Dennis and J.R. shot photos and videos as we worked. I had brought an artisan crafted erhu that I had purchased on a trip to Hong Kong nearly a decade earlier, as I anticipated it was going to be a special evening. Dolly and I were about to attempt something new and very unique—playing a melody on an ancient Chinese instrument to complement an American country song.

After listening to the demo, I said to Dolly, "That's lovely. Do you have my part of the score?"

"I have no score for your part," she replied.

"Okay, can I see the score for your part?"

"I don't have a score either."

So we had no score for my instrument. Dolly knew the song so well, she simply sang it from memory.

I realized I wasn't here just to play, but to compose as well. The last song I ever wrote was "Little Bird," which I did on the train ride to the University of Science and Technology in China at the end of the Cultural Revolution. Prior to that, I had mainly just composed music as a teenager with Tian-ma to try to avoid deportation and a lifetime of poverty and hard labor. Thinking back to those days, I realized we were actually lucky we weren't arrested because some of our songs—like "The Prisoner's Song"—described our longing for freedom from communist oppression, so we could have gotten into deep trouble if the government had ever found out about them.

Nearly three decades later, I was now composing once again but this time, the mood, purpose, audience, and location could not have been more different. The only similarity was the longing expressed in both songs, a desire for freedom and love that endures.

The erhu was the perfect instrument to express longing. Tom, Dolly, and I started playing around with the melody, trying to figure out a sound combining East and West that hadn't yet been heard. We wanted to create something very special that would bring harmony to two very divergent styles of music that operate on entirely different scales. Chinese music uses mostly the five-note scale (the black keys on the piano), whereas Western music uses a seven-note scale (both black and white keys). We listened to the demo of "The Cruel War" over and over, breaking it into many different segments, and experimenting with notes on the erhu's two strings.

For several hours we strung a variety of notes together until we finally had a workable score for the erhu. While we were waiting for the engineers to set up for recording, I felt like celebrating. I was elated by how the East and the West had come together and had produced such a lovely harmony with each other.

"I'll play a song if you'll sing with me," I said to Dolly, as we waited in the sanctuary.

"Let's see; what Chinese song do I remember?" Dolly said to herself with a mischievous laugh.

"Oh, this one you will know for sure," I replied.

Since my first days in America, my favorite song to play on the erhu was the Irish tune "Danny Boy." Sitting in that vast room, the memories of a century of singers hovering overhead, I began to draw my bow across the strings.

Dolly jumped right in and started singing. She had such immense talent and so many years of experience that she needed no preparation. As I played the main notes of the famous melody, she sang in harmony, complementing the erhu's plaintive sound. As the song came to an end, I played toward the high end of the scale and Dolly followed right along.

"I didn't know where you were going, but I was heading there anyway!" she said with a laugh.

My whole being radiated with happiness. I had just played an Irish hymn on an ancient Chinese instrument with an American country music icon. There was magic in the way the music transcended the cultural differences. We were about to begin recording my first erhu composition in decades, after following a fascinating creative process. I was thrilled to experience the transformation and redemption of my erhu playing from a fear-driven task when I was young to a celebration of life and love thirty years later.

After we completed the recording, Dolly walked us out, and I told her how much I appreciated the evening, and how much I enjoyed the songs on her new album. "Those sure were the days," I said, alluding to the album's title track.

"Yes," she said with a smile, "those were the days."

She waved goodbye and we pulled out of the parking lot. I smiled at Dennis, who had thoroughly enjoyed observing our East-meets-West collaboration. As for his request for an autograph, Dolly didn't take it lightly. She found the sheet paper on which we had written our original composition, and she signed it in large, swirling cursive. I would remember that afternoon with Dolly some years later when I found myself an advocate for artists in the middle of a battle for their rights.

Chapter 20

Giving Back

The room was filled with tension and I could barely sit still. I was surrounded by songwriters, music-industry executives and congressional leaders, all gathered to discuss how to combat music piracy in China. At first I wasn't sure why I was even in the room, since I was just an eye doctor and not a music professional. But as I listened to the arguments being presented, something began to stir inside of me. I couldn't keep quiet any longer.

I have lived in the United States since 1982, so my entire adult life has been shaped and formed here in America. I am immensely grateful to America for all the opportunities it has given me. From the moment I landed in Washington, D.C., I have fallen in love with America, and I have been blessed to be able to live the American dream.

My childhood was filled with the traditions of the East. I grew up with loving parents and grandparents who taught me the family value, to work hard and believe in myself. But America has taught me how to look to the future, dream big, and lead. My success in medicine and my ability to impact lives has been uniquely fashioned at the intersection of my Eastern roots and Western education. The combination of these experiences has given me the insight and ability to lead in my medical profession, and to help resolve issues of conflict in our society. I have always been interested in political dialogue and cultural exchange between the East and West. From my experience as a child meeting President Nixon during his visit to China, to my social activism during the Tiananmen Square tragedy, to meeting with President Reagan and Vice President Bush at the White House, I have interacted with some of the great political leaders of our time. I have learned a great deal from those experiences, which has fostered my interest in engaging in societal and political issues, and giving back to America.

The hearing about music piracy in China took place in a large auditorium inside the BMI building on Music Row. The primary topic of discussion was how to protect American songwriters from the piracy of songs running rampant in China.

One of the congressmen proposed enacting sanctions against China. "Tell the Chinese we won't take this anymore! We will enforce our laws using any measure necessary, including economic sanctions."

I winced as I listened to him speak. Strong-arming China on this issue was not a good idea and wouldn't be effective in supporting American songwriters. This was my moment to give back and to contribute. I stood up and offered a different approach.

"Consider the state of music and movie piracy in Hong Kong thirty years ago," I said. "Back then, fifty percent of music sold there was pirated. But now that number is down to less than a few percent, which is the Western standard. That's what we would like to see happen in mainland China. Do you know why the change has occurred in Hong Kong over the last thirty years? It wasn't because the U.S. threatened economic sanctions. It was because Hong Kong's own artists—international stars like Jackie Chan—realized it was in their own best interest to stand up and protect artists' intellectual property. So in my opinion the key here is to work together and communicate with the artists and the government in China in order to help them realize that reducing music piracy benefits not only America, but China itself as well."

There was a silence in the room after I spoke. I sensed that the audience was reflecting on and considering what I had just said. Then the executive director of the Nashville Songwriters Association, Bart Herbison, said, "I completely agree with Dr. Wang. We should strive to follow his suggestion."

A wave of excitement rushed through me. I realized I was making an impact on protecting the intellectual property of American songwriters while maintaining sensitivity and respect for different cultures and people. I knew in that moment that I wanted to help even more, so I joined the Nashville Songwriters Association as an advisory board member and became active in helping with the dialogue and interactions between musicians in China and the United States.

Beyond bolstering Nashville's music and creative community, I felt increasingly drawn to improve cultural understanding between my American compatriots and the Chinese, especially by helping local Tennessee companies to sell their products overseas. I was troubled by the fact that America buys so much from China, so I wanted to encourage trade traffic in the opposite direction—exports from Tennessee to China—while also encouraging Chinese manufacturing firms to relocate to Tennessee to create jobs here.

In 2007, I founded the Tennessee Chinese Chamber of Commerce (TCCC) to help Tennessee businesses sell products to China. Later on I also became the honorary president of Tennessee-American Chamber of Commerce (TACCC). As an American business owner who was born in China, I know both the cultural perspective of the East and the business mindset in the West. I believe a vital part of selling a product—for any business—is understanding the customer. Hence, learning about other cultures such as that of China is no longer just the right thing to do as a citizen of the world today; it's actually now an economic necessity, since if we want to increase our exports to China, we need to learn about our customers. Through educational forums, TCCC and TACCC taught Tennessee businesses owners about our potential customers—the Chinese—including the history, people, and culture of China.

At a recent chamber meeting, I was asked by some local business owners what their next step should be in finding a way to work with Chinese businesses.

"What's your unique value proposition?" I asked. "If you want to collaborate with Chinese businesses to produce and sell goods in China domestically, what are you bringing to the table that your Chinese business partner does not have and most needs?"

"I can offer capital," responded one of the local entrepreneurs.

"America actually owes China two trillion dollars, and our annual trade deficit with China stands at 318 billion dollars," I said. "China doesn't need our capital."

"Okay, if not money, how about technology?"

"Well, China adopts technologies rapidly," I said. "They have extremely smart engineers."

"Then how about management skills?"

"U.S. business management is good, indeed, but China has reasonably efficient managers of its own, and they learn these skills very quickly."

At that point, the meeting attendees seemed to be at a loss for any other ideas, so I repeated and emphasized my initial questions.

"What do the Chinese need from us? What is our unique value proposition? We have to have answers to those questions in any business collaboration. Although China doesn't need our capital, technology or management, they do need something that they consider very important...something that can only be provided by us."

The room fell silent as everyone waited for my punch line.

"What they need is our American brand," I concluded. "The Chinese have historically regarded American products as being of a much higher quality than goods made in China. If a product in China has an American label, it might fetch three times the price in China's market than a product made domestically in China. The next five to ten years will be a golden opportunity to do business with China and capitalize on the reputation of the American brand."

"Our unique value proposition is simply this . . . we are American!"

As president of TCCC, I was invited to join a 2009 trade mission to China, led by former Tennessee governor Phil Bredesen. Beginning in late October of that year, our group of business and government leaders spent ten days visiting Beijing, Xian, Hangzhou, and Hong Kong, meeting with Chinese leaders in business, technology, and healthcare. The goal of the delegation was to do a follow-up visit to the 2007 founding of the Tennessee-China Development Center in Beijing. This economic development office was established to foster business exchange between the two countries with the hope of encouraging Chinese firms to relocate to Tennessee, which would create new jobs here. My involvement in the delegation was yet another step in my own personal vision to give back to America.

* * *

There remains a lot of room for improvement in our understanding of diverse cultures, not just overseas but also with respect to the immigrant groups living right here in America. To this end, I partnered with Galen Spencer Hull, PhD, an educator who has had a long-standing interest in uniting immigrant and minority businesses. We co-founded the Tennessee Immigrant and Minority Business Group (TIMBG), whose first meeting was held on September 16, 2013. The mission of TIMBG is to facilitate communication between immigrant and minority businesses, and to identify and discuss issues of common interest. One in four businesses in middle Tennessee is immigrant- or minority-owned, representing the fastest-growing sector of our business community.

In recent years, I also began to sense a longing to reconnect with China. When I left China in 1982, I was twenty-one years old and had already endured more hardship and suffering than some people experience in a lifetime, and I wanted nothing more to do with communist dictators. I came to America for freedom, and I have loved and embraced its language, culture, and Christian faith. As I got older, however, I began to appreciate more of the values of my ethnic origin, such as the importance of family, education, and respect for elders. So I wanted to give back to China as well. On August 22, 2005, I performed China's first bladeless, all-laser LASIK procedure, the first surgery of its kind in a country of 1.4 billion people! In 2006, I became the international president of the Shanghai Aier Eye Hospital, the flagship hospital of the Aier Eye Hospital Group, the largest private eye hospital system in China. Among the eight textbooks in ophthalmology that I have published, five have been translated into Chinese. Chinese eye doctors are also regular visitors and many fellows have been trained at Wang Vision Institute in Nashville. I have done these things throughout the past decades to help the country of my birth using knowledge that I have learned here in the West.

Beyond medicine, I have also been interested in helping China spiritually. America gave me not only a world-class education, but also a life-changing belief and trust in God. As my Christian faith continued to grow, I wanted to do something worthwhile to help spread faith and belief in God to China. As material wealth has increased in China, corruption has risen significantly as well. This needs to change, but I do not believe the law alone is enough to solve this major problem. China as a society today needs more emphasis on individual accountability and ethics, attributes which are the cornerstone of the Christian faith.

When I first arrived in America, I often heard people say, "You're not supposed to do that." As simple as the phrase sounds, it's not one that is used in China very often because it is embedded with a moral compass, an intrinsic sense of right and wrong, which characteristically is heavily influenced by America's historical roots in Christianity. China, on the other hand, is a country that is predominantly atheistic. At least half of American citizens profess to be Christians, and those who are living a truly Christian life are guided by their belief in God, and consider themselves accountable to His higher standards of personal conduct. Without faith and accountability to a higher power, a person may not hesitate to act corruptly as long as no one will find out. Though one can strengthen laws and legal system, but without faith, we could never hire enough police. I believe what China needs the most is for its people to believe in God.

In 2008, I founded the Wang Foundation for Christian Outreach to China, which funds the China Bible Pen Pal Project. Our goal is to deliver ten thousand Bibles to China and to obtain email addresses from the Chinese people who receive the Bibles. We then disperse these email addresses to their Christian brothers and sisters in America, so they can become pen pals with these budding Chinese Christians in order to fellowship with them and nurture their faith. One person at a time, I want to give to the people of China the Christian faith that was given to me, a faith that has blessed my life richly. I am excited about the immense opportunity the China Bible Pen Pal Project has of recruiting a quarter of the human race for God's kingdom!

* * *

My unusual transformation from atheist to Christian has also inspired many others because I have been able to share the lessons I have learned about the compatibility of faith and science. In recent years, I have travelled around the country giving lectures in the hope of bridging the gap between the two. I truly believe faith and science are friends, not foes. As my experience with the amniotic membrane contact lens shows, faith and science can indeed work together. It is in the uniting of the two, not splitting, can we find new, often unexpected and more powerful solutions to the problems in our lives.

In the fall of 2012, Rice Broocks, pastor of Bethel World Outreach Church in Brentwood, Tennessee, approached me about including my story in his book, *God's Not Dead*, which presents evidence for the existence of God. I was delighted to be a part of it. Following its publication, the book inspired a movie with the same title that illustrates the story of a freshman college student who challenges his philosophy professor's atheist beliefs. One of the characters in the movie, a Chinese student who is considering Christianity, was inspired by my life story. At the time of the first print of this book, the film had grossed nearly $100 million worldwide, and more than 25 million Americans had seen it. Now the sequel to the original movie, *God's Not Dead 2*, has also come out in which my Chinese student character decided to return to China to spread the Gospel, a story line modeled after our current China Bible Pen Pal Project. I believe the movie's success is due in large part to the hunger many of us have for a connection with the divine, a longing that we were created with that runs through all mankind, and to every part of the globe from East to West.

No matter where we have come from and where we are going, we all desire the same things—love, peace, and security—and we all appreciate the beauty of God's creations. So we don't have to be at odds with one another because, like faith and science, people with seemingly polarized perspectives can indeed still work together in creative, mutually beneficial ways. As a proud American with Asian roots, I hold a hand out to both the East and the West, in the hopes of bringing them a little closer together.

President John F. Kennedy put it best when he said, "Ask not what your country can do for you; ask what you can do for your country."

I have taken these words to heart, and I believe the idea of giving back is an ongoing mission of paying it forward to the next generation. This is a way of life for me, a lens, if you will, through which I see the world. I am not perfect and do not believe I have all the answers, but of this I am sure: the harder I work and the more my own actions inspire others—even those I have just met for the first time—to have a heart of gratitude for the freedom this great country has blessed us with, the greater chance we have to begin to lay a mighty foundation for change, and to appreciate much, much more the freedom we enjoy as Americans! With gratitude, our hearts will be primed and motivated to find ways in our own local, civic, religious, and family communities to help and to give back. This will undoubtedly build strength in our families, in our workplaces, and in our places of worship. This heart of giving back will effect positive change in our own spheres of influence and beyond, and it will lead to more fruitful and fulfilled lives.

This sense of appreciation and the desire to give back has been the bedrock of my drive to build the Wang Foundation for Sight Restoration, the Wang Foundation for Christian Outreach to China, the Tennessee Chinese Chamber of Commerce, and Tennessee Immigrant and Minority Business Group, as well as the inspiration for all my social and community work over the years. I am honored and humbled to receive many awards over the years for my charity and community work, including NPR's Philanthropist of the Year Award, the Outstanding Nashvillian of the Year Award from Kiwanis Club and an honorary doctorate degree from Trevecca Nazarene University. I want to do everything that I can to assist each person seeking to come out of darkness and go into the light, both physically and spiritually.

Part Five

I'm So Pretty!

Chapter 21

Maria, Part 2

At noon on Thursday, November 7, 2013, friends and supporters around the world were praying for Maria . . . and for me. I was facing the most difficult reconstructive eye surgery of my entire career.

It seemed like an impossible situation. At church the Sunday after I first evaluated Maria, I tried to listen to the sermon, but instead I kept going over the details of her upcoming surgery over and over in my mind. Her chance for healthy sight had been slim from the start to begin with, as Maria had been born prematurely, weighing only two pounds. Growing up in a Moldovan orphanage, she had also lacked access to basic medical care and essential nutrition. Maria had retinopathy of prematurity. The accompanying detached retina in her left eye was never treated, so she had lost all hope of any sight in that eye. She also had only light perception vision remaining in her right eye, but even that was compromised by the eye's severe damage and chronic inflammation. So since her right eye was all we had to work with, we had only the slimmest chance of restoring any sight at all for Maria.

I was honest with Maria and her host family and Steve and Lynn Hendrich, in explaining to them that the surgery on Maria's right eye could fail, and if it did, she could lose even the little bit of sight she had left in that eye. And if there were any surgical complications—such as an infection—then we might have to remove her entire right eyeball altogether. That would be a disaster, since an eye that at least has light perception vision is still much better than facing the rest of her life in total darkness. Additionally, if the eye had to be removed, the tissues and bone structure around her eye socket would deteriorate, so her pretty, young face could be permanently disfigured.

Furthermore, what if I opened up Maria's eye and found even more damage, like I had with Kajal? Could I handle another heartbreak like that? I felt tense and unsettled.

And to add insult to injury, my third marriage was unraveling as well. I had met Ye-jia Xue about five years earlier at a social gathering in Shanghai. She was beautiful, an elegant dancer, and one of the smartest people I had ever known. We fell in love, and Ye-jia moved to the U.S. to be with me. We were married a short time later, but the ongoing stress of work took its toll on our marriage over the next several years. As I spent more and more time at work, Ye-jia grew increasingly unhappy, and our marriage suffered as a result of each of us focusing on our own issues, instead of working to strengthen our relationship.

The burdens I was carrying with another declining marriage, and the tremendous risks and high expectations related to Maria's surgery, caused me so much stress that I felt like I was going to completely fall apart. I had nowhere else to turn but to God. Sitting in the church pew, I bowed my head and prayed.

"God, why do I have to go through all these trials all at once? It is unbearable. With Maria's upcoming surgery, if someone could create the absolute worst-case scenario regarding amount of intensity, risk, and uncertainty, this would be it! This is too stressful for me. Everyone has such hopes for her surgery, and on top of that, my own life is falling apart at the same time! Now God, this is really the time I need you, Lord . . . I need you desperately! You're my only hope to survive through all of this. Lord, I am not scared or fearful of the failure for myself or how hard my situation is right now, I have seen stress and failures so many times in my life. Rather, I am scared and fearful of possibly letting down Maria, someone who is so innocent, precious and vulnerable. God, please help us!"

On the day of Maria's surgery, I had a moment to myself while I scrubbed in. Despite seemingly insurmountable difficulties, my earnest prayers over the previous few days had brought me peace. I finally sensed that God was with me, and I was able to put my personal stress aside long enough to focus exclusively on Maria, and on her surgery. Even though the surgery seemed impossible, I knew God had already carried me through other unimaginable surgeries—Francisco, Joel Case, Brad Barnes, and Kajal—so I was confident He would come through for me again with Maria.

Perhaps God had allowed my personal and professional lives to be so stenuously tested so I would fall to my knees and be humbled enough to realize how much I need Him. Perhaps He wanted me to fully realize that even my best human efforts would not be enough to help these patients . . . or myself. I needed to listen to Him, and submit to His much greater power and will. Only through a combination of hard work and true faith in Him could I have a chance to persevere through these most difficult situations.

I walked away from the scrub station with my hands held high, feeling refreshed, at peace, and completely determined. Before I walked into the operating room, I told Steve and Lynn that we had arrived at the point of no return. We were all well aware by this time that the surgery was going to be very risky and in the end, Maria may regain some vision or she may lose her sight completely. We prayed for God's guidance, strength, and wisdom. Because the chance for success was so slim, I prayed that God would help us all to accept whatever His will was with the outcome. I knew deep down that truly having faith doesn't mean asking God for what we want and then expecting Him to give it to us, but rather faith is presenting your prayer request to God with a humble attitude of "not my will, but yours be done," and then accepting whatever His decision is for our situation.

I was going to give it my best...and the rest was up to God!

Inside the operating room, the surgical team prepared the surgical instruments as I secured my gown and gloves.

We were ready to begin.

There were at least ten significant barriers to restoring sight in Maria's right eye, and we had only overcome one so far—the ultrasound had indicated that her right retina was still intact. The next barrier was that her pupil wouldn't dilate and would have to be manually pried open, which increased the risks of the surgery. The goal was to get behind her constricted pupil to break up the rock-hard, opacified cataract, excavate, and implant an artificial lens. All of that had to be accomplished through a scarred cornea—which gave me only a very limited view of the eye's content—and a chronically inflamed eye with a distorted anatomy. In addition, I wasn't sure whether I would encounter an unstable lens or the capsular structure would be firm enough to support the removal of the dense cataract and the implantation of the lens. Finally even if we were successful with all these steps, I would still have to face dealing with the distorted iris, trying to reconstruct her pupil, and after this surgery, managing potential retinal and optic nerve issues.

As I attempted to manually open her pupil, I realized that her iris was stuck to the capsule containing the lens, which was why the pupil couldn't dilate. I was going to have to separate the stuck tissues, which was an extremely delicate procedure because of the high risk of damaging the capsular tissue in such a chronically inflamed eye. And if the capsule was damaged, the removal of the rock-hard cataract would become much more difficult. To separate the iris from its tight adherence to the capsule, would be like gluing two pieces of plastic wrap together, and then using a surgical blade to cut all the way through the middle of the two pieces without tearing or puncturing either one...except for the fact that the iris is even thinner than plastic wrap! I felt like I was attempting an impossible feat.

I looked at the nurse and whispered, "It's going to be a long day."

I looked through a large surgical microscope and used the tips of the finest forceps to stretch the tissue slightly until it was taut, and then sliced it with an ultra-thin scalpel with the utmost care and precision. After about an hour and a half—which felt like an eternity—I made it through about seventy-five percent of the stuck tissue, which was only a few millimeters in length. But as the iris was separating from the capsule, the capsule and lens got free and began to move all around and sideways. Since it was no longer tightly anchored to the iris, the lens started to shake and threatened to fall into the eye cavity. At this point, the detaching work became even more difficult, like cutting through those same two pieces of glued plastic wrap, except now they were blowing back and forth in the wind.

Faced with even more difficulty in an already unfeasible situation, I finally felt that I had to give up. It just wasn't humanly possible to go any further. Sadly, it looked like we wouldn't be able to help Maria, and the situation would end just like Kajal's did!

I injected some gel to stabilize the content in the eye, and then pushed the microscope to the side and rolled my chair away from the operating table. The gravity of the situation had caused me to sweat all over, and I needed a break, a chance to refresh myself. The nurse pulled down my surgical mask and held a paper cup to my lips so I could take a sip of water.

I had reached that familiar place of angst where I had done my best, but was at the limit of my surgical capabilities and couldn't go any further on my own.

Suddenly, the first prayer I had ever prayed—thirty years ago at the University of Maryland as I stood over the atom collider—came flooding back to my mind. "God help us!" I thought about how I felt that night in the Harvard quad, about my struggle to find meaning in science and a solution to the moral dilemma of fetal tissue research. God reminded me that at the times in my life when I thought there was no hope or solution, He demonstrated His power again and again, just as He had when He revealed the solution to the fetal research dilemma.

Now I knew I needed to do what God had encouraged me to do in every one of those previous difficult situations—humbly submit to Him and ask for His help in pushing through this extremely narrow passage in Maria's eye surgery. The spiritual symbolism of the moment was so profound that it brought to my mind the Bible verse from Matthew 7:14: "Narrow is the road that leads to life, and only a few find it."

I took a deep breath, and lowered my head to pray.

"God, *I am done*," I said. "You've given me a challenge that is beyond the knowledge and skills I have acquired up to this point in my life. Please reveal *your* plan! You've carried me this far, so will you please help me through this most difficult part? Will you please steady my hands because I really cannot afford to make a single mistake now. I ask this in the most powerful name of Jesus Christ, Amen."

Though it had only been about a ten-minute break, that can feel like an eternity to an operating room staff, so I knew the nurses and technicians were wondering what was going on. Since the surgery looked like a lost cause, one nurse was actually getting ready to turn the lights back on as soon as I declared the surgery a failure and confirmed that we were done. But I just remained in prayerful stillness, listening for God's leading.

The operating room was quiet, very quiet, interrupted only by the monotonous beeping of the cardiac monitor.

Gradually, a sense of calm came over me as it had in all the other situations where I had let go and let God be in charge, and I felt His presence within me increasing.

With renewed confidence, a refreshed mind and steady hands, I rolled my surgical chair back into place.

For the next two hours, I worked with "laser focus" and determination to separate the last, most difficult bit of stuck tissue, all while facing the added challenge of the unstable moving lens.

When I finally made it through the remaining tissue and the pupil was finally open, I was amazed to see that the capsular tissues were still entirely intact. It was a miracle! When I asked for a new instrument, the staff knew the dangerous dissection was finally and successfully completed, so the relief to the whole team was palpable.

The hardest part was over, and I felt immense relief, but I had to stay on task. Next, I had to maneuver through the stretched pupil to carefully break up the rock hard cataract without damaging the back part of the lens capsule or the already weak supporting structure, then stabilize the lens capsule and implant the artificial lens. The rest of the procedure including the removal of corneal opacities went quickly and after I finished, I rotated my chair around, glanced contentedly at the staff, and gave them two thumbs up.

"We got it!" I exclaimed, then cheers and applause broke out throughout the operating room.

God had come through for me, and for us, once again!

Routine cataract procedures typically take only about ten minutes, but Maria's surgery was so arduous and multi-layered that we were in the operating room for over four hours. The surgery had gone as well as I could have hoped, but the results were yet to be determined. I had restored the anatomical structure of her eye, but I didn't know yet if Maria would be able to see at all. There still remained several obstacles to overcome.

What if her retina or optic nerve didn't function properly? We would have a better idea once we removed her bandages, but even if all the parts of her eye were healthy, we still had to contend with whether or not her brain would be able to process visual stimulation after a lifetime of blindness.

As Maria slowly came off the anesthesia, the nurse came to me and said, "Dr. Wang, she asked for you."

In that moment, I had a decision to make. I could remove her patch and test her sight all by myself, so no one else would witness the letdown if the surgery had failed to restore her sight. But if she was able to see, I would be the only one to witness this once-in-a-lifetime moment of miracle of God. Few of us know someone attempting to go from darkness to sight, but even fewer of us are present at the very moment when a person comes out of that darkness, and enters the amazing world of sight!

I decided to put my ego aside and accept that if the results weren't what we had all hoped for, I had the peace of knowing I had done all I could. But if Maria regained any sight at all, the experience was something everyone would remember for the rest of their lives.

This was too precious an opportunity for anyone to miss. To be present when a blind person is finally able to see is truly a miraculous moment.

I asked Maria if her host family, supporters, and the staff could be in the room when I took off her patch. Maria agreed, and the entire team that had labored for nearly two years on her behalf gathered around her. I was too exhausted to go into much detail about the surgery, so I simply told them that it had been a close call.

"This is the moment of truth," I said. "God has carried us this far. This is the moment for Him to shine. God, please help us accept whatever your will is."

Maria lay listlessly on the bed, still wrapped in a light white blanket with large sunglasses that dwarfed her delicate features. Lynn stood to Maria's right, teary and nervous. She and her family had poured so much of themselves into this young girl's life. If Maria couldn't see when the patch was removed, Lynn and Steve had already decided they would care for Maria for the rest of her life. This is, in fact, the foundation's biggest challenge—finding host parents willing to provide lifelong care for an orphan who may or may not regain sight, even with our best efforts.

But I knew Lynn wasn't crying because she feared the task in front of her. She was nervous and hopeful. She loved Maria so much and wanted nothing more for her than to receive the gift of sight that would transform her life. We all longed for the same thing.

While everyone watched, I took off the sunglasses and then the patch over Maria's right eye. She had very limited light perception vision left before surgery, so my first test would be to see whether she still had the same amount of vision, or if the surgery had in fact reduced her already very limited sight even further. "Maria, is the light in the room on?" I asked.

She nodded. I was relieved that at least we hadn't lost anything!

I then summoned up the courage to continue testing her sight while her host family and supporters looked on. I had no idea what to expect; the results were up to God.

The first indication of improved sight would be her perception of hand movement, so I waved my hand back and forth in front of her face.

"Maria, can you see my hand moving?"

She nodded again.

I was elated! Her eyesight had actually improved! As excited as I was, I wondered if I should stop right there and end the testing on a high note, or take the risk of going on to the next test and face a possible negative response. There was only one more test I could do without a vision chart, so after a moment of thought, I decided to go for it. I held up my pointer finger and asked her how many fingers she could see.

Everyone in the room seemed to be holding their breath.

Maria squinted toward my hand. There was a pause.

Then she whispered, "*Unu*," which is "one" in Romanian.

Maria could see my finger!

The room erupted in shouts of joy, laughter, and sobs of relief. We were each overflowing with elation born of a Herculean effort that had spanned nearly two years and five thousand miles, and included the contributions of hundreds of people.

We had witnessed a miracle, something only God could accomplish.

At long last, Maria could see.

Maria's vision continued to improve as the swelling went down. The Hendriches took her home so she could rest and recover. Later that evening, when Maria had come out of her groggy haze from the anesthesia, Steve, Lynn, and their daughter Casey stood with her in front of their large bathroom mirror. She clutched her dark glasses in one hand as her patch was removed.

Maria looked quizzically into the mirror. She was noticing something. Steve perceived an expression of uncertainty and disbelief on her face.

"Can you see yourself, Maria?" he asked.

Maria started putting her dark glasses back on, almost poking herself in the eye.

"Oh, oh, be careful," Steve responded as he gently pushed the glasses away from Maria's face.

Maria looked into the mirror again, except this time when she moved, the image in the mirror moved too! Her expression transformed into a big smile as she realized that the person she was seeing in the mirror ... was in fact herself!

"*Sunt frumoasa!*" she squealed in an elated, high-pitched tone. Her Romanian declaration was, "I am so pretty!"

Casey moved closer to Maria and asked her, "Can you see me?"

Maria turned to Casey and looked at her intently. "Yeah!" she cried, and then the two girls hugged tightly.

Maria looked back at the mirror again. She was quiet, studying the lovely image reflecting back at her, and contemplating what had just happened.

Maria had just seen herself, and the world around her, for the very first time!

* * *

At one of her first post-op visits, Maria received an amniotic membrane contact lens to help her cornea heal after the removal of her corneal opacities. It had only been a few years since the amniotic membrane contact lens had emerged on the commercial market. After being granted the two U.S. patents for this technology in 1999 and 2000, I had spent the next decade trying to develop a viable product before eventually licensing the patent to a company in California. So after sixteen years of research and development by our team, the amniotic membrane contact lens was finally available commercially in November of 2011. The breakthrough technology was rapidly adopted, and more than a thousand surgeons have used them to restore sight in countless number of patients throughout the world.

My experience with the amniotic membrane contact lens is powerful proof that science and faith can indeed work together. I believe God loves all of us and He wants us to do research, since our quality of life is improved by what is reaped through research. But He wants us to do it the right way. The amniotic membrane was a godsend opportunity for us to conduct fetal tissue research without harming an unborn child. We can now help blind patients without compromising our moral, ethical, and spiritual principles.

The amniotic membrane contact lens allowed Maria's eye to begin to heal, and the vision in her right eye improved from one percent to twenty percent.

By early 2014, we were faced with another unique challenge. Until recently, there was little evidence that a teen or adult brain could learn to see—to interpret visual stimulation—if the person had been blind since birth or early infancy.

But in Maria's case, the surgery had actually been done on a unique human being whose physical age was fifteen, but whose visual age was only a few months. So based on all we knew, Maria should not have been able to interpret visual images. However, defying all previous scientific assumptions, I was amazed to see that Maria's brain began to actually adapt. With vision therapy and the help of renowned optometrist and a foundation doctor Dr. David Shen, Maria was able to gradually learn to interpret what she sees. She can now put jigsaw puzzles together, and with the help of a magnifier, she can do math. In fact, when I play card games with Maria that require math skills, she sometimes beats me! She also learned to ride a bicycle. Maria is a straight-A student in school now. She learned to play the piano and gave her first public piano recital. It was such a blessing to see Maria, who has gone from being a blind orphan at the brink of being subjected to human trafficking and prostitution, to now a happy teenager who can see, who is loved and lives in Franklin Tennessee with her host family the Hendriches!

On Saturday, October 11, 2014, the Wang Foundation for Sight Restoration held its ninth annual EyeBall fundraiser at the Massey Concert Hall at Belmont University. It had been two years since Maria's pictures first filled the giant screens at the 2012 EyeBall, inspiring many of the event's attendees to rally around her to offer assistance.

Since it was founded in 2003, the Wang Foundation for Sight Restoration has helped patients from more than forty states in the U.S., and over fifty-five countries around the world. Foundation doctors donate their services, and other supporters have helped cover all other costs. As the foundation decided to take on more blind orphans, we realized that our greatest need and challenge was to find dedicated host families like the Hendriches, so we offered free admission to the 2014 EyeBall. Although the event has historically been mainly a fundraiser, we wanted as many people as possible to hear about this need for host families so the foundation is able to help more blind children.

More than 700 guests showed up for that event, the theme of which was "A Gift of Sight for Our Children." Rather than our usual ballroom dance gala, this time we hosted a concert. I played the erhu along with Carlos Enrique on classical guitar, Deidre Emerson on cello, and David Fischer singing tenor. Acclaimed producer Robert Swope created the show. Halfway through the program we showed a video of Maria's remarkable journey, and then Steve, Lynn, and Maria came on stage. Steve shared with the audience how they met Maria at the summer camp in Chişinău, Moldova, and how they were moved to help her. Lynn then spoke about how deeply Maria had impacted her family, and helped her children realize how blessed they are living in America today and how much they should appreciate it.

When our guest of honor, Maria, came to the microphone, she shared the deep joy and gratitude she felt for receiving her sight back and for being rescued from impending destitution.

"Thank you for being here," she said. "I love you all very much!"

Then, just as Kajal had done, Maria surprised us with a song. Steve later told me Maria had fallen in love with "Lord, I Need You,"—initially recorded by Matt Maher, a Canadian contemporary Christian artist—and that she now sings it all the time.

She sang each word full of emotion. "Lord, I need you, oh, I need you. Every hour I need you. My one defense, my righteousness, oh God, how I need you."

Maria had overcome more adversity than many of us will ever comprehend, yet she has remained very sweet, kind, and tender in spirit. Like Kajal, Maria had a profound impact on the people who knew and supported her, and on the over a quarter million others from around the world who have watched the incredible video footage of Maria seeing herself for the very first time, exclaiming "*Sunt frumoasa!*" Maria entered all of our lives with a purpose of which even she was unaware. She pointed us to God and reminded us that He comes through for us when we reach the end of ourselves, and when no human option remains to pull us through.

As Steve, Lynn, and Maria left the stage, Maria gave me a big hug. We then resumed the music and before we began our last song, "Amazing Grace," I spoke to the audience. The guests present that evening included supporters of different nationalities, cultures, and faiths—Christians, Jews, Muslims, Buddhists, and also many Hindu Indians who had supported Kajal. They all gathered at EyeBall 2014 for the same purpose, to do their part to bring sight to blind orphans. I wanted this final performance to include everyone, to help all of us transcend our differences and barriers, and unify us in the common goal of serving the poor and vulnerable.

"The EyeBall is an occasion for all of us to celebrate the spirit of giving and to show that we love those who need our help," I said. "We are celebrating the remarkable journey of one young orphan girl who has gone from darkness to sight. The world today is not always a very friendly place, but being among the loving, generous people here tonight reminds us that there is still hope for humankind. This last number is a song that, no matter what your ethnicity, culture, or religious beliefs are, reminds us of our vulnerability, our mortality, and our need to believe in an immortal, eternal, almighty Creator."

Then one at a time, the members of our ensemble began to play, each musician rendering an interpretation of "Amazing Grace" that reflected his or her own life experience, as well as the eternal quality that transcended them all.

From Deidre's cello came deep, melancholy tones whose mournful sound recalled the pain of Maria's former darkness, as well as the pain that many blind orphan children from around the world still suffer today. It reminded me of the pain I myself had sustained, and how far I had come to be sitting on that stage and performing for the people and country I love.

Next, Carlos's classical guitar strummed out a lively and joyful South American interpretation. His version of the song reminded me of the feats our team had achieved, my own life's light and happy moments, and all the wonderful people I have known, those who have helped me and those I have been blessed to help in return.

David's was the only vocal rendition of the song, and it was full of his compassion and love for God. "Amazing grace! How sweet the sound, that saved a wretch like me. I once was lost but now I'm found, was blind, but now I see."

Next I played the song on my Chinese erhu violin, deliberately slowing down the melody, extending each note. I wanted the two strings to convey the essence of life, the adversity I faced during the Cultural Revolution, the pain of discrimination, the hard work, the moments of joy, and the emotions and love that connected all of us.

Finally, all the musicians joined together to play the song for the fifth and the last time, inviting all the EyeBall guests to sing along. Many people stood up, singing in worship and full of emotion. I could feel the resonance throughout the auditorium, each person expressing the song in his or her own way, based on his or her own life experience, everyone aspiring to be part of something greater than all of us. EyeBall reminds us that no matter what our culture, religion or ethnicities are, we as human beings share more in common than we are different. We all desire the same thing, to love and to be loved.

Following the EyeBall, we held an after-party at Nashville's Sunset Grill for key patrons. As I entered the restaurant, I greeted a group of about eighty people that included Wang Foundation board members, participating physicians, medical counsel, musicians, artists, photographers, and event volunteers. At my side throughout the evening was a special woman named Anle Ji.

As I've gotten older, I have finally learned that life is not just work; it is also and more importantly about family, and about finding a proper balance between work and those relationships that mean so much to us all. I have also learned that in order to truly love others, we must first love those who are closest to us, such as our own family members. As I've matured in this area, I now spend more time with my son Dennis, my brother Ming-yu and his family, my parents, and my godparents Misha and June. I have come to realize how deeply I love my family. They are my backbone and strength, and their love sustains me in my work. My parents are in their eighties now, and Dad has severe Parkinson's. In order to better take care of them, I moved both of them in, to live with me, for the rest of their lives. In my youth, my parents have done so much to help me. In their sunset years, I want to take good care of them.

I also understand now what it is that I truly need to be as a man. After my divorce from Ye-jia, I met Anle, a Chinese-American woman who is beautiful, mature, gentle, caring, supportive, and a dedicated Christian. She is also well-educated and comes from a strong academic family like my own. What Anle brings to my life is what I have always lacked—balance with work, responsibilities, and family time. With Anle's help, I am learning what it means to support one another and approach life as a team. For the first time in my life, I have been able to be with someone with whom I share a deep and loving connection, and a lifelong passion of wanting to make not only our own lives better, but also the lives of people around us.

With Anle's hand in mine, I walked to each group of guests and thanked them for the contributions they made to both the foundation itself and the 2014 EyeBall. When I approached Steve and Lynn Hendrich, we shared with each other the deep gratitude and joy we felt about all God had allowed us to witness and accomplish together during the long two-year journey since they first showed me Maria's photo.

And finally I walked up to Maria, who was walking around, chatting with everyone.

"Would you like to dance?" I asked. "Do you remember the swing dance I taught you?"

She smiled and nodded, and then handed her glasses to someone. As we started dancing to the big band music playing in the background, most of the guests circled around us. In the presence of everyone who had helped her, it seemed fitting for Maria to have an opportunity to showcase her newfound joy. At first, she was shy and timid with so many people watching, but then she bravely took her first step. As Maria warmed up to the music and the rhythm of the dance, she became steadily more comfortable and light on her feet, and her burgundy dress twirled as I spun her around.

She began to laugh as she danced more and more with abandon. It seemed the cork had finally popped on the joy inside of her that had been bottled up and suppressed by the darkness in which she had lived all these years. Her newly restored sight had already started transforming her life. She was no longer living in an orphanage or facing a destitute life on the streets of Moldova. Instead, she was living in a free and prosperous country, among God's people and with a family who loved her. She could finally be the fun-loving teenager she was meant to be.

As we danced, I enjoyed every moment that Maria's laughter filled the air. I had never seen her laugh so much! Her joy reminded me of what I had felt so long ago when China's deadly Cultural Revolution finally came to an end. Gone was the darkness, fear, and looming dread of deprtation that hung over me constantly. Gone was the hardship and suffering I endured as I fought against ethnic prejudice. Gone was my impulse to run from the ghosts and darkness in my life.

My whole life's experiences—both good and bad—made so much more sense to me now. My character had been shaped by my Eastern origins and my heart and soul had been healed through the faith I received from the West. I was now free to love more fully. By doing what it took to come out of my own darkness, I was able to help others out of theirs. God had blessed me with gifts and abilities that I will continue to use to give back to others in need, especially the blind orphans who need it the most. Maria tossed off her heels and danced with an energy that I found difficult to match. It dawned on me that the surgery that I performed on Maria not only restored her sight, but also liberated her spirit as well.

Once she was blind, but now she is free.

About the Author

D r. Ming Wang, a Harvard and MIT graduate (MD, *magna cum laude*), is a world-renowned laser eye surgeon, philanthropist and Kiwanis Nashvillian of the Year. He is one of the few cataract and LASIK surgeons in the world today who holds a doctorate degree in laser physics. Dr. Wang has performed well over 55,000 procedures, including those on over 4,000 doctors, so he has been referred to as the "doctors' doctor."

Born on October 24, 1960, Ming grew up in Hangzhou, a city in southeastern China. At age fourteen, his education was suddenly cut short and he faced deportation and a life sentence of hard labor and poverty, a devastating fate that fell upon millions of youth in China during the Cultural Revolution (1966-1976). To avoid deportation, Ming learned to play the Chinese violin— called the erhu—and to dance, with the hope of being accepted into one of the communist government's song-and-dance troupes. Unsuccessful because the government discovered his plan, he then studied medicine illegally and composed songs expressing his longing for the chance to go back to school and have a future. With the death of the dictator in 1976, the disastrous Cultural Revolution ended and China reopened its colleges after ten years. Ming learned three years of the high school curriculum in just a few months and gained a coveted admission spot in the University of Science and Technology of China. Ming eventually made his way to the U.S. in 1982, with only $50 and a Chinese-English dictionary in his pocket, but a big American dream in his heart.

Ming completed his PhD in laser spectroscopy and atomic collision dynamics in 1986 from the University of Maryland at College Park. In 1987, he enrolled in the joint Harvard Medical Shool/MIT MD program and a postdoctoral fellowship. Together with Professor George Church, he developed a new way to study DNA-protein interaction *in vivo* and published a paper in the world-renowned journal *Nature*. Dr. Wang graduated in 1991, with his MD (*magna cum laude*) from Harvard and MIT and a first place award for his graduation thesis in biomedical sciences.

Dr. Wang completed his ophthalmology residency at Wills Eye Hospital in Philadelphia, followed by a corneal fellowship at Bascom Palmer Eye Institute in Miami. In 1997, he was named the founding director of the Vanderbilt Laser Sight Center, and became a full-time faculty member and director of the residency program in the Department of Ophthalmology and Visual Science at Vanderbilt University in Nashville, Tennessee. From 1997 to 2002, Dr. Wang also worked as a panel consultant for the U.S. FDA's Ophthalmic Device Panel.

In 2002, Dr. Wang opened his private practice, Wang Vision Institute, which was later renamed Wang Vision 3D Cataract and LASIK Center. He performed the state's first bladeless all-laser LASIK, laser cataract surgery and KAMRA procedure, the U.S. first Intacs procedure for advanced keratoconus, and the world's first laser-assisted artificial cornea implantation. Dr. Wang has published eight textbooks and over one hundred papers, and holds several U.S. patents for his inventions of new biotechnologies to restore sight, including the world's first amniotic membrane contact lens. He is the recipient of the Honor Award from the American Academy of Ophthalmology and the Lifetime Achievement Award from the Association of Chinese American Physicians.

Dr. Wang is currently the only surgeon in Tennessee who performs 3D LASIK (18+), 3D Laser KAMRA and Raindrop (45+), 3D Forever Young Lens Surgery (50+) and 3D Laser Cataract Surgery (60+).He established two 501(c)(3) non-profit organizations, the Wang Foundation for Christian Outreach to China and the Wang Foundation for Sight Restoration, which to date has helped patients from over forty states in the U.S. and over fifty five countries worldwide, with all sight restoration surgeries performed free of charge.

Dr. Wang is the founding president of the Tennessee Chinese Chamber of Commerce, the honorary president of Tennessee American-Chinese Chamber of Commerce, the co-founder of the Tennessee Immigrant and Minority Business Group, and co-owner and international president of the Shanghai Aier Eye Hospitals in Shanghai, China, the largest private eye hospital group in China today, with over one hundred locations and a ten percent share of China's eye care market. In 2005, Dr. Wang performed China's first bladeless all-laser LASIK, the first in 1.4 billion people.

A champion amateur ballroom dancer, Dr. Wang is a former finalist in the world ballroom dance championships in the Pro/Am International Open 10-Dance. He still plays the erhu today, and was invited to accompany country-music legend, Dolly Parton, on her CD *Those Were the Days*. Dr. Wang also used the dance skills he learned during the Cultural Revolution as inspiration for his foundation's annual sight restoration fundraising event—the EyeBall—which features classical ballroom dance. The EyeBall is now in its tenth year and has drawn attendees from all over the U.S. and around the world.

An internationally known philanthropist, a conservative activist, and a community leader, Dr. Wang regularly travels throughout the country and around the world to do work related to his two 501(c)(3) non-profit foundations. He is a sought-after public speaker for his two favorite topics, "Appreciating Freedom in America" and "Faith and Science: Friends or Foes?"

Dr. Wang was recognized for his charity contribution and community service with many awards including NPR's Philanthropist of the Year Award, the Outstanding Nashvillian of the Year Award from Kiwanis Club and an honorary doctorate degree from Trevecca University.

Dr. Wang lives in Nashville, Tennessee with his wife, Anle Ji, and his parents, Dr. Zhen-sheng Wang and Dr. A-lian Xu.

Acknowledgments

This book would not be possible without the dedicated efforts of David Dunham, the Dunham Group, and especially Heather Ebert, who dedicated countless hours to this project, laboring hard and guiding me patiently through the process. Their professionalism, artistry, and counsel were invaluable. Thank you, David and Heather!

I am grateful to David Fischer, who contributed many valuable ideas, and thoroughly read and assisted in revising the manuscript. I hope to work with David again soon to turn this autobiography into a feature film.

I appreciate Senator Bill Frist, MD, for contributing the foreword for this book, and for the advice and mentoring he has provided me through the years.

A very sincere thanks goes to those who endorsed this book, including Dolly Parton; Charlie Daniels; Senator Lamar Alexander; Senator Bill Frist, MD; Mayor Karl Dean; Governor Bill Haslam; Governor Winfield Dunn; and many other friends and colleagues.

I would like to express earnest gratitude for my friends who spent many hours reading and offering suggestions for this book: Dr. Richard Nelson, Dr. James Hiatt, Charles Grummon, Larry Tomczak, David and Megan McCullough, Jerry Moll,

Tony Roberts, Tony Ashley, Tim Skow, Dave and Jan Dalton, Suzanne Gentry, Kip Dodson, Steve Ludwig, John Bransford, Kane Harrison, Shirley Zeitlin, Lynda and David Evjen, Rudy Kalis, and Robert Swope.

I am thankful to all the teachers, mentors, and colleagues that I have had through my career, including James McNesby, PhD; John Weiner, PhD; George Church, PhD; Larry Donoso, MD, PhD; Scheffer Tseng, MD, PhD; Richard Forster, MD,; William Culbertson, MD; Don Gass, MD; Spencer Thornton, MD; Arun Gulani, MD; Ilan Cohen, MD; David Chang, MD; Aleksandar Stonjavic, MD; Francis Muier, MD; Guy Guzerin, MD; Li Li; Bang Chen; Bao-sung Liu, MD; Michael Zhou, MD; Xiao-bing Wang, MD, Tracy Swartz, OD; Helen Boerman, OD; Amy Waymire, OD; Shanna Hill, OD; Dora Mathe, OD; Ara Sudtelgte, OD; Megan Blemker, OD and Gretchen Blemker, OD. If they had not challenged me constantly to pursue knowledge and make new discoveries, I might not have fulfilled my dream of becoming a doctor.

I would like to acknowledge the entire team at Wang Vision 3D Cataract & LASIK Center: Dr. Sarah Connolly, OD; Dr. Nathan Rock, OD; Dr. David Zimmerman, OD; Heather Brown; Leona Walthorn; Tammy Cardwell; Ana Martinez; Suzanne Gentry; Cameron Daniels; Scott Haugen; Eric Nesler; Crystal Micillo; Ashley Patty; Beth Riley, COA; Skyler Nelson; Kayla Sinyard, COT; Clare Stolberg, RN; Haley Wilson; James Wright; Chloe Jenkins; Amanda Knight; Shannon McClung, COA; Anle Ji; Dr. Li Jiang, MD, Dr. Hui Zhao, MD and Dr. Benyamin Ebrahim, MD. Each of you holds a special place in my life and work. We are changing lives together, and I am so thankful for all of you.

I am so appreciative of the Wang Foundation for Sight Restoration board of directors, and of all the foundation's medical council doctors who have donated their time and resources to help rescue so many of the foundation's patients from darkness.

I am deeply thankful for the foundation's patients and their families, who have entrusted their eyesight to me and traveled on the journey with me from darkness to sight: Francisco; Carole Klein; Clementina; Brad and Jackie Barnes; Kajal and Grace; Bobby Joel Case; Margarette, Dave, and Melody Snodgrass; Anna, Lisa, and Jeff Post; Anna and Beth Ann; Matthew and Mrs. Higgins; Wade and Mrs. Cook; Chris Dixon; Thomas Brewington; Randy Mathenia; and finally Maria, Steve, and Lynn Hendrich. With God's grace, together we have achieved the impossible!

I want to extend my most heartfelt thanks to my family, whose love and support made all of this possible: my father Dr. Zhen-sheng Wang, my mother Dr. A-lian Xu, my brother Dr. Ming-yu Wang, his wife Peggy and his daughter Yong Yong, my son Dennis and his sweetheart Alisa, my god parents Misha Bartnovsky and June Rudolph, and my wife Anle Ji, without whose thoughtfulness, care, and love I might never have been able to accomplish what I have done and to write this story. Anle also spent countless hours helping to organize the photos for this book. Family and friends are an important lifeline in one's journey, and I have continued to think about and remember each one of you fondly as I have encountered my triumphs and failures in life. We have stuck together and supported one another through it all, and I love each one of you dearly.

Finally, and most importantly, I want to thank God for delivering me from darkness and surrounding me with such glorious light!

Ming Wang, MD, PhD
Nashville, Tennessee, USA, 2016

How to Help the Sight Foundation

Founded in 2003 by Ming Wang, MD, PhD, and located in Nashville, Tennessee, USA, the Wang Foundation for Sight Restoration is a 501(c)(3) non-profit organization. The foundation's mission is to provide reconstructive eye surgeries to restore sight to indigent patients who otherwise could not afford such procedures.

The foundation consists of a team of medical council doctors (ophthalmologists and optometrists) who donate their services, and a board of directors made up of community leaders and philanthropists.

There are several ways in which you can help the foundation:

Host families: The foundation's current focus is helping blind orphan children. It is hard to imagine anyone more deserving of assistance than these children. For example, Maria's life has changed dramatically as a result of the help we have been able to provide. She has gone from being a blind orphan in Moldova who was at the brink of becoming a victim of human trafficking and prostitution, to a happy teenager who now lives in Franklin, Tennessee, is loved, and can see! Maria's host family, the Hendriches, made all of this possible. If you are interested in being a host family, or you know someone who may be interested in serving as a host family, please inform us through our foundation's website (www.wangfoundation.org). You can specify the age preference of the orphan(s) you would like to host, and how long you can host. The foundation works with several Christian missionary groups who travel around the world, so when we identify blind orphans that we may be able to help, we do our best to place them with the best matched host families.

Placentas: The foundation continues to conduct active research to further study the healing effects of the amniotic membrane and to improve the technology of the amniotic membrane contact lens based on our U.S. patents. The processing of these lenses involves fetal tissue research that does not touch or harm any part of an unborn child, as it utilizes post-birth placentas which are otherwise typically discarded after delivery.

If you know any pregnant women who are interested in donating their placentas after their babies are born, please inform us through our foundation's website (www.wangfoundation.org). One placenta can be processed into nearly one hundred amniotic membrane contact lenses, and therefore has the potential of helping restore sight to one hundred older people!

EyeBall: Each year the foundation hosts its annual fundraiser gala—the EyeBall—which showcases the beauty of classical ballroom dancing, reminding attendees how precious the gift of sight is. Without sight, we would not be able to appreciate the elegance of this style of dancing. It is important to do what we can to help those who have lost the gift of sight. We need volunteers for future EyeBall events, as well as in-kind service and silent auction item donations.

Donations: Though the foundation's doctors donate their services, there is still a significant need for funds related to other aspects of caring for these patients, including travel, lodging, clothing, and other medical care that is outside the range of specialties of the foundation doctors.

Therefore, any financial support is much appreciated! Helping blind patients, especially orphans, go from darkness to sight is the mission of the Wang Foundation for Sight Restoration. Together, we can all make a difference!

Wang Foundation for Sight Restoration
A 501(c)(3) non-profit charity
1801 West End Ave, Ste 1150
Nashville, TN, 37203
615-321-8881(O)
615-321-8874 (fax)
www.wangfoundation.com

Additional Endorsements
for This Book

"I thought I knew Dr. Wang well, but reading this book gave me the full picture of the struggles he's occasionally alluded to, but never dwelled upon. I didn't know the details of how he learned his music and dancing skills to literally save his life during the Chinese Cultural Revolution, nor how he had to qualify for a university spot or face a life of labor. It sheds light on his focus and work ethic, things he admits have been costly yet helpful. From Darkness to Sight is for anyone who wants to know the man behind the surgical mask, or just to know more about the struggles of one determined immigrant who fled a bleak future and created a life of success and service in his adopted home country."
—Charles G. Grummon, CFP®,
Associate Vice President – Investments, Wells Fargo Advisors

"I have personally never known a better student of dance and of life than Ming Wang. His openmindedness and willingness to learn are matched only by his intellect, desire and talent. I have learned as much from Ming as he has ever learned from me... wisdom about life and the inspiring example he is of determination and generosity. Our partnership is unique and special; we both see dancing as the ultimate activity that is stimulating intellectually, physically and emotionally, and Ming has taken this tremendous love of dance and has found ways to not only share his passion, but to *utilize dancing as a way to help others. I couldn't ask for a better partner and friend."*

—Shalene Archer, former U.S. Professional American
Ballroom Champion

"I am honored to be publishing From Darkness to Sight. *Dr. Wang is a real visionary and self-made man whose story of dedication, perseverance and hope will inspire millions. It is the honest and compelling story of a young man who escaped cruel and inhumane communist deportation in China by coming to America, overcoming racial discrimination, earning degrees from Harvard and MIT, and becoming one of America's leading LASIK surgeons."*

—David Dunham, Dunham Group, Inc., Publisher
From Darkness to Sight

"In the Bible, Proverbs 16:9 reads: 'In his heart, a man plans his way in life, but it's the Lord who directs his steps.' To me that encapsulates Dr. Ming Wang. All the challenges in his early life gave him an understanding and compassion for others, and the determination to make a difference. Couple that with brilliant wisdom and remarkable talent, and you have the makings of a man who God can use in a mighty way. He is driven by a never-ending thirst to find new ways of relieving pain and giving hope through the miracle of sight. The day will come when he will stand before his maker, who will say 'Well done, good and faithful servant.'"

—Rudy Kalis, Anchor, WSMV/Channel 4/NBC

"Ming Wang has a remarkable story, overcoming incredible odds to realize his dreams here in the United States. He has dedicated his life to helping people around the world, and I'm proud to know him."

—Beth Harwell, Tennessee Speaker of the House

"Dr. Ming Wang is what I consider to be a modern Renaissance Man. While he is an accomplished musician, ballroom dancer,

and certainly a profound man of science and medicine, he lives out daily his faith, and is an example of how we as followers of Christ should live our lives — not simply in words, but in deeds as well. He generously gives away his time, resources and medical skills to those who cannot see. He is a friend and someone I truly admire."
—Glen Casada, Tennessee House Majority Caucus Chairman

"There are few people who influence my life as positively as Dr. Ming Wang. His personal friendship spurs me to continue pursuing my God-given dreams. His tenacity inspires me to trust God fully when mountains seem insurmountable. His fearlessness in proclaiming the connection of God and science helps countless people reach beyond their own humanity to a greater faith in The Divine."
—David McCullough, Mayor, Cheatham County, Tennessee

"It is a real privilege to be able to comment on Dr. Ming Wang and his life. I have had the opportunity to hear him speak of how God has influenced his life, and I have seen it occur. He not only talks about God influencing his life, but I have listened to his testimony and have seen it in action. What a great opportunity to see him use his great gift in our city."
—Joe Greene, Founder, Christian Executive Officers Fellowship

"A tornado in a hurricane! Ming is a world-class eye surgeon whose commitment to introduce breakthrough technology despite the restrictive medical atmosphere is paralleled in his personal life, where his relentless passion to help mankind is undeterred by the repeated storms that life throws in his way. A simpleton at heart with an IQ of an impatient genius, I believe what he has achieved is only testimony to his capacity which is yet to be called for a higher function."
—Arun Gulani, MD, Gulani Vision Institute

"From Dr. Ming Wang's struggle to survive as a young man in China to his great success and conversion to Christianity in the

United States, Ming's life story contains many lessons for all of us. It is not only Ming's brilliant mind but also his love of Christ and servant's heart that are propelling him forward with a life of passionate purpose."

—Jerry Moll, MA, MPA, IOM, AOM, Founder, President & CEO, Living Sent Ministries

"Having been taunted and bullied as a kid growing up in the projects wearing Coke-bottle glasses, when the opportunity to undergo LASIK became available nearly a quarter century ago, I thought it was too good to be true. It was a life-changing miracle, which occurred again recently when Ming replaced my cataracts with Forever Young lenses. Miracles do happen, especially when a gifted surgeon humbles himself, kneels down and prays with his patients. The Word as stated in Jeremiah 29:11 is appropriately applied to this gifted man of God: 'I know the thoughts that I have for you,' declares the Lord, 'and they are plans to prosper you and to keep you from harm and to give you a hope and a future.'"

—Michael Sheppard, CEO/Chairman, NMC Inc. and Founder of The Sheppard Group

"Ming Wang was one of the first people we met in Nashville. His energy, faith and kindness have made us friends for life. As a board member of the Wang Foundation, I have been blessed to work for the cause of providing sight to those who could have never dreamed of ever seeing at all. Countless children and adults alike have been given this gift. Ming gave me the 'sight' to want to work tirelessly for others and to be an example of his deep commitment to faith and healing. His love of country and his struggles in life give him a dedication and love for what he does that is to be admired and honored. In countries where people already have so little, the gift of restored sight that the Wang Foundation can give will mean the gift of life as well. For many it means being able to work again, look after their families again, and regain their dignity. Ming's life is a tribute to what is good and sane about humanity. God bless you,

my dear friend, and thank you for being in my world."
                                        —Lynda Evjen, Evjen & Associates

"In 2010, due to mistakes of another specialist eye surgeon, I was going blind. At the last moment of hope, I met Dr. Ming Wang on a Friday morning at an event where he was a speaker. Booked for months, he instantly put all aside for me. I was in his office by noon, where he and his team worked on me until 5:00 that afternoon. By the next day, the invasive infection had been arrested, and my frightful experience began a steady reversal from its impending darkness towards full sight. Today, I see clearly, with thanks to God and to Dr. Wang. When I visited China in 1979, as one of the earliest Americans who was allowed to visit China after Mao Zedong began his rule in 1949, the young Ming was not far from where I visited. He was still in his years of struggle and searching. This year, I was able to read his life story several times as it was being written. Both then and now, perhaps because of what I saw in China and because I witnessed some of what he experienced, I found myself emotional again and again as I read passages of anguish, hope and eventual consummate victory, success, and spiritual blessing! My wife and I feel continually honored to be in his company, whether in his home or supporting him at public events. Together with his beloved Anle, he has become a treasured, intimate friend...worthy of my best love and highest respect! This book will be inspiring to any person who reads it...it has my enthusiastic recommendation!"
                                    —Dr. Richard A. Nelson, Pastor/Writer/Builder

"Dr. Ming Wang's engaging account of his struggle to find faith and freedom in the United States gives us an insightful glimpse into the travesties of the Cultural Revolution in China. Understanding this peculiar period of history is important for all Americans interested in developing relationships with the Chinese in business, education, medicine or ministry."
                                    —William H. Slater, MEd, JD, Headmaster,
                                        Hendersonville Christian Academy

"Over several decades, Dr. Ming Wang has brought to Tennessee and the nation a level of skill and excellence in surgical care that has restored sight to many and has inspired other physicians to follow his lead. He is a teacher, author, and mentor to a new generation of eye surgeons, making the future brighter. Dr. Wang's life story is one of overcoming obstacles, mastering the excellent and making the science of eye care an art second to none. Having known and admired him over the years, I have been pleased to see him achieve the recognition that he so richly deserves. I predict more honors and recognition in the years ahead."

—Spencer P. Thornton, MD, FACS, Past President, American Society of Cataract and Refractive Surgery; Clinical Professor, Department of Ophthalmology, University of Tennessee

"Engaging stories of inspiration and timeless truth must be told! From Joseph in Genesis to Disney's Cinderella, *we are enthralled by grand tales of heroes and heroines confronting massive hardships, and in the face of incredible odds, accomplishing great things and rising to unbelievable heights. We cheer as goodness and faithfulness, as well as courage, persistence, and honest hard work prevail. From* Darkness to Sight *is such a story! Invest a few minutes with Dr. Ming Wang and be enlightened, encouraged, and entertained!"*

—James T. Hiatt, JD, MBA, Associate Vice President for Academic Programs, Dean, Skinner School of Business and Technology, Trevecca Nazarene University

"As the producer of the EyeBall, I have the blessed experience to know and appreciate Dr. Ming Wang on a level most may not. While Ming is probably the most talented man I have ever had the pleasure to know, from ophthalmologist to concert performer to competitive ballroom dancer to physicist, I have noticed he also shares a kindness with the world that you very rarely find these days. From Darkness to Sight *is a brilliant read, encapsulating how this one man has struggled to become the world-class expert he is on a multitude of levels, while simultaneously finding the inner peace through God to share*

those talents with humanity in a very real and remarkable manner. It is a pleasure and an honor to call Ming my friend."
—Robert Swope, Producer, EyeBall, President/CEO, Sunrise Entertainment

"I had the pleasure of spending a year with Dr. Wang, as a fellow learning advanced laser eye surgery. His dedication to using technology to help people see is incredible, and he has made more contributions to our profession than I am able to count. He is a tremendous mentor and valued friend."
—Lance Kugler, MD, President, Refractive Surgery Alliance

"We have known Dr. Wang for almost twenty years. He is a gifted scientist, clinician, and entrepreneur—an inspiring Renaissance Man. The title of his book, From Darkness to Sight, *is a perfect metaphor for his life. He transformed personally from darkness to faith, freedom and generosity of spirit. And we, his friends and patients, are the beneficiaries."*
—John Dayani, President and CEO, Vanderford Capital Advisors
—Elizabeth Dayani, Founder and Vice Chairman, Cardiac Care Group

"Dr. Ming Wang is a truly unique person with a mix of talents and principles rarely found in a single individual. He is a superb and caring physician, a visionary and entrepreneur, an innovator and a philanthropist, a role model for immigrants seeking the 'American Dream.' Never mind that he dances a lot better than I do."
—Harry Jacobson, MD, former Vice Chancellor of Health, Vanderbilt University

"As an immigrant to this country from Cuba, who knows firsthand the oppressiveness of communism, Dr. Ming Wang's story is particularly moving to me. And like Dr. Wang, I too have been blessed to live in this country that honors hard work, liberty and freedom of religion.

Dr. Wang is an inspiration to us all, especially the immigrant community, because he reminds us that this country is truly a place where anything is possible. I consider Dr. Wang a close friend and know that he is a man of God committed to public service. I encourage everyone to pick up a copy of From Darkness to Sight *because it is one of the best personal accounts of the 'American Dream.'"*

—Raul Lopez, Executive Director for Latinos for Tennessee, a nonprofit organization promoting faith, family, and fiscal responsibility to Latinos in Tennessee

"Dr. Ming Wang is one of the premier pioneers of our time in surgical innovation and techniques. His surgical skill and magic touch have transformed the lives of the many patients who have sought his help and expert advice. He does not cease to amaze by introducing or embracing surgical techniques that are at the forefront of cornea and refractive surgery. I had the honor to watch his surgeries and to scrub with him on numerous occasions, and I can comfortably say that I would rank him among the top five surgeons in the world. His prolific career extends from helping patients with extremely disabling eye diseases (using basal stem cell transplants) to those who choose elective procedures (such as the Kamra implants) that are designed to provide a better lifestyle. His contributions to the field of ophthalmology as a surgeon, author, inventor and teacher will immortalize his name."

—Ilan Cohen, MD, Ophthalmologist and Cornea Specialist

"It is a rare yet precious occasion when one encounters a person who can truly be described as 'extraordinary.' I can attest that I have met the embodiment of the word in Dr. Ming Wang. His remarkable life story, beautifully chronicled in his recent autobiography, From Darkness to Sight, *is inspiring. His harrowing escape from the clutches of China's Cultural Revolution and the Gang of Four is riveting. Dr. Wang's accomplishments as a preeminent scientist and eye*

surgeon are only surpassed by his acts of philanthropy, which are inspired by his strong Christian faith. He is the embodiment of the harmony between science and religion. I am grateful to know Dr. Wang and honored to be among his friends."

—Farzin Ferdowsi, CEO, MRCO, LLC

"Dr. Ming Wang is a generous man who has overcome much adversity to become a world-renowned eye surgeon and philanthropist. His powerful life story has the potential to impact and change the lives of millions of people who will be inspired and motivated by his remarkable story. I highly recommend this book to anyone who needs a reminder about the greatness of America and the sovereignty of God."

—Carol M. Swain, Professor of Political Science and Professor of Law, Vanderbilt University

"More than any other immigrant to the Nashville area, Ming has raised the profile of the immigrant community. With his numerous contributions—both professional and cultural—as well as his business leadership, he has left his mark on our community. I am pleased to have collaborated with Ming in the founding of the Tennessee Immigrant and Minority Business Group. As a keen observer of Ming's various and sundry activities, I once asked him when he ever had time to sleep. His quick response was: 'Oh, I do get two or three hours every night.' Apparently enough to keep the Energizer Bunny running!"

—Galen Hull, PhD, Co-Founder of Tennessee Immigrant and Minority Business Group and CEO of Hull International, LLC

"Dr. Ming Wang and I have been friends and colleagues for nearly 20 years. We first met while in training at the world-renowned Bascom Palmer Eye Institute. It was on those few occasions when we had some free time that we would always talk about our dreams of taking our hard-earned education and using it to make a great and lasting impact in our community, close to home and beyond. In many ways, we spoke of the 'American Dream.'

All these years later, Dr. Wang embodies the realization of this Dream, whether it be through his work as a visionary of the Wang Vision Institute, his committed involvement in community and faith-based organizations or his Foundation for Sight Restoration, where I had the privilege of being asked to be one of the founding members of the Medical Council. This foundation, which has given us the opportunity to care for patients from all over the United States and 55 countries worldwide is, I believe, one of Dr. Wang's greatest achievements to date. What will be even more extraordinary are the gifts he will share with us that have yet to come. I am proud to call him a lifelong friend."

—David J. Shen, OD, Director of Eyecare Services,
Vue Optique, PLLC

"Dr. Wang and I frequently co-manage patients with corneal diseases, utilizing our respective expertise in both surgery and contact lenses through a unique, patient-centered approach called the Keratoconus Center. His dedication to patient care and near-obsessive pursuit of excellence translates to his outstanding surgical results. He is genuinely concerned for each and every patient, not as 'eyeballs on which to operate' but as human beings who have needs, wants, expectations, and emotions. It is unique to have a colleague who will treat mutual patients the way that everyone should be treated, and to know that they will be receiving the best care known to medicine."

—Jeffrey Sonsino, OD, FAAO, Diplomate, Cornea,
Contact Lens and Refractive Technologies,
American Academy of Optometry

"I have known Dr. Ming Wang for over a decade as a patient and close friend. Now to see his story put into this book is so exciting! I encourage everyone to read it to derive fresh inspiration and hope for their lives. If you need encouragement for a fresh start or simply to persevere toward your goals, read this book!"

—Larry Tomczak, Bestselling Author and
Cultural Commentator

"Dr. Wang's story is an amazing testament to the human spirit, and reflects—like an amazing painting—the awesomeness of its creator. While his many accomplishments are appreciated, the boldness of his faith is what I admire most."

—Mark Green, MD, Tennessee State Senator
and President/CEO of Align MD

"Over my twenty-eight-year career in publishing, I have had the honor of working with the leaders in medicine. Ming Wang is at the top of the list of skilled surgeons, while also being a towering intellect and a humanitarian. Add to this his compelling life story: he is a true original that one is not likely to meet more than once in a lifetime."

—John Bond, Chief Content Officer, SLACK Inc.

"Through the stages of study during my tenure at the University of Tennessee, I had the privilege to travel and study abroad. I saw the sad faces of poverty in Liechtenstein, the ruins of Italy, the Summer Palace of Peter the Great of Russia, and the many palaces of the rich of Europe. In Russia I encountered the distaste of the communist rule that limited one's ambitions, and freedom through diminishing the tools needed for innovation and creativity. My studies and travels never prepared me for the world that Dr. Ming Wang experienced in the Communistic world of China. The reading of his life story placed me in his world of sustaining ambition and creativity that pushed through the world of darkness and blindness. The book explored the world of darkness that opened up an insight of what can be, in spite of what is. It explored the pathway to freedom, and the achieving of it against all obstacles."

—Tony Roberts, BA, BS, MBA